The Extreme Right in Franc 1789 to the Present

The Extreme Right in France, 1789 to the Present surveys the history of a fascinating but contentious political and intellectual tradition. Since 1789 the far right has been an important actor in French political life and in different eras has taken on a range of guises, including traditionalism, ultra-royalism, radical nationalism, anti-Semitism and fascism.

This book is structured around five main phases of extreme-right activity, and the author explores key questions about each:

- Counter-Revolution – what was the legacy of Joseph de Maistre's writings?
- Anti-Third Republic protest – how was the 'new right' of the 1880s and 1890s different from the 'old right' of previous decades?
- Inter-war fascism – how should we characterise the phenomenon of *le fascisme français*?
- Vichy – why did Pétain and Laval collaborate with the Nazis?
- Post-war agitation – what is the relationship between *Algérie Française*, Poudjadism and Le Pen's FN?

The Extreme Right in France, 1789 to the Present provides the key to an understanding of this vivid and long-standing feature of France's political history, with its amazing ability to reinvent itself and to appeal anew to important sections of the French population.

Peter Davies is Senior Lecturer in Modern European History at the University of Huddersfield. He is author of *The National Front in France* (1999) and *France and the Second World War* (2000).

The Extreme Right in France, 1789 to the Present

From de Maistre to Le Pen

Peter Davies

First published 2002
by Routledge
11 New Fetter Lane, London EC4P 4EE

Simultaneously published in the USA and Canada
by Routledge
29 West 35th Street, New York, NY 10001

Routledge is an imprint of the Taylor & Francis Group

© 2002 Peter Davies

Typeset in Sabon by Prepress Projects Ltd, Perth, Scotland
Printed and bound in Great Britain by The Cromwell Press, Trowbridge, Wiltshire

British Library Cataloguing in Publication Data
A catalogue record for this book is available from the British Library

Library of Congress Cataloging in Publication Data
Davies, Peter, 1966–
    The extreme right in France, 1789 to the present : from de Maistre to Le Pen / Peter Davies.
        p. cm.
    Includes bibliographical references and index.
    1. France–Politics and government–1789– 2. Right-wing extremists–France. 3. Right and
left (Political science) 4. Conservatism–France–History. I. Title.
DC252.D25 2002
320.52´0944–dc21   2001048497

ISBN 0–415–23981–8 (hbk)
ISBN 0–415–23982–6 (pbk)

This book is dedicated to my Mum and Dad

Contents

Preface

I am very grateful for the support I received from the University of Huddersfield during the preparation of this piece of work. In addition, I would sincerely like to thank Rainer Horn and Malcolm Crook for their time and advice, Gillian Oliver and Victoria Peters at Routledge for their encouragement, and all the people I have met in France who have aided me in my research.

Peter Davies
November 2001

Introduction

Paris — Dreux — Mantes-la-Jolie — La Vendée — Vichy — Orange — Le Cimetière de Chambière — Paris — Marignane — Toulon — Orange — Carpentras

Not so long ago I made a very special kind of pilgrimage. It was not a trip that would have appealed to many other people, if to anybody at all, but for me it was a journey that I had always wanted to make. It was a *Tour de France* with a difference.

I travelled to London, bought a Rail Rover ticket (France), and hopped on the Eurostar to Paris. I stayed in the French capital for a couple of days and did all the things I usually do. I visited the spacious but heavily guarded headquarters of the Front National (FN) at 4 rue Vauguyon on the banks of the Seine at St Cloud. After conducting a lengthy interview with passionate *Lepéniste* Cyril de Beketch, I popped into the FN *boutique*, where I bought a few right-wing tomes and a sample of cut-price memorabilia – all in red, white and blue, of course. As I exited the building I picked up a selection of complimentary party newsletters from a table in the foyer. Once outside I looked for the mansion of FN leader Jean-Marie Le Pen, which I knew was located in the plush neighbourhood nearby. I thought I could see it in the distance, but I could have been mistaken.

I also took in Dreux, an unremarkable town to the west of Paris that witnessed the FN 'breakthrough' of 1983, and Mantes-la-Jolie, a depressed, high-immigrant suburb of the capital that – all on its own – seemed to illuminate the plethora of socio-economic problems that were aiding the continuing emergence of Le Pen's movement. Back in the capital, I traversed the streets. My antennae were sharp. I was looking for any sign of the far right: posters and graffiti – whether friendly or hostile – on the walls of the city; journals – whether pro- or anti-Le Pen – on display in the pavement news-stands; maybe even billboards screaming out the latest FN-related news. As usual I had a lot to keep me occupied.

From Paris I took the train to Angers, a peaceful provincial town two-thirds of the way to Nantes in the west. I stayed there for two nights, in a small hotel on the main street, and I was delighted to be out of the busy capital. But Angers was not my destination, just my headquarters. It was an ideal base from which to discover the beauty and historical profundity of the Vendée – the region that had rebelled so violently against the Revolution in the mid-1790s.

During my stay in the West, I travelled to all the places I had read about in Tilly's celebrated study of the conflict.[1] Saumur, Cholet, La Roche-sur-Yon – I went everywhere. It was a stirring experience to visit all these small, unassuming towns that had been at the centre of the most famous counter-revolutionary revolt of all. It had always been drummed into me that there was something unique about the Vendée, and as I toured the region in person – rather than via Tilly's powerful narrative – there was no mistaking the expanse of rolling farmland and the great sense that this was an area that guarded its history and heritage to a remarkable degree. I visited a museum dedicated solely to the 'heroic' revolt of 1793 and bought lots of picture postcards celebrating the event. I even did a bit of on-the-spot research into the 1995 presidential candidate Philippe de Villiers – a maverick right-winger and proud Vendéan – who was very much the personification of that arch-conservatism associated with the West.

Leaving Angers, I headed east towards the centre of France. I was aiming for Vichy, the spa town made infamous during the Second World War. When I arrived in the town it was raining. Given what I knew already about the Vichy regime of 1940–4, I thought this was highly symbolic. Almost sixty years on, Pétain's capital struck the first-time visitor as sleepy and unspectacular. My hotel was mid-range but it had real classical style. This reminded me that the puppet regime of 1940 had chosen Vichy as its headquarters because of the town's excellent communications and its lavish repertoire of hotels. In 1940 it was Pétain, Laval and Co. who had enjoyed the town's hospitality. Six decades on, it was me.

There was virtually no sign at all of Vichy's infamy – and believe me, I was looking. There were sporadic marks on occasional buildings, but nothing to write home about. I reflected on the fact that the rewriting of history has gone on in countries other than the former Soviet Union. As I walked around the town, I realised that it was a lovely, tranquil and pleasant place. It was difficult not to contrast the town with the administration that it had been home to. I sipped the spa water, bought a book about the town's history, and purchased some high-quality *Pastilles Vichy – Source Citron* as a memento of my visit.

From Vichy I headed south, not to the usual tourist locations of Nice, Cannes and St Tropez, but to Orange, where Le Pen's party had just won a dramatic mayoral contest. As I approached the place on the train, images of a run-down, estate-ridden new town with a severe immigration problem flickered across my mind.

The reality could not have been more different. What I found was a classical Roman town, Mediterranean in feel and looks, comfortable, middle-class, and home to a giant amphitheatre and well-heeled tourist industry. I checked into my hotel and went for a stroll. I found it hard to believe that 'sophisticated' Orange had succumbed to the 'jackboot' of Le Pen. There were no giveaway clues at all. When I located the local party headquarters – a converted garage – I spoke to two officials who were obviously used to people like me asking the six million franc question: 'Why Orange? What's "wrong" with Orange? How come the FN has conquered Orange – of all places?' I received a well-rehearsed answer: 'Monsieur, Orange is a normal place. It is not an immigration thing. It is just that we have a committed, enthusiastic set of party workers and our leader, M. Bompard, is an effective politician who gets himself involved in issues like road safety, refuse collection and the quality of the local pavements.' I grabbed a selection of local FN literature and left, my learning curve in Midi politics already steep. What I had heard had to make sense – because in Orange there was no immigration crisis to exploit. It was just an ordinary, and very beautiful, tourist town. This was a huge eye-opener. If Le Pen can win in Orange, I thought to myself, he can win anywhere. Of course, the local newspapers were full of FN-related stories, as were national publications. The republican left was organising a boycott of Orange as a protest against what they saw as the ascendancy of the anti-republican right. I got back to my hotel and meditated upon what I had just discovered.

Orange to Strasbourg was a colossal journey. Strasbourg was a city that had only recently witnessed a significant FN vote and, as a result, one wag had pinned a swastika to the top of the *hôtel de ville*. But I was in Alsace for other reasons. The day after I arrived in the north-east I visited the military cemetery at Chambière that the late-nineteenth-century nationalist Maurice Barrès had eulogised in one of his most lyrical pieces of writing.[2] I followed in his footsteps and inspected the same cemetery on the outskirts of Metz. Even for me, there was something incredibly powerful about the rows and rows of military graves. It was difficult not to have some conception of how Barrès must have felt in 1902. I returned to Paris on the night train. The FN was holding its annual *Fête Bleu-Blanc-Rouge* in the city and the new political year was just about to start.

After several trips to France during which I had visited only Paris, my 'far-right tour' had been both refreshing and illuminating. The following year I added to my collection of political hot-spots. I travelled to the airport town of Marignane, in the Marseilles conurbation, where local FN activist Daniel Simonpieri had only recently captured the *hôtel de ville*; just down the Mediterranean coast in Toulon I interviewed a close associate of the new FN mayor Jean-Marie Le Chevallier and went for a seafront lunch with a municipal official who had been charged with implementing the new *Lepéniste* agenda in the city; I revisited historic Orange and located the woman at the head of the anti-FN movement Alerte Orange, as well as noting the amount of pro- and anti-FN literature on sale in the town's only bookshop; and I also took a trip to nearby Carpentras, where Le Pen's party had been implicated in an unpleasant scandal involving the exhumation of

Jewish graves. My education on the extreme right was not complete, but my eyes had been opened further.

This book is not primarily about people or events, but ideas. It has several key aims. It seeks, firstly, to illuminate a rich, interesting and controversial political tradition. It could be argued that the history of the French far right is a slightly neglected topic because, when the spotlight turns to extreme-right politics, it is usually Germany and Italy that gain most attention. But France also has a vivid tradition. The Counter-Revolution of the 1790s gave birth to a range of right-wing ideas, and 200 years later the FN emerged – one of the most compelling examples of neo-fascism in action. In between times there were regular eruptions of far-right activity: in the 1880s and 1890s 'pre-fascist' ideas took root; during the inter-war years France was home to hundreds of extra-parliamentary fascist *ligues*; and in the early 1940s Vichy not only collaborated with the Nazis but launched the National Revolution – an ultra-traditionalist right-wing crusade. If the French right has been under-studied, this book should be viewed as a corrective.

Moreover, this study will consider France's right-wing history in a non-polemical fashion. Its aim is not to examine the extreme right in order to denigrate or undermine it, or to be overjudgmental or pejorative. Rather it seeks to understand and explain right-wing ideas and movements, both in their own terms and in our terms. There is no 'agenda' – and I hope that this will be a refreshing feature of the book. It will be as 'neutral' and 'objective' as it possibly can be.

The book will draw on a wide array of sources from a variety of eras. In addition to conventional historical texts it will, where appropriate, draw upon literary extracts and pictorial evidence to help us explain and understand the topics on which it focuses. And given the scope of the study, it will refer to the work of both historians and political scientists. Throughout, the aim is to present the 'state of the debate' on key topics, and so prominence will be given to secondary sources. But, where appropriate, primary sources will be utilised to give the reader a flavour of the 'raw history' and to help generate debate. A combination of English and French secondary sources will be used, and from this mixture the reader will hopefully get the best of both worlds. With regard to primary sources, a variety will be cited and referred to. Some I have translated into English, but most have been translated by others and now feature in edited collections of texts. We will handle diaries, charters, press cuttings, speeches, parliamentary decrees and propaganda posters. In my view, the book will benefit from this rich amalgam of sources.

The aim is also to mix a thematic approach with a conventional chronological approach. Chapter 1 introduces a range of underpinning issues; Chapters 2–6 investigate specific eras in turn. But, in these five sections, the focus is less on the 'story' of the extreme right than on the ideas and debates associated with the topic in question. Thus, an individual timeline will accompany each chapter, to act as an aid to context-building and understanding.[3] Overall it would be fair to say that this book should be catalogued under 'History of Ideas' rather than 'History' or 'Political History'.

Finally, this study will add to the available literature on the far right. Of course, the tradition already has its historians in English and French. To begin with, in English there are some excellent analyses of individual movements and periods. On the Counter-Revolution, for example, there are Roberts, Godechot, Carpenter, Mansel, and Tilly;[4] on early Third Republic nationalism, Tombs, Sternhell, and Mazgaj;[5] on inter-war fascism, Soucy, Sternhell, Paxton, and Passmore;[6] on Vichy, Rousso, Halls, and Fishman *et al.*;[7] and on the FN, Declair, Simmons, Hainsworth, and Marcus.[8] This is only a selection. If we add to this the many specialist studies in French, we have an impressive and growing library.

There are, furthermore, several good survey histories of the right and extreme right. In French we should be aware of the work of Sirinelli, Winock, Milza and Petitfils. The most impressive volume in terms of size and scope is the collection of essays edited by Sirinelli. *Les Droites françaises* – published in 1992 – is a thorough, authoritative and comprehensive work that presents the history of right-wing politics in all its variety and richness.[9] Its structure is partly chronological and partly based on themed analysis. Sirinelli is interested in *idées*, *intérêts* and *tempéraments*, and in *politique*, *cultures* and *sensibilités*.[10] As the title of the book indicates, he contends that the key to understanding the right in France is to pluralise it.

Winock's 1994 study, *Histoire de l'extrême droite en France*, takes a similar approach, moving from the 1780s to the 1880s and on to the 1980s with due care and clarity. The edited collection comprises eight themed essays on the far right, and Winock concludes by noting 'the regularity of its resurgences'.[11] The survey history written by Milza – *Fascisme français*, published in 1987 – has a tighter focus than the other two studies. It is concerned exclusively with French fascism and is constantly posing questions: 'La France de Vichy a-t-elle été fasciste?' 'Le Front national est-il fasciste?'[12] It is impossible to reach any definitive conclusions on issues such as these, but Milza is certain that, since the late nineteenth century, France has been home to a variety of fascist-style movements and ideologies.

Much less ambitious is Petitfils' study, *L'Extrême droite en France*. It is almost a 'pocket guide' to the French far right and, thus, does not have enormous depth. But it is interesting that this tradition is deemed to be worthy of such a study – evidence, surely, of its importance and topicality.[13] It is a clear, well-focused and accessible guide and, for a book published in 1983, is strangely prescient in its concluding remarks: 'The French extreme right is dying – all political observers are in accord on this matter. But... it is not on the verge of disappearing.'[14] When he wrote this, Petitfils could not have known that on 4 September 1983 Jean-Pierre Stirbois of the FN would win 16.72 per cent of the vote in the first ballot of a municipal by-election in the small town of Dreux. The mainstream right – the Rassemblement pour la République (RPR) and the Union pour la Démocratie Française (UDF) – asked Stirbois to join their list for the second ballot, and the new coalition emerged victorious with a 54.33 per cent share of the vote.[15] Political scientists are generally agreed that the 'Le Pen phenomenon' was born at Dreux in 1983; and, thus, Petitfils was right to be sceptical about the demise of the tradition.

In English we are served by Rémond, Anderson, McClelland, Winock, and Arnold. Rémond's work, *The Right Wing in France*, is a classic and a point of reference for all students of the French right, but it does not delve into the pre-1815 era and only examines developments up until the early 1960s.[16] Anderson's study, *Conservative Politics in France*, is incisive, informative and provocative. But, even though it does examine a range of far-right movements, its focus remains, quite tightly, 'conservative politics'. Published in 1974, it limits itself to a consideration of French political history after 1880. So, as with Rémond, it does not deal with the Counter-Revolution as an era, or contemporary developments on the right.[17]

In contrast, McClelland's volume, *The French Right from de Maistre to Maurras*, is a collection of key texts. The major works of de Maistre, Drumont, Barrès and Maurras are included but, on the whole, McClelland is more interested in the right than the extreme right. As such, he also includes extracts from Taine, Sorel, Le Bon and Claudel and, for good reason, offers only a minimum of commentary. His book was published in 1971, so modern far-right thinkers such as de Benoist, Le Pen and Mégret do not get a mention.[18] Winock's recently translated volume, *Nationalism, Anti-Semitism and Fascism in France,* is a welcome addition to the available literature in English.[19] This study is interested less in the 'extreme right' as a specific concept than in exploring 'the national self and its diseases' (*le Moi national et ses maladies*); but clearly, in doing so, Winock investigates a range of apposite themes, including national-populism, anti-Americanism, decadence and Bonapartism.[20]

The Development of the Radical Right in France: From Boulanger to Le Pen, edited by Arnold and published in 2000, is the most topical survey. The history of the radical right is divided into four periods – 1887–1914, 1914–40, 1940–4 and 1944–98 – and contributors explore topics such as anti-Semitism, fascism and neo-Nazism. Arnold notes in his introduction that the discourse of the far right is dominated by notions of 'conspiracy', 'decadence' and 'mythology' and also indicates that these ideas help to explain the 'continuing success of this political formula'.[21]

One of the merits of the present study is its scope. It is comprehensive, broad-ranging and brings the story of the French far right up to date. Overall, it deals with two centuries and more of political and intellectual history. It starts with the Counter-Revolution, finishes with the FN and the Mouvement National Républicain (MNR), and in between times deals with the new nationalism of the 1880s and 1890s, the reactionary right associated with the Action Française (AF), the agitation of the fascist *ligues* in the 1920s and 1930s, the politics of Vichy and collaboration, the Poujadist phenomenon and *Algérie Française*, among other things.

In focusing on the extreme-right tradition we are confronting a complex, fascinating and varied strand of politics.[22] In the course of seven chapters, I will turn the spotlight on to a myriad of political ideas, most notably anti-Semitism, collaboration, collaborationism, conservatism, fascism, national-populism, nationalism, neo-fascism, populism, pre-fascism, proto-fascism, reaction and traditionalism. It should be said that this is not a comprehensive list! We will also deal with some movements and thinkers that, to some commentators, are 'left-wing' or 'of the left', and others that almost defy classification. This should not worry us. It just illuminates the wonderful richness of France's political and intellectual history.

We should also be aware of the intense opposition that far-right activity in France has provoked, on the left, in the centre, and even on the right. To cite a selection of examples: the wartime government of Pétain was obstructed by de Gaulle's Resistance movement; the Anti-Dreyfusard Movement of the 1890s was confronted by the full force of republican France; the modern-day FN has had to deal with the threat of a legal ban and the ambiguous posturings of the mainstream right; the *ligues* of the inter-war period were eventually outlawed by the 1936 Front Populaire; and two centuries ago, the first right-wing extremists were forced into combat with Jacobinism, dechristianisation and liberalism. Clearly, these confrontations help to define the far right, and thus we will pay due attention to them and to historical context more generally.

The title of this study is *The Extreme Right in France, 1789 to the Present*, but the fact is that 'extreme right' is almost synonymous with such terms as 'far right',[23] 'hard right',[24] and 'ultra-right',[25] and these phrases will be used in forthcoming chapters where appropriate.

The book is structured chronologically around five main sections: 1789–1830, 1870–1918, 1919–39, 1940–4 and 1945 to the present day. In one sense, these demarcation dates are slightly artificial – obviously, the far-right tradition does not neatly compartmentalise itself into these blocs – but, in another, they will help us to trace the evolution of right-wing politics over time. Each chapter is self-contained and each depicts a different and distinct type of extreme right but, clearly, the chapters are connected in the sense that there are continuities running through the full history of far-right politics. There is the occasional element of overlap, but I would hope that if any historian of ideas was asked to split the history of the far right into five chronological (and, at the same time, thematic) segments, they would concur, in general terms, with my choice.

There are periods of French history that do not warrant our attention. The four decades between the July Revolution of 1830 and the Franco-Prussian War of 1870 are crucial in terms of the general political history of

France, but it is clear to even the most casual observer that these years were devoid of 'extremist' activity on the right. After the fall of Charles X in 1830, right-wing radicalism went into hibernation. The royalist right was still active of course, but it represented a moderate brand of conservatism. More light will be shed on the 1830–70 era in Chapters 1, 2 and 3.

Likewise we would be hard pushed to argue that Napoleon III's imperial regime (1851–70) was either of an extreme-right persuasion or threatened by forces of a far-right character. That said, no understanding of extreme-right politics is possible without first comprehending the essence of Bonapartism – and this fact will become clear at several junctures throughout the book.

The dates associated with Chapter 2 on the Counter-Revolution are 1789–1830, but in reality this should be 1789–99 and 1814–30. Not only would it be inaccurate to label Napoleon I's 1799–1814 regime 'far right' (in any sense of the term), but it is clear that the Counter-Revolution was generally in abeyance during the empire years. It was neutralised, and only reignited by the fall of Napoleon and the Allies' desire to put the Bourbons back on the French throne in 1814.[26] This is why the period 1799–1814 will not detain us.

To sum up, this book is a history of the extreme right in France rather than a history of France per se. The focus is tight – that is why we are leaving aside periods in which there was little or no far-right activity to speak of. This relies on my judgement of course, but I have endeavoured to reflect the consensus view among historians. The book examines two centuries of political and intellectual history, and it would be accurate to assert that for most of this time France was home to a vigorous far-right tradition. Chapter 1 will set the scene.

1 The extreme right in France

An enduring political tradition?

La politique, ce sont des idées.[1]

The far right in France is not the easiest political tradition to pin down and comprehend – if it is in fact one single tradition at all. It is complex in its lineage, chameleon-like in its evolution and often contradictory in its discourse;[2] Winock argues that the extreme right is 'a hard political tendency but a soft concept' (*une tendance politique dure mais un concept mou*).[3] Hainsworth, hinting at the rationale behind the present study, says: 'France has experienced various cycles of extreme right-wing activity... sparking off much debate about the nature and essence of this political family'.[4] Thus, we have to be very careful about the terms we use. Throughout this study we will utilise the terms 'right' and 'extreme right', but we must remember that any attempt to delineate political labels and categories will always be open to criticism.

Defining the right and extreme right

The words 'left' and 'right' are 'central to political debate'.[5] It is customary to begin a study like this with a qualification that indicates both terms are inadequate, but also quite useful in the absence of any better nomenclature. And it would be sensible to keep faith with tradition, because there are plenty of doubters where conventional political terminology is concerned. Sirinelli suggests that the left–right cleavage is almost passé, while O'Sullivan says the term 'right' is 'vague' and 'unfocused'.[6] Moreover, O'Sullivan and Winock argue that labels such as 'the right' are prone to abuse and misuse, and it is difficult to disagree with this general point.[7] Over time, the term has lost much of its value and integrity (in much the same way as 'fascism' has), but, having said this, it is clear that the word 'right' has come to denote a series of definable political attitudes: realism, conservatism, and the belief in established authority and traditional values such as religion, monarchy and hierarchy.

The language may be problematic – and even flawed – but it still has wide currency. Rémond explains its enduring appeal:

Right, Left... the oscillation of these two terms, indissolubly linked by their opposition, paces by its rhythmic tempo all the political history of contemporary France. Men of the Right, men of the Left, parties of the Right, parties of the Left, Leftist bloc, Rightist coalition, Right-Centre, Left-Centre, the persistent hammering of these twin words punctuates 150 years of political struggles... A fundamental principle of French political life, this traditional division of public opinion into two great contrary points of view today remains the key which opens the door to an understanding of France's recent history. This history is bewildering and incoherent if left in an arbitrary and fortuitous disorder.[8]

Rémond might have been writing in 1971, but his point retains validity today. How do we even begin to understand the complexities of France's history – both political and intellectual – without the aid of the 'right–left' political spectrum and its accompanying vocabulary?

As regards the present study, we are at something of an advantage because the term 'right' (just like the term 'left') does have innately French origins. It was during the early years of the Revolution that the distinction emerged, with nobles and clerics sitting on the right-hand side of the National Assembly and representatives of the Third Estate sitting on the left.[9] Those on 'the right' came to be associated with efforts to preserve the King's authority and the established social order and, in time, with counter-revolution. McClelland says the French right 'attacked rationality, universality and democracy and in so doing worked out an opposing position of great coherence and force'.[10]

Many books have been written about the French right – as distinct from the right in general or the French far right – and it would be fair to say that commentators have identified not just one right-wing tradition in France but many, and the Revolution is invariably the starting point and key reference point. McClelland continues: 'If, as the right argued, all France's troubles can be attributed to the Revolution, then it follows that to save the nation, the Revolution and its mythology in the present must be destroyed'.[11] From the last years of the nineteenth century to the first years of the twenty-first, this has been a fact of life.

But, what of the extreme right? What does *it* stand for? Billig outlines the scale of the problem:

The term 'extreme right' is a particularly troubling one to use in political analysis. In ordinary speech and in journalistic writing one could use the term without being misunderstood, and intuitively there seems to be a set of political parties, movements and tendencies which 'go together', for example all outwardly Nazi parties. However, in an academic context this is not sufficient: one would have to justify why such parties are being called both extreme and right-wing. And it is here that the problems start.[12]

Needless to say, it is the aim of the present study to make sense of these 'problems' in the French context. Hainsworth refers to the same issue:

> The concept of the right… is elusive and, by extension, so is that of the extreme right. Of course, it would be wonderfully convenient – though academic wishful thinking – if leaders, parties and movements labelled themselves extreme right to make easier the task of comparison and analysis. Instead, organisations studiously avoid and reject extreme right labelling.[13]

Thus, we are left in a difficult situation. We want to attach labels to 'leaders, parties and movements', and also to political traditions, in a relative and comparative way, but there is always the danger of being simplistic, subjective and even pejorative.

Anderson suggests that moderates on the right probably have more in common with moderates on the left than they do with extremists on the right and seems to imply that the gap between 'right' and 'extreme right' is greater than we think.[14] This is interesting but it should not bother us unduly. We are more interested in the nature of the far right in France rather than its proximity to other traditions, but here we encounter more problems. Is there one extreme right or several? De Maistre, the *émigrés*, the Vendée rebels, the Ultras, Charles X, Boulanger, Barrès, the Ligue des Patriotes, the Anti-Dreyfusard Movement, the AF (Action Française), the fascist *ligues*, Vichy, the Paris Nazis, *Algérie Française*, Poujadism, the FN (Front National). All these individuals and movements have, to a greater or lesser extent, been saddled with the label 'extreme right' over the last 200 years. Do they really have anything in common? And if so, what?

On balance, Hainsworth says the extreme right in France is almost indefinable,[15] and given this fact we must take Winock's advice and not get too hung up on the precise definition of the term. He accepts the term is problematic but says it is still 'used by everybody', and as such is an aid to understanding.[16] Another difficulty comes in the fact that the far right in France is consistently stigmatised and demonised by political opponents, historians and social scientists. It is as if 'extreme' political traditions are devoid of ideas and theory, and exist only as battering-rams for politically correct observers. This kind of polemic is unhelpful and certainly does not assist our quest for a working definition.[17] McClelland counters this negativity and refers to 'the intellectual respectability of extreme right-wing thought in France'.[18] This is a significant statement to make and gives our study a clear rationale.

Historians such as Sirinelli and Winock have explored the extreme right tradition in full.[19] There are no easy answers as to what is of the extreme right, and what is not, but it is clear that the far right possesses many characteristics of the right, but to a more intense and radical degree. On the far right there is also an intransigence and a willingness to resort to extra-parliamentary tactics that are not features of the conventional right.

It is difficult, if not impossible, to construct an 'identikit' extreme right. In every generation the far right seems to re-emerge, often in a new and totally different guise, but a helpful starting-point is Winock's assertion that, whatever the overlaps and complexities, there have been continuities in the extreme right over the last two centuries. He alludes to five: the rejection of parliament, the attachment to strong government, the hatred of socialism and communism, the belief in the closure of frontiers, and a consistent desire to 'rebuild *la maison française*'.[20] We might add others as well: the ability to exploit crisis conditions, the belief in direct action, the use of violence (sometimes), a constant trust in 'charismatic' cult leaders, a tendency to communicate in both populist and intellectual terms (occasionally at the same time) and, more often than not, failure. Billig seeks to distinguish the extreme right from the extreme left, the non-extreme right and fascism. However, he acknowledges a clear overlap between the 'extreme right' and 'fascism' and distinguishes three common features: nationalism/racism, anti-Marxism/communism, and a hostility to democracy.[21]

Anderson, talking about the 1880–1970 period, also moves towards some kind of general characterisation:

> The extreme Right has had its own themes expressed continuously but with varying degrees of vociferousness since the end of the nineteenth century. These have related mainly to various conspiratorial views of politics including Jews, Freemasons, foreigners, bankers and the 'two hundred families'. *Anti-Etatisme* has been a common platform, at various times, of groups threatened by economic change and the fiscal policy of the State. But all the continuities are vague and tenuous. The content of the common attitudes or traditions has been so ill-defined and so much disputed that they have not provided symbols around which durable political organisations could be built.[22]

On the basis of such views, it is possible to argue that there *is* a single extreme-right tradition in France – in effect, a linear progression, through a variety of movements and ideas, from 1789 to the present day. Winock agrees with this general line of thinking, arguing that even though the extreme-right tradition is a 'kaleidoscope', there are important elements of continuity.[23] He says that in each generation the extreme right has a newness about it, but also an element of heritage.[24]

Today's FN is a good example of a far-right movement that is both 'new' and 'old'. It has developed distinctive positions on modern issues such as Europe and immigration, embraced twenty-first century technology in the shape of the internet, and adapted seamlessly to the world of 24-hour news. The ultimate in *mediatique* politicians, Le Pen is in many ways the personification of modernity. That said, it is also true that the FN situates itself in line with tradition. Whether knowingly or unknowingly – and for most of the time it is the former – the movement still honours the memory of *Algérie Française*, still makes use of Poujadist vocabulary, still emphasises Vichyite themes, still talks a rabble-rousing language reminiscent of the inter-war *ligues*, still imitates the populism of Boulanger, still apes the 'rooted' nationalism of Barrès, and still associates itself with anti-revolutionary and counter-revolutionary politics. The same could be said of Pétain's wartime regime and the radical right of the late nineteenth century, for they too adapted themselves to a new political context and defined themselves in modern terms, but at the same time were not frightened of drawing on elements of the past to help expand their appeal.

Historians and the French right

In Europe and America Eatwell and O'Sullivan identify five 'types' of right: 'reactionary', 'radical', 'moderate', 'extreme' and 'new', and this typology will be a useful reference point for the duration of this study.[25] Eatwell says it is 'difficult to find a common linking strand in right-wing thought' because there are 'significant differences' and 'contradictions' across the spectrum.[26] Again, this point is worth bearing in mind as our examination of the French right-wing tradition progresses.

In his classic study, Rémond pinpoints three 'families' within the main tradition of the French right: Orleanism, nationalism/Bonapartism and Ultracism.[27] Interestingly, though, he rarely talks explicitly about 'extremism', nor does he give much credibility to the notion of a French fascist tradition.[28] Sternhell, Milza and Soucy disagree with Rémond in that they do identify a fascist tradition. Sternhell says that France offered 'particularly favourable conditions' for the growth of fascism (as movement and ideology, rather than regime).[29] He views French fascism as a cocktail of nationalist and socialist elements and in the period 1880–1920 discerns the birth of 'a mass movement' (*un mouvement de masse*) – in effect, a new 'revolutionary right'.[30] Soucy locates a fascist tradition that in its early phase owed a significant debt to Barrès and by the middle of the twentieth century had given birth to a 'definite ideology' and was 'highly moralistic, highly serious-minded'.[31] Milza, meanwhile, traces the history of French fascism from the 1880s to the 1980s.[32]

Arnold's edited volume highlights the diversity of the 'radical right'. This political family is depicted as broad-ranging and home to anti-Semitic, fascist, collaborationist, neo-Nazi, new-rightist and extreme-right currents.[33] For his part, Sirinelli refers to *Ultracisme*, and then Legitimism, as the 'true right'. He argues that a new right was born in the late nineteenth century and, in this regard, talks about 'the dawn of political modernity'.[34] During the last century he identifies both a parliamentary and an anti-parliamentary right; in the post-1945 period he refers continually to *les droites*, and after 1965 he pinpoints an 'extreme right' and also a 'new right'.[35] Anderson examines the political and intellectual history of France after 1880 and locates conservative, counter-revolutionary and nationalist strands to the broad tradition.[36] He attempts to sum up the essence of the right:

> A simple prejudice has been widely shared among French politicians, since the failure to restore the monarchy in the 1870s, that to be of the Right implies association with the forces of the past... Groups accrete to the Right as a result of changing circumstances. No issue or theme defines the Right for any extended period of time but there nevertheless have been threads running through the politics of the Right since the late nineteenth century. These are clericalism, nationalism, regionalism and the defence of property.[37]

In his 1994 study, Winock identifies two main subtraditions: counter-revolution ('over two centuries it has kept its vigour and its unity of thought')[38] and populism/national-populism ('the goal is not to restore the monarchy but to found a firm-handed regime').[39] He is also happy to countenance a third tradition – fascism – from the 1920s onwards.[40] The title of his 1990 book – *Nationalisme, antisémitisme et fascisme en France* – would suggest that he also conceives of an independent and autonomous anti-Semitic tradition.[41] Austin's exclusive focus is the inter-war period and he recognises a powerful far right and conservative right. He concludes that the 'ideological differences' between these two factions was 'often buried, especially between 1934 and 1938 when conservatives and extremists shared a common commitment to recapturing political power'.[42] This example helps us to understand the way in which right-wing traditions can fuse.

Petitfils talks about the extreme-right tradition as a combination of *le nationalisme français* and *la tentation fasciste*, but underpinned by 'the old traditionalist and counter-revolutionary current'.[43] He argues that these three traditions are very different and that, over time, far-right activists have had their fall-outs but, he says, what is undeniable is the 'permanence and renewal of ideological themes' and 'the multiple points of convergence that go to form the unity of this political family'.[44] The dichotomy at the heart of the extreme-right tradition is clear. There may be many different phases but there is also a 'tradition of thought unbroken since the Revolution'.[45]

Although historians are divided on how to break down and classify the right, it is possible to synthesise their ideas, and it is clear that we should talk in the plural rather than the singular. And as we will discover, some right-wing traditions are particularly relevant to a study of the extreme right, while others are less so.[46]

Right-wing 'families': the counter-revolutionary right

The counter-revolutionary – or reactionary[47] – tradition is the most enduring on the right and, at the same time, is crucial in helping us to understand the essence of the extreme right. As we noted earlier, McClelland argues that the most important characteristic of the right in general, and thus of the extreme right, is its hostility to the French Revolution and, more specifically, the values that emerged from the events of 1789.[48] On an intellectual level, Joseph de Maistre fired the first shots:

> There is a *satanic* element in the French Revolution which distinguishes it from any other revolution known or perhaps that will be known. Remember the great occasions – Robespierre's speech against the priesthood, the solemn apostasy of the priests, the desecration of objects of worship, the inauguration of the goddess of Reason, and the many outrageous acts by which the provinces tried to surpass Paris: these all leave the ordinary sphere of crimes and seem to belong to a different world.[49]

It is because of passages like this that de Maistre is commonly viewed as the founding father not only of the counter-revolutionary right, but of the right and the far right in France. O'Sullivan describes him as the personification of 'reactionary conservatism'.[50]

In terms of action, the main players were the Vendée rebels, the *émigrés* and members of the Court (primarily, the King and Queen) – actors who exhibited an 'excessive sentimentality'.[51] It is a mistake, however, to associate counter-revolutionary values with the decade 1789–99 alone, for the Counter-Revolution is an idea rather than a period of time. In the early nineteenth century the torch was passed on to the Ultras (the 'pure' *émigrés* of the 1790s) and they put their faith in a 'mystic conception of the monarchy'.[52] Extreme royalism reinvented itself as 'Legitimism' following the anti-Ultra revolution of 1830, and it was to trade under this name right up until its demise in the last quarter of the nineteenth century. *Ultracisme* is examined in depth in Chapter 2, but the impact of this political force can be seen throughout the book, and throughout French history.

Extreme-right movements in the twentieth century also exhibited a strong dislike of the Revolution: from the pro-restoration Action Française through to Vichy – which banned the 1789 *Déclaration* and replaced the revolutionary triptych of *Liberté, Egalité, Fraternité* with *Travail, Famille, Patrie* – and the FN, which in 1989 campaigned against the idea of 'celebrating' the 200th anniversary of the event.[53] McClelland says that, 'what unites the right ideologically in France is the fundamental attack on reason and the rights of man'.[54]

Out of this basic position – an inbred mistrust of the Revolution and all it stands for – have emerged other related standpoints, most obviously a critique of the left. Those on the far right have viewed nineteenth- and twentieth-century socialists and communists as the chief benefactors of the Revolution's inheritance and, as such, they have demonised ideas and movements of the left. This has been consistent, and in different eras different organisations have suffered: the Jacobins in the 1790s, the liberals and constitutionalists during the Restoration, Dreyfusards in the 1890s, the Cartel des Gauches and the Front Populaire in the inter-war period, Resistance forces during the Second World War, and the Parti Socialiste (PS) and Parti Communiste Français (PCF) in the contemporary period. At the height of the Cold War, Le Pen explained his antipathy towards the left:

> Today the USSR and communism constitute the main threat to our liberties and our lives… Communism is an economic system of stupidity and imbecility and this has been demonstrated to good effect by the material results of almost 70 years of slavery and brutality.[55]

Others have couched their anti-leftism in more sophisticated terms, but the message has invariably been similar. Hainsworth recognises that anti-communism is not the sole preserve of the extreme right, but in his view it still remains 'a longstanding attribute'.[56]

In addition to anti-leftist political warfare, movements of the far right have also engaged in attacks on basic concepts like democracy. Vichy banned elections and the *ligues* of the inter-war years yearned for the complete overhaul of the democratic system. Some individuals on the far right have engaged with the democratic process – Le Pen since the 1970s, Poujade in the 1950s and Boulanger and Barrès in the 1880s and 1890s – but their main instinct has always been to oppose it and campaign instead for some kind of Utopian alternative. Barrès is a good case in point. Campaigning as a Boulangist in 1898, he demanded: 'Revision of the Constitution with the aim of giving universal suffrage its full and complete sovereignty, particularly by means of the municipal referendum'.[57] The intention here is noble, but the language is vague.

The far right's hatred of the Revolution resurfaces in its virulent anti-republicanism. Just as today the FN offers an in-depth critique of the Fifth Republic – and actually proposes the establishment of a 'Sixth Republic'[58] – so the Poujadists and *Algérie Française* activists of the 1950s campaigned against the Fourth Republic on account of: (a) its 'insensitivity' to small businesses; and (b) its weakness in the face of Arab nationalists. Likewise, the Third Republic was dogged from birth by protest and agitation on the radical right. The Ligue des Patriotes condemned the regime's lack of interest in claiming back the 'lost territories' of Alsace and Lorraine, while Boulanger criticised the corruption and selfishness of parliamentary *députés* and Barrès condemned the 'anti-national' policies of successive governments. The anti-Dreyfusards of the 1890s synthesised these ideas and were close to bringing the regime to its knees. Their *coup d'état* failed, but their assault on the hated Republic was a milestone and left a significant legacy.

Nonetheless, it was probably Maurras who crafted the most compelling critique of republicanism. In 1899 the AF leader contrasted the Third Republic with the royalist regime he yearned for:

The ridiculous republic, one and indivisible, that we know so well, will no longer be the prey of ten thousand invisible, uncontrollable little tyrants; instead thousands of little republics of every sort, 'domestic' republics like families, 'local' republics like towns and provinces, 'intellectual' and 'professional' republics like associations, will freely administer their own affairs, guaranteed, coordinated and directed as a whole by one sole power which is permanent, that is to say personal and hereditary and with an interest in the preservation and development of the state… Whereas the citizen of the French Republic is left only with his own meagre individual powers to protect him against the mighty state machine, the citizen of the new kingdom of France will find himself a member of all kinds of strong and free communities (family, town, province, professional organisation etc.) which will deploy their strength to protect him from any injustice.[59]

The *ligues* of the 1920s and the 1930s shared Maurras' dislike of the Republic, but argued for some kind of firm executive government rather than the return of the kings.

Pétain and his acolytes blamed the pre-1940 regime for the Fall of France and in so doing absolved the military. They talked about the 'decadence' of the Third Republic and one pro-Vichy writer spoke of 'this hovel we have lived in for 70 years'.[60] For Pétain, the Republic was the Revolution by proxy, and it is no surprise that Vichy propaganda played so heavily on the weakness and fragility of the pre-1940 regime and the intrinsic stability and strength of the post-1940 regime – or so things were perceived.[61]

At certain junctures, the corollary of this critique has been a call for 'Conservative Revolution'.[62] The AF patented this slogan but Pétain and others also took it on board. The belief was that France, somehow, had to go backwards to go forwards. However, in saying this, we should note the fact that since 1880 many groups on the far-right fringes of French politics have viewed themselves not as conservatives and reactionaries, but as radicals. At one point or another, Boulanger and Le Pen have defined themselves as 'revolutionaries', and have even placed themselves explicitly within the French revolutionary tradition.[63]

As a footnote to this discussion, it should be said that extreme nostalgia sometimes substitutes itself for counter-revolutionary zeal. In the 1950s Poujade looked on small-town, pre-supermarket France as a 'golden age', and in the same decade the hardline Algerian rebels displayed a powerful attachment to France's imperial past. But in general terms it is accurate to characterise the far-right tradition as, first and foremost, counter-revolutionary. McClelland claims that, 'if, as the right has argued, all France's troubles can be attributed to the Revolution, then it follows that to save the nation, the Revolution and its mythology in the present must be destroyed'.[64]

Nationalism and national-populism

The national-populist tradition is younger than the counter-revolutionary tradition, but equally imposing. Nationalism is not exclusive to the extreme right – on the contrary – but it is nevertheless a core element of its heritage.

It is tempting to argue that, since 1880, nationalism has been an ever-present characteristic of the far right. Anderson writes:

> The beautifully expressed and eclectic nationalist sentiments of Maurice Barrès have been very widely held. Many of his ideas were typical of a European wide intellectual climate of the 1890s. The sense of decadence, hostility to liberal democracy and big city civilisation, and condemnation of corrupt and unheroic modern society were attitudes... [that] reached their apotheosis in the Vichy regime.[65]

Winock goes further and argues that 'two hundred years of uninterrupted "decadence" ' has had profound consequences for *la nation française.*[66]

Indeed, since the late nineteenth century, those on the far right have generally championed a bi-polar conception of the world. There is 'France' and there is 'Anti-France'. *France pour les Français* nationalists have aligned themselves with some or all of the following: 'language', *le peuple*, 'culture', 'roots', *le tricolore*, 'religion', 'soil', *la terre*, 'blood', 'Joan of Arc', *enracinement*, 'the military', 'eternal values', *les petits gens*, 'agriculture', 'Empire', *le chef de l'état*, 'ancestry' and 'the regions'. At the same time, they have attacked all evidence of 'Anti-France', whether 'Jews', 'socialists', 'immigrants', 'cosmopolitans', 'foreigners', 'internationalists', 'gypsies', *metèques*, 'revolutionaries', 'freemasons', 'Germans', *philosophes*, 'Arabs', 'half-castes', 'disease', 'mosques', *foulards*, 'the French Revolution', 'protestants' or 'AIDS'. This conceptualisation is graphic but at the same time simplistic and reveals much about the black-and-white mentality of the extreme right.

According to Winock and Hainsworth, the national-populist tradition encapsulates movements of the late nineteenth century and the late twentieth century (and many in between).[67] With the advent of the Third Republic and mass politics in the 1870s, a new type of right emerged – modern, radical and embodied by the new icons: Barrès, Boulanger and Déroulède.[68] It sought to adapt itself to the circumstances of the moment and to engage with democratic politics. Winock talks about the 'era of the masses': when 'the people' were viewed as the source of all authority and legitimacy and when anti-Semitism emerged as a new defining characteristic of the far right.[69] This new radical right was populist and nationalist, and in line with Woods' typology it viewed the 'existing social order [as] decadent' and in need of removal.[70] It is possible, without too much trouble, to view three twentieth-century phenomena – the *ligues*, the Poujadist movement and the FN – as part of the same family. The language used by these groupings is significant. In the 1980s an FN propaganda poster stated simply: LE PEN, LE PEUPLE.

National-populism, in the view of Winock, is the product of three core attitudes: 'we are in decadence'; 'the guilty are known'; 'the Saviour has arrived'.[71] And Hainsworth is happy to lump together national-populists from different generations:

> The political rationale of Barrès, Boulanger, Paul Déroulède's Ligue des Patriotes and Le Pen is premissed upon the perceived decadence and moral decline of France, attributable to political mismanagement and retreat from traditional values. Furthermore, Barrès evoked the will of a great country to rediscover its destiny, a theme echoed by Le Pen in his major speeches and writings.[72]

Today, the FN is the embodiment of a virulent brand of closed nationalism and it is strong in its patriotism and vitriolic in its hatreds: North African immigration, 'Americanisation' and the 'Brussels-dominated' EC among others.[73]

In the 1950s Poujadism was both anti-immigrant and pro-empire, while the *Algérie Française* movement was completely loyal to the idea of France as a pro-active imperial power.[74] In the 1940s Vichy stood as the embodiment of ultra-nostalgic patriotism. Although it was fatally compromised by its collaboration with Nazi Germany, Pétain's regime put great emphasis on 'eternal' French values. The Marshal – France's most famous soldier and 'Victor of Verdun' – was the ultimate role-model.

In many ways the backward-looking National Revolution launched by Vichy was the natural sequel to the integral nationalism of Barrès and Maurras. These two writers developed a way of thinking about France that was to influence many, not just Pétain. In the later years of the nineteenth century and the early decades of the twentieth century, they argued that France had to withstand all external pressures and 'threats' (which Maurras grouped together under the epithet 'Anti-France'). They viewed patriotism as 'unconditional' and set great store by the preservation of the *moi national*, even if this meant erecting 'barriers' (more metaphorical than real). Neither Barrès nor Maurras had any truck with the notion of a 'cosmopolitan' France and yearned instead for an integral, homogeneous nation, entirely free of 'alien' influences.

Although Revisionist[75] politicians like Boulanger and Barrès resorted to socialist-sounding platitudes when appropriate (when they needed working-class votes), their obsessive nationalism – and, at times, racism – placed them firmly on the far right. As such, in the decades after 1880 'patriotism' became intrinsically associated with the new radical right. This was a significant change, for before 1880 the left had claimed to be the 'patriotic' party and the monarchical right had given them plenty of ammunition. During the Revolution the princes and aristocrats had shown themselves to be more concerned with cross-monarchical solidarity than the future of the nation, and in 1871 it was the left that wanted to carry on the war and the right that wanted to retreat. So, in this sense, the 1880s were a landmark. Nationalism was now associated with the far right and, what is more, it became a defining characteristic.

Having said that, a couple of important qualifications need to be made: the inter-war *ligues* were pro-German in general outlook, and the policy of collaboration pursued by the Vichy regime was obviously a very unnatural agenda for a 'patriotic' regime.

We could also suggest that blame-allocation is a long-standing feature of the far right.[76] Hainsworth says that, 'nourished by defeatism and anxious for redress, the extreme right has found little difficulty in pinpointing scapegoats for France's failures: Jews, Freemasons, foreigners, communists and other allegedly alien influences'.[77] This kind of mentality is a continuum. Barrès' view that foreign workers were 'parasites' (espoused in the late 1880s)[78] finds an echo in Le Pen's belief that France is suffering an 'invasion' of North African immigrants (expounded throughout the 1980s and 1990s and in the first years of the twenty-first century). There have been other graphic illustrations of nationalism veering off into xenophobia: the insularity of the AF and Vichy, the ideology of 'superiority' advanced by the *ligues*, and the anti-Arab discourse of Poujade and the *pieds noirs* in the 1950s.

Likewise, anti-Semitism: a key ingredient in national-populist ideology but not exclusive to it, and not so much a characteristic as a tradition or, in Winock's words, a 'current'.[79] Byrnes explains how Drumont – arguably the most notorious anti-Semite in French history – was able to connect with people in the 1880s:

> [He] brought into his antisemitic books both the racy, journalistic style and the eagerness to bluster and offend which had been characteristic of some of his earlier writings... Drumont's volumes were not only skilfully written, but they were an expert blend of true and false. He scattered attractive anecdotes throughout his works, giving them an interesting concrete and personal element... Provincial readers were attracted by his intimate descriptions of Paris society at its worst, while romantic souls enjoyed his musical treatment of mediaeval France and of the beauties of the countryside... *La France juive* not only became the most widely read book in France, but it also prepared the way for a whole series of books by Drumont on the same theme.[80]

In many ways Drumont viewed anti-Semitism as an ideal way of tapping into people's preoccupations and, thus, a means towards the ultimate end of making a name for himself. This helps us to understand the essence of national-populism.

Sternhell emphasises the importance of anti-Semitism in the late nineteenth century, arguing that it was instrumental in the emergence of a 'new intellectual climate' and eventually paved the way for fascism.[81] From Drumont and the radical right of the 1880s and 1890s through to the

Maurras, the *ligues* and Pétain, Jew-baiting has been ever present. Even in the post-war period when the extreme right should have known better, the anti-Semitic dimension to Poujadist and FN rhetoric has been there for all to see, and it is for this reason that Wistrich entitles his chapter on French anti-Semitism, 'From Dreyfus to Le Pen'.[82]

The trap we should not fall into is to view all these instances of anti-Semitism as identical. The fact of the matter is that over a period of 120 years several main 'types' have been evident. We should not set too much store by the labels, nor should we assume that the 'families' are mutually exclusive, but it is possible nevertheless to identify a 'cynical' anti-Semitism (as advanced by the anti-Dreyfusards and Laval), a 'xenophobic' anti-Semitism (Barrès, Maurras), a 'sensationalist' anti-Semitism (Drumont, Le Pen) and an 'opportunistic' anti-Semitism (Boulanger, Poujade). Overall, Wistrich confirms that 'the ideological continuity in French antisemitism has shown remarkable persistence'.[83]

We should note finally that it is not just in France that traditions of national-populism and extreme-right politics overlap. Hainsworth talks in global terms:

> Central to the extreme right's discourse is the question of identity, national identity drawing upon language, religion, culture, history and other aspects. Nation, national identity, ethnocentrism: these are at the core of the extreme right's value system. The rhetoric of the extreme right is based upon a vision of the nation supreme, heroic, pure and unsullied by alien forces such as Third World immigration and communist ideology... National-populism, although not simply a preserve of the extreme right, helps largely to differentiate the extreme right from the moderate or traditional right, with the former often able to attract a significant number of voters – working-class, ex-left wing, unemployed, disaffected youth, former abstentionists and first-time voters – temporarily (or otherwise) denied to the latter.[84]

It would also be true to say that many assumptions associated with the national-populist tradition are replicated on the fascist right.

Fascism

Fascism, without doubt, is the most controversial political phenomenon in France. In the words of Winock: *Fascisme à la française ou fascisme introuvable?* ('French fascism or fascism nowhere to be seen?')

Rémond is notoriously sceptical about the existence of fascist movements, never mind a fascist tradition,[85] but other historians are willing to countenance the idea. Eatwell argues that French fascism was more an intellectual phenomenon than a practical political proposition and also identifies a buoyant neo-fascist tradition in France in the decades after 1945.[86]

Sternhell and Soucy are committed to the notion of a French fascism. The former is particularly interested in the period between 1880 and 1914, in which he detects the emergence of a 'pre-fascism' that anticipated the emergence of 'full-blown' fascism in the 1920s and 1930s. His two main theses are that twentieth-century French fascism was an indigenous phenomenon and that, in its 'full-blown' state, it synthesised leftist and rightist assumptions. Soucy's research ties in with much of this, but he puts particular stress on the political ideas of Barrès, 'the first French fascist'.[87]

For his part, Milza identifies a rich, varied and perplexing orbit of movements and ideas. Writing in 1987, he talks about fascism in the past and the present tense and characterises the contemporary species as a product of post-Vichy 'fantasies, obsessions and hatreds'.[88] His main conclusion is that fascism has been remarkably unsuccessful, mainly because of its lack of numbers and the formidable 'republican culture' that exists in France.[89] Winock concurs on this last point – he talks about the 'republican spirit' and the 'reflex of "republican defence" in the face of the far right' – but he delineates a fascist tradition in France beginning only in the 1920s.[90]

Nolte's contribution to the debate is important. He recognises the Action Française movement as one of the 'three faces' of inter-war European fascism, and remarks:

> In spite of all its doctrinal rigidity, the system of Maurras' ideas is of an extent, acuteness, and depth without parallel in the Germany or Italy of that time. The practice of the Action Française anticipates, in the clear simplicity of the rudimentary, the characteristic traits of the infinitely cruder and more wholesale methods used in Italy and Germany. Seen by itself, the Action Française is not an epochal phenomenon. Yet it is, as it were, the missing link demonstrating fascism as a stage in an overall and much older struggle.[91]

This comment helps to put French fascism in a European context and, at the same time, demonstrates the significance of 'early fascism'.

So, from 'early fascism' and 'pre-fascism' – when the idea of fascism existed but the word itself did not[92] – through to 'semi-fascism' and 'neo-fascism', France is an important field of study and, whatever the caveats and qualifications, there is a strong case to be made for the existence of an independent, autonomous fascist tradition running through her intellectual history.

Warner says that 'only a major catastrophe could bring fascism to power in France', and pinpoints 1940 as the moment.[93] However, *fascisme français* was never a reality in the same sense that Italian or German fascism was, but, ironically, this has tended to increase historians' fascination with the subject, rather than lessen it. Griffin states:

> France provides a major case study in the often subtle distinctions which

separate fascism from new forms of radical right that emerged after 1870 such as the anti-Semitic leagues, prototypes of national socialism associated with Boulanger and Barrès, the mainstream *Action Française* or the veteran anti-socialist leagues such as the *Croix de Feu*, which were such a feature of inter-war France.[94]

More rights

The Bonapartist tradition will be of interest to us in the present study, but most historians would agree that, as political leaders, Napoleon I and Napoleon III were devoid of real political ideology and were interested mainly in power and jingoism, and as such could not seriously be considered as being of the 'right' or 'extreme right' in any meaningful sense. However, as Winock notes, Bonapartism did have a significant influence on individuals such as Boulanger and Déroulède and movements such as anti-Dreyfusardism and the inter-war *ligues*. In more specific terms, he identifies a strong plebiscitary, anti-parliamentary continuum.[95] Rémond thinks in the same kind of way, and in Boulangist agitation he locates a Bonapartist-style nationalism.[96]

The Gaullist right was born with General de Gaulle and outlived him. The significance of Gaullism has to be understood, but no-one could argue that it was (or is) 'of the extreme-right'. Indeed, in many senses, it was (and is) unusually hostile to the far right. Not many *Algérie Française* veterans would agree that the Gaullist Party is, to quote Anderson, 'the long-awaited culmination' of right-wing politics![97] There are some significant overlaps between the Gaullist right and the extreme right (for example: 'cult' authoritarian leadership, nationalism and an intense belief in the *grandeur* of France), but we must keep things in perspective.

In the modern era – the 1980s and 1990s in particular – we should acknowledge the emergence of a new right tradition. On a global scale Eatwell interprets the new right as an amalgam of libertarian, *laissez-faire*, traditionalist and mythical thinking, underpinned by a powerful anti-communism.[98] In France *la nouvelle droite* is difficult to pin down, but in de Benoist, the Groupement de Recherche et d'Études pour la Civilisation Européenne (GRECE) and the Club de l'Horloge, France has given birth to a new, distinct and progressive type of right that, over the years, has impacted significantly on Le Pen's FN.[99]

The liberal right – heir to Rémond's Orleanist right – is a significant continuity in French history, but it is of only limited relevance to a study of far-right politics. If it has importance it is in the sense that it contrasts so sharply with the extreme-right tradition.[100] This has not been an exhaustive survey – far from it – but it does help us to understand the main traditions that have underpinned right-wing discourse over the last 200 years.

Given the parameters of this study, it would be fair to say that, of the subtraditions referred to so far, Counter-Revolution (incorporating

Ultracism), nationalism/national-populism, fascism, nationalism/ Bonapartism and the new right are of most relevance. By contrast, Gaullism and the liberal/Orleanist right are of only marginal importance to us. The parameters of this particular study dictate that we leave these two subtraditions on one side. As we will discover, the counter-revolutionary, national-populist and fascist traditions are omnipresent on the far right, and we will now focus on these three 'families' almost exclusively.

A plethora of questions is raised with regard to these central traditions. Which is the most dominant? At what point does each subtradition reach its apogée? In which individual or movement does each subtradition find its best, most graphic embodiment? Which individuals or movements crystallise, in themselves, *all three* subtraditions? Are all three subtraditions alive today? In this chapter, and in the book as a whole, we will touch on all these issues.

It should be reiterated that the nature of these traditions is certainly not cut and dried. On the subject of nationalism, for example, Winock talks about an 'open nationalism' (associated with the left) and a 'closed nationalism' (associated with the right), and also speaks of 'variations and contradictions' within the French nationalist tradition.[101] Similarly, with regard to fascism, Sternhell talks about a 'heterogeneous' and 'ambiguous' phenomenon.[102] These remarks should serve as a warning to us as our investigation proceeds and becomes more detailed.

We should not assume either that these main subtraditions are mutually exclusive. Quite the contrary, in fact, for there are junctures at which all three appear to intersect: most notably, in Barrès (anti-Dreyfusard, arch-nationalist and, arguably, 'the first French fascist'),[103] in the extreme right of the 1930s ('a complex galaxy', according to Winock),[104] and in Vichy (anti-rights of man, personified by super-patriot Pétain, and, to some observers, the best example of authentic 'French fascism').[105]

McClelland also makes an interesting point about inter-tradition relationships. He says that to link someone like de Maistre (in the late eighteenth century) with fascism (in the mid-twentieth) would be absurd. But he goes on to claim that, in reality, there is a connection in that both early nineteenth-century conservatives *and* twentieth-century fascists were reacting to, and rebelling against, the French Revolution and 'certain assumptions about the nature of man and political society'.[106] Likewise, Steiner refers to the way in which counter-revolutionary ideas can emerge 'under the dubious aegis of proto-fascisms or outright fascism'.[107] We should certainly take this point on board, for it is certainly true that relationships may exist where we least expect them. Nonetheless, the fascination of the extreme right lies in the fact that, for most of the time, subtraditions have existed in parallel with each other, each with different emphases and starting-points.

Another way of thinking about the whole issue is to conceive of a political spectrum with a 'space' or 'void' on the extreme right that has been filled by a succession of different parties, movements and ideas. The advantage of this conceptualisation lies in the fact that it takes account of the way in which the extreme right has changed and evolved over time. It also stops us trying to make erroneous connections and linkages between extreme-right movements in different eras – movements that, in reality, have little in common. It is always tempting to think in terms of an extreme-right 'tradition', and we will do exactly this in the course of our investigation. However, it could also be argued that every individual or group in France labelled 'far right' has been unique, and has had very little in common with previous manifestations of this 'thing' we call the extreme right.

Moreover, at times it would seem to be more accurate to talk in terms merely of 'protest' and 'agitation' – and to forget all notions of a specific type of political ideology or a full-blown political tradition. But that is not to deny the validity and usefulness of the schema put forward by Eatwell and O'Sullivan, Rémond, Sternhell, Milza, Soucy, Sirinelli, Anderson, Winock, Petitfils, Hainsworth, and McClelland. Indeed, the frameworks advanced by these commentators will not only help us to focus on the key issues in forthcoming chapters, but will also supply us with vital points of reference.

2 1789–1830 – the Counter-Revolution

Providence and plotting

No revolution is unanimous.[1]

1789   14 July: Fall of the Bastille
1790   July: Civil Constitution of the Clergy
        November: Publication of Burke's *Reflections on the Revolution in France*
1791   21 June: Flight to Varennes
        27 August: Declaration of Pillnitz
        9 November: Law against the *émigrés*
1792   20 April: France declares war on Austria
        9 February: Sequestration of *émigré* land
        22 September: Monarchy abolished
        September: Savoy and Nice occupied by revolutionary armies
        November: Savoy annexed by France
1793   21 January: Louis XVI executed
        March: Vendée revolt begins
        October: Lyon revolt; dechristianisation begins
        4 December: Vendée rebels defeated
1795   February: Vendée pacified
        July: *Émigré* army defeated at Quiberon
1796   Publication of de Maistre's *Considerations on France*
1799   Napoleon's coup
1800   Pacification of the West
1804   May: Proclamation of Empire
1814   Allies invade France
        6 April: Napoleon abdicates
        4 June: Charter proclaimed
1815   Napoleon's 'Hundred Days'
        August: Election of 'Incredible Chamber'
1816   September: Chamber dissolved
1821   Ultras enter government

1824   March: Ultra election victory
        September: Death of Louis XVIII; Charles X succeeds him
1825   Sacrilege Law; Émigré Indemnity Law
        May: Coronation of Charles X
1828   Martignac government
1829   Polignac government
1830   25 July: Charles X issues Four Ordinances
        28–30 July: Revolution in Paris
        2 August: Abdication of Charles X

In *Les 50 Mots clefs de la Révolution française*, Péronnet pinpoints three terms of special relevance to this chapter: *Contre-Révolution*, *émigrés* and *Vendée*.[2] It is doubtful whether this selection does adequate justice to the significance of the anti-1789 revolt, but it is at least a start. One thing is for sure: if Péronnet is limiting himself to only three words on 'opposition to the Revolution', he has probably chosen the three most obvious and illuminating.

The story of the extreme right begins with the Counter-Revolution. Cobb says it was 'always highly fragmented and regionalistic', but as an era it endured longer than the Revolution.[3] Roberts claims that in many ways the Counter-Revolution anticipated the Revolution, and did not merely respond to it. Opposition to reform, he argues, began in the 1770s.[4] Thompson agrees:

> The counter-revolution was not a new thing: it was as old as the revolution itself. It rested upon the discontents of a nobility deprived of titles, exemptions, and privileges; of a church robbed of its wealth, and resentful of secular control; and of a magistrate ousted from profits and emoluments. There was, indeed, a sense in which the counter-revolution was even older than the revolution.[5]

In Chapter 1 we described how the opening shots of the Revolution provoked one party – dominated by nobles and clerics – to distance itself from the representatives of the Third Estate, and in so doing create a 'right' and a 'left' for the first time. We will now move on to consider how the right developed and evolved, and eventually metamorphosed into the movement we know as the Counter-Revolution. But in using the term 'movement' we should not look upon the Counter-Revolution as a united and homogeneous phenomenon. The truth is quite the opposite. What we find is something of a rag-bag: a collection of failed campaigns, badly thought-out crusades and would-be saviour figures. There was agitation, but no real overall framework.

The era of sustained counter-revolution can be split in two. Clearly, the decade following 1789 witnessed the opening burst of counter-revolutionary action, and this chapter will focus predominantly on these years. The Restoration era (1814–30) was the second main phase of counter-revolutionary activity, when, after the Napoleonic era, the Bourbons were restored to the throne and the Ultras were allowed to exert influence at the apex of French political life.[6]

In this chapter we will examine the writings of Joseph de Maistre, the man now viewed as the founding father of the French right (and extreme right) and the most important representative of the Theocrats – those who, in Muret's words, 'hated the Revolution and all its works indiscriminately, and hoped to bring about a complete return to the past'.[7] We will also analyse the main aspects of the Counter-Revolution 'on the ground': the actions and attitudes of King Louis XVI and his Queen, Marie Antoinette; the nature and rationale of the emigration; the origins and importance of the Vendée revolt; and the essence of ultra-royalism as a political creed.

At this point it is necessary to make some general introductory remarks. First, 'Counter-Revolution' is not just a period, but an idea. Obviously in this chapter we will be discussing the counter-revolutionary era, but we should not be blind to the fact that the idea of counter-revolution outlived Louis XVI, Joseph de Maistre and Charles X. The Revolution remained a battleground throughout the nineteenth and twentieth centuries, and into the twenty-first. McClelland says, 'the French right has been complaining about the French Revolution ever since it happened... [it] has always had to confront that original and startling victory of the left'.[8] Needless to say, individuals and movements on the extreme right retained their counter-revolutionary zeal, even when the period of revolution was over.

Over two centuries and more, the term 'counter-revolutionary', like many others in the historical lexicon, has lost precision. Roberts states: 'Distortion and misunderstanding were built into the revolutionary conflict from the beginning. Who was, or was not, a friend of the Revolution lay very much in the eye of the beholder so that at some stage or other almost everybody could find themselves denounced as a counter-revolutionary agent.'[9] It is a fact that during the 1790s individuals could be denounced as a 'counter-revolutionary' *whatever* their political affiliations. Forrest argues that the word is deceptive, while Péronnet suggests that the terms 'revolution' and 'counter-revolution' are always going to be relative.[10] Equally, we should not confuse 'anti-revolutionary' and 'counter-revolutionary' attitudes.[11] The former entailed hostility, while the latter presupposed sustained opposition. Lewis talks about the 'anti-' position in derogatory terms, equating it to 'apathetic or sporadic resistance', arguing that, by contrast, the 'counter-' standpoint attracted 'a minority, albeit a very dedicated one'.[12] Roberts looks at things in a different way, arguing that the Anti-Revolution was 'directed *against* the Revolution' while the Counter-Revolution was '*for* the restoration of the structure of the *ancien régime*'. He implies that many popular rebellions within France in the 1790s were just *anti-revolutionary* outbursts.[13] Hufton points out that this debate about nomenclature carried on into the bicentenary celebrations.[14]

Moving on, we should be aware of the religious 'continuity' at work within the Counter-Revolution and, in addition, the importance of the 'theocratic school' – thinkers who 'deduced the principles of their system from religious considerations such as the will of God, the workings of Providence, and the good of mankind'.[15] Individuals such as de Maistre and Bonald were at the forefront of this group and, with good reason, Anderson claims that 'religious belief was inextricably involved with the counter-revolution'.[16] However, we need to be aware that a 'historical school' of counter-revolutionary theorists stressing 'positivist and experimental analysis' also existed, and this faction came to the fore in the early twentieth century with Maurras.[17]

But there was also change and evolution on the reactionary right. The Counter-Revolution was not a static or homogeneous phenomenon but rather fluid and ever-changing. As Doyle makes plain, in and around 1790 it metamorphosed from Court-based intrigue into genuine popular rebellion.[18] In time it would acquire significant European and intellectual dimensions, and also encapsulate swathes of women – 'modest personages who were prepared to turn their backs on the national line'.[19] By the time of the Directory, the Counter-Revolution was a significant domestic force, advancing 'in the Councils... [and] at a varying pace, in the provinces'. *Émigrés* and priests were welcomed back into the country, the White Terror acquired its victims, and anti-religious legislation was repealed.[20] This fluidity was an asset but also perhaps a problem.

Finally, Godechot puts forward the distinction between 'doctrine' and 'action' in the Counter-Revolution.[21] This is a useful device that emphasises the difference between 'thinkers' and 'doers', and is echoed by Péronnet, who defines the Counter-Revolution as an amalgam of 'movements of ideas and action led against the Revolution'.[22] This is an interesting way of conceptualising the French right, and will be referred to throughout this chapter and others.

Doctrine: de Maistre and *Considerations*

Steiner says that 'the most rigorous foundation for a doctrine of counter-revolution is theological'.[23] Forrest states: 'Just as the Revolution had its theorists and intellectual defenders, so did the counter-revolution.'[24] Godechot argues that the counter-revolutionary movement was 'first of all ideological and doctrinal'.[25] Thus, any discussion of the period 1789–99 must begin with Joseph de Maistre, whose key work, *Considerations on France*, was published in 1796. Parker interprets de Maistre's treatise as 'a mystical, God-fearing response to the upheaval of the Revolution'.[26] Beik argues that the book crystallised ideas for the French right (and thus, by extension, for the extreme right).[27] And Soltau says that 'the world has never been without people who thought the clock of time could be put back, who saw in the rejected past the true goal of mankind'.[28] Whatever the verdict, it is clear that de Maistre viewed the Revolution as a seminal event, a turning-point, a 'chance for regeneration'.[29]

As a piece of literature, *Considerations* was of profound significance. The French Revolution had 'met its intellectual match',[30] but de Maistre was not the only individual to offer a concerted critique of 1789. Bonald, Chateaubriand, Lamennais, Mallet du Pan, Rivarol, Ferrand, d'Antraigues, Barruel, and Duvoisin also offered their own specific counter-revolutionary insights,[31] and so did writers outside France – most notably Burke.[32] These theorists may have been 'aloof' from the action, but they gave the Counter-Revolution an important extra dimension.[33]

There is no doubt that de Maistre's influence was long-lasting. His impact in the late 1790s was marked, but it was during the Restoration that his writings assumed pivotal importance.[34] The Ultras of the 1820s might have 'distorted' the essence of his doctrine[35] – de Maistre would not have agreed with everything that was done in his name – but writers like Murray view him as the unofficial theorist of the Restoration and 'spokesman' for the Bourbon Reaction.[36] Others argue that his influence stretched into the second half of the nineteenth century.

De Maistre was born in 1753 and came from Savoy, an Italian province later to be incorporated into France.[37] It is ironic that the founding father of the extreme-right tradition in France should hail from outside her borders, but it is easy to empathise with his situation. The French invasion of Savoy in 1792 forced him into exile and meant he had to 'take sides' on the Revolution.[38] Other aspects of de Maistre's early life are also interesting. He was born the son of a recently ennobled father and a devout mother, and as a young man he pursued legal studies. Aristocracy, Catholicism, law – these were to become central values in his thought system. Phillips says the circumstances of de Maistre's life had a 'profound' impact on his thinking.[39]

Interestingly, de Maistre's attitude to the Revolution evolved over time and was not always a negative one. During the period 1789–91 he could accept much of what the revolutionaries wished for. As a lawyer he was always going to understand the aspirations of the upper Third Estate; indeed, as a young man de Maistre was a liberal conservative, and was actually disciplined for his radicalism by the King of Sardinia. But war and terror – the bywords of 1792–4 – were totally alien to his temperament and placed in jeopardy the peaceful society he yearned for. Greifer suggests that he evolved from conservative to reactionary in a short period of time.[40]

De Maistre felt that France had been punished by Providence for her 'sins' in 1789 and, even though he himself came to personify counter-revolutionary thinking, he was sensible enough to acknowledge the weaknesses and failings of the *ancien régime*.[41] As Murray states, 'de Maistre's apparently impossible request for the re-establishment of the monarchy was not a request for the monarchy which immediately preceded 1789'.[42] This is a good indicator of the Savoyard's realism. But, at the same time, de Maistre puts unquenchable faith in Providence, believing that the Counter-Revolution will come and triumph, just like the Revolution came and triumphed. He never puts a date on it, but he is confident he will be proved right. As such, it is extremely difficult to argue against de Maistre.

So what were the main themes in de Maistre's work? Winock suggests that *Considerations on France* should have been renamed *Religious Considerations on France*.[43] The first line of the book sets the tone: 'We are all bound to the throne of the Supreme Being by a flexible chain which restrains without enslaving us. The most wonderful aspect of the universal scheme of things is the action of free beings under divine guidance.'[44] De Maistre was in awe of God and his work constantly invokes religious imagery. The Revolution is likened to 'evil' and 'original sin', order is viewed as 'angelic' and chaos as 'diabolic', and the author was aghast at the dechristianisation policy pursued by the revolutionaries.[45] In essence, what de Maistre offered was a 'theological interpretation' of events.[46] At the apex of his 'new society' was the Papacy – an institution that unifies earthly and spiritual power.[47] De Maistre argued that French society was in desperate need of 'Pope and Executioner';[48] in other words, more religious devotion (order) and more 'policing' (less disorder). There is a constant emphasis on discipline and control, and it was in this sense that de Maistre and the Theocrats were viewed as 'anti-Revolution authoritarians'.[49] According to Muret they based their doctrine on religious authority rather than compromise.[50]

De Maistre displayed an 'unflagging' belief in Providence.[51] In his mind, Providence, and nothing else, caused the French Revolution:

> Every nation, like every individual, has a mission which it must fulfill…
> [France] was at the head of the religious system, and it was not without
> reason that her king was called *most Christian*… However, as she has
> used her influence to pervert her vocation and to demoralise Europe, it
> is not surprising that terrible means must be used to set her on her true
> course again.[52]

He uses coded language – the phrase 'terrible means' equates to 'revolution' – but he was sure that Counter-Revolution would follow Revolution, just like night follows day. Again, God would be responsible. Steiner says that 'Maistre takes it as self-evident that divine providence commands the lives of nations and of individuals'.[53]

The author of *Considerations* believed in the 'natural' social and political order. He argues for inequality, privilege and hierarchy, and also acknowledges the role of 'intermediate' social bodies such as family, commune and province. In this sense his doctrine was 'strongly anti-individualistic'.[54] Furthermore, he believed that man has 'duties' rather than 'rights': a position that marked him out as an arch-exponent of the traditionalist, counter-revolutionary right and signalled his profound opposition to 1789 (and the 'rights of man').

Moreover, de Maistre placed a special premium on the restoration of hereditary kings. He viewed the monarchy as a kind of social cement, but was realistic enough to know that it must become less corrupt and more religious. Reform was always going to be a problematic idea for him to embrace but he knew that, in the aftermath of 1789, limited and measured change was essential. On the one hand, he wanted to make the monarchy less arbitrary; on the other, he wished to establish a new theocratic regime. Either way, de Maistre knew the *ancien régime* was finished. But he still believed that the monarch had God-given power and that within certain parameters he, or she, had absolute authority.[55] He remained convinced that monarchy was 'natural' for France.[56]

The corollary of de Maistre's belief in 'divine' monarchy was his contempt for 'man-made' constitutions, abstract ideas and 'philosophisme'.[57] Murray says that de Maistre wanted 'stability, unity, and continuity' – three things the *philosophes* put in doubt.[58] The Savoyard believed that constitutions were 'natural' and 'organic' and thus, by implication, condemned the written constitutions of 1791, 1793 and 1795.[59] In one of the most compelling parts of *Considerations*, he states:

> What a prodigious number of laws has resulted from the labours of three French National Assemblies! From July 1st to October, 1791, the National Assembly passed 2,557. The Legislative Assembly passed, in eleven and a half months 1,712. The National Convention, from the first day of the Republic until 4 Brumaire year IV (October 26, 1795), passed in 57 months 11,210. Total 15,479... Astonishment must quickly change to pity when the futility of these laws is recalled... Why are there so many laws? Because there is no legislator.[60]

In the light of this, de Maistre demanded that assemblies and conventions give way to God and King. He poured ridicule on the individuals at the vanguard of the Revolution: 'It has been said with good reason that the French Revolution leads men more than men lead it... The very villains who appear to guide the Revolution take part in it only as simple instruments; and as soon as they aspire to dominate it, they fall ingloriously'.[61] It does not need stating, but he had very little faith in human beings.

More fundamentally, de Maistre attacked intellectuals, reason and the very notion of universal rights. He viewed the Enlightenment as a dangerous and foolhardy enterprise and the Revolution as 'the political manifestation of this Satanic revolt'.[62] But de Maistre was convinced that in the end Christianity would triumph over philosophy.

In its own terms, de Maistre's thought system is coherent. But weaknesses do abound: for example, the over-reliance on Providence – what Steiner calls 'theological fatalism'[63] – and the paradox inherent in an intellectual criticising intellectualism and other intellectuals. There are other criticisms too. De Maistre exaggerated key aspects of the Revolution in order to legitimise his own ideas, and similarly it is clear that he paid scant attention to the Revolution's social and economic dimensions – a serious flaw. Overall, the author of *Considerations* peddles a fairly simplified interpretation of history: one in which the monarchy could do very little wrong. Winock says that de Maistre was impotent – a 'spectator' with 'no programme', a man happy just to 'wait' for things to happen.[64] Soltau says he 'destroys better than he builds'.[65] Lebrun, summing up, states: 'Joseph de Maistre's status as a symbol of reactionary opposition to the spirit of modern civilisation is possibly beyond revision.'[66]

Action I: the Court and the *émigrés*

It is doubtful whether there was much interchange between de Maistre and the other main players in the Counter-Revolution. Of course, the writers and intellectuals known as the Theocrats would have traded ideas and influenced each other, but it is another thing entirely to establish some kind of definite relationship between de Maistre and, say, the *émigrés*, even though he himself was one. No doubt, after the publication of *Considerations* in 1796 some nobles and clerics would have been aware of de Maistre and his ideas, but the book was not a blueprint for action; the fact that it was published in 1796, and not earlier, suggests that it was merely a *cri de coeur*. As if for therapeutic purposes, de Maistre wanted to make a statement.

Counter-Revolutionary 'action' started seven years earlier. The various events of 1789 each had a knock-on effect; and by 1790 the Counter-Revolution 'was everywhere'.[67] Even though counter-revolutionary activity achieved very little and was in many senses shambolic, the nature of this activity and the rationale behind it is significant. 'At the top' the Counter-Revolution incorporated two main elements: the Court and the *émigrés* (although there was a clear element of overlap). There was also agitation from small counter-revolutionary groupings inside France, such as Salon Français and Vivarais.

The Court comprised the King, the Queen and the 'Austrian Committee' (*Le Comité Autrichien* – the name given by opponents to the group of plotters at work within the Court).[68] The Court put up a front: it gave the impression that it was 'of' the Revolution, or not necessarily against it, but at heart, and by instinct, it was fundamentally opposed to it. This, as one can imagine, was a tricky pose to strike, and we should probably applaud the fact that the Court was able to maintain the façade for so long, rather than criticise it unduly for eventually succumbing and collapsing.

It is helpful to distinguish between the attitudes and actions of the King and those of the Queen. Louis XVI had his weaknesses and failings, but on the whole he was well liked. Throughout the period June 1789 to September 1792 he remained the nation's figurehead, even though the Revolution was evolving and radicalising. Many of his actions, however, are open to interpretation. In April 1791, he announced to the foreign powers that he counted the French Revolution and the Constitution 'among his titles to glory' and was honoured to be known as the 'Restorer of French Liberty' – but this was deemed to be a pre-Varennes stalling tactic.[69] He accepted the 1791 Constitution – but 'with his tongue in his cheek',[70] and he signed

France's declaration of war in 1792 against Austria – but at the same time he and his wife were pleading with monarchs around Europe to come and rescue them. So, behind the scenes Louis was playing a double game.

There were two key moments when Louis did reveal his hand. In November 1791 he vetoed a decree prescribing death to all *émigrés*, but the turning-point in the Revolution had come five months earlier when the King and Queen had tried to escape the country. This was not their first effort to flee, but it was certainly the most celebrated. They were caught at Varennes in north-east France on 22 June 1791, and thereafter had no real legitimacy left.[71] Louis' diary entry for the 22 June does not really convey the profound significance of the date:

> Departed for Varennes at 5am/6am,
> Dinner at Saint-Menehoul,
> Arrived Châlons 10am,
> Took supper and slept at *l'ancienne intendance*.[72]

The King may not have known it, but – in the words of Rudé – Varennes 'had an electrifying effect and destroyed many illusions'. Most notably, it brought European war closer and convinced some monarchs of the merit of not intervening in French affairs.[73] After Varennes, Louis was suspended and his prerogatives withdrawn, and the consensus among historians is that he 'died' in the eyes of his subjects after the escape attempt. In January 1793 he was executed. By way of a footnote, Godechot argues that all escape efforts were 'fiascos'.[74]

It would be pushing it to say that the King was an ideological creature – particularly as some on the right saw him as a 'dupe' of the Jacobins[75] – but between 1789 and 1791 he was definitely the pivot around which the Counter-Revolution revolved. However, events moved quickly, and Murray argues that, following Louis' acceptance of the 1791 Constitution, the centre of counter-revolutionary activity shifted from Paris to Koblenz.[76]

The Queen met the same ultimate demise, but her story is different. As a fairly intransigent political operator and a foreigner – she was known pejoratively as *l'Autrichienne* – Marie Antoinette was never well liked in France. She was more overt than Louis in her political attitudes, and on the revolutionary side hatred of her went hand in hand with hatred of Austria.[77] Letters written by the Queen, and found later in the Tuileries, confirm the fact that throughout the early 1790s she was actively seeking foreign rescue as de facto head of the 'Austrian Committee'. Blanning puts its actions in perspective:

> As one of the most reliable of contemporary memoirs recorded, everyone professed to know the country's foreign policy was being run by an 'Austrian Committee' headed by Marie Antoinette, that all of France's ambassadors at foreign courts were supporters of the old regime, that

secret emissaries were being sent from the Tuileries to Koblenz (the headquarters of the *émigrés*) and Vienna to plot counter-revolution and that 'in short, the Court had a constitutional exterior and an anti-constitutional interior'. Although paranoia was one of the most common and potent of revolutionary emotions, these convictions were well founded. The court *was* conspiring against the Revolution and *was* seeking the armed intervention of the European powers.[78]

Historians are agreed on this matter. Rudé, for example, talks about the 'desertion' of the Court, arguing that 'the King – and still more the Queen – could not be trusted'.[79]

The King and Queen were not only divided – Louis, allegedly, was not very interested in his wife's anxieties[80] – but in Vovelle's words did not have enough 'elbow room' or political nous to follow an effective counter-revolutionary strategy.[81] Even so, their attitudes had significant ramifications. For a start, the Court's tactics gave revolutionary factions an excellent opportunity to play on the 'treachery' of the King. The Brissotins, as the pro-war faction, were particularly interested in Louis' posturings, and once they sensed his loyalty was in question they argued even more enthusiastically for the merits of European war. They felt that war would eradicate the Revolution's enemies within both Europe and France, and would also expose the King and his 'real' attitude. Louis, meantime, felt that he could not lose: if the military campaign went well, he might benefit as the man who signed the official declaration of war; if it went badly, the Revolution might begin to crumble and, again, he might emerge stronger as a result.

The monarchs of Europe were 'extras' in the drama of the Revolution and, as noted earlier, were viewed as potential saviours by the King and Queen.[82] But they were strangely quiet for most of the time. Each European leader seemed to have his or her own reasons for not wanting to become involved. The monarchs signed the Declaration of Pillnitz – announcing that they would intervene in France with the agreement of all signatories – but this document was not worth the paper it was written on.[83] There were constant rumours of invasion, and of joint military ventures with the *émigrés* and the rebels in the Vendée, but nothing of substance occurred. Robespierre talked about 'enemies within and enemies without'; however, he was in serious danger of flattering his opponents.[84]

It is difficult to separate out the Court and the *émigrés* because there was a clear overlap in terms of personnel and attitudes, but Thompson helps us to understand the specific nature of emigration:

The French word *émigré* has the same derivation as the English word 'emigrant', but a different meaning. Both languages have another word – *réfugié*, 'refugee' – for one who is driven abroad by political or religious persecution. An 'emigrant' is one who leaves his native land to better his condition elsewhere. An *émigré* leaves his native land because he dislikes its government. An *émigré* works for the overthrow of the new regime. An *émigré* is ready to join in a foreign invasion of his country in order to regain his position and power. The *émigré par excellence* was the French aristocrat of the revolutionary period. He had been demoralised by lack of political responsibility. He was cut off by his caste from every-day contacts with other classes. He was often unfit to adapt himself to the ideas and institutions of a regime which asked him to share liberty and equality with his banker and his baker.[85]

It is also the case that, while at large, the *émigrés* saw themselves as a kind of 'Court-in-exile' or 'Court-in-waiting'. Their sense of their own importance was clear, but they were to impress no-one on their nomadic trek round Europe. In Pasquier's eyes the whole enterprise was flawed:

> Who... reasoned out the emigration? It has oftentimes been asked how so extraordinary a resolution came to be taken; how it had entered the minds of men gifted with a certain amount of sense that there was any advantage to be derived from abandoning all the posts where they could still exercise power; of giving over to the enemy the regiments they commanded, the localities over which they had control.[86]

On the whole the *émigrés* were spurned by the foreign powers and kept at arm's length by the King. Louis' attitude is particularly interesting. In the early days – 1789–91 – he showed disapproval and demanded that the *émigrés* return immediately to France, but as the Revolution progressed and attitudes intensified on both sides, he became more confrontational.[87] After Varennes he was actually encouraging army officers to defect.[88]

For good reason the *émigrés* have been mocked by onlookers, but the irony of the situation is that they were taken extremely seriously by the revolutionaries in Paris. The Brissotins, for example, supported the idea of military action against the *émigrés*; Blanning says that 'while the enemies without were allowed to carry on their wicked work, it was argued, the enemies within would continue to flourish'.[89] In addition, the Paris authorities enacted an enormous range of laws and decrees: on 6 August 1791 (banning emigration), 31 October 1791 (ordering the Comte de Provence to return to France), 9 November 1791 (delineating *émigrés* as traitors), 1 February 1792 (demanding the use of passports), 12 February, 8 April and 6 September 1792 (ordering the sequestration of property), 25 October 1792 (banishing *émigrés* 'in perpetuity'), and 28 March 1793 (a package of 'final' measures).[90]

As well as defining in the minutest detail what an *émigré* was (and was not), the March 1793 decree stated that *émigrés* were 'civilly dead'.[91] This was a landmark in anti-*émigré* legislation but pressure on the authorities had been building up. Eighteen months earlier, the revolutionaries had announced:

The National Assembly, considering that the peace and security of the kingdom bespeak it to take prompt and effectual measures against Frenchmen who, in spite of the amnesty, continue to plot abroad against the French Constitution, and, considering that the time has come when those who have not responded to leniency and returned to the duties and sentiments of free citizens must be severely restrained, has declared that there is urgency for the following decree...[92]

The law they framed in this instance was never enacted, but its wording helps us to understand how the *émigrés* were perceived by Paris.[93] They were suspected of 'conspiracy against the *Patrie*' (Art. 1), and in fact the word 'conspiracy' features in each of the first three articles. The *émigrés* were to be punished with death for their 'anti-national' plotting.[94]

Counter-revolutionaries branded the anti-*émigré* decrees 'premature' and 'barbarous', but the vindictiveness of the Paris authorities was understandable.[95] They were sensitive, if not paranoid, about threats to the Revolution – whether real or imaginary. The existence of a large group of roaming aristocrats and clerics obviously alarmed them, but the fact of the matter is that the Revolution grossly exaggerated the danger. The *émigrés* were intent on wining and dining and not much else. Thompson talks about their 'smart, expensive and disorderly life'.[96] Cobb says they engaged in 'pleasure, women, drink, gambling, romance and boastfulness... what the Revolution so much lacked'.[97] And one *émigré*, the future Madame de Gontaut, referred to the 'illusions' with which the folk in Koblenz comforted themselves.[98] This seemed to say it all.

Of course the *émigrés* established their own intelligence networks, and even formed their own army (of sorts), but they were not serious people.[99] The Marquis de Falaiseau described the *émigré* army as 'a confused mass of grown men, greybeards and children fresh from their dove-cotes... It presented a picture of the old monarchy, the final scenes of a world that was passing away.'[100] It was all fairly predictable. On his departure from France, the Comte d'Artois – the *émigrés*' leader – stated, famously and foolishly, that he and his aristocratic brethren would be 'back in three months'. Greer comments: 'Three decades would have been a better forecast, but the outraged seigneurs of 1789 contemplated only a temporary withdrawal from a scene unworthy of their presence.'[101]

Who were the émigrés?

In many ways the *émigrés* were a standing joke. But how many were there? Where were they based? What motivated them? And what was their philosophy or ideology? Greer and Vidalenc estimate that, in total, there were around 130,000–150,000 *émigrés*, and they equate this figure to 0.5 per cent of the French population.[102] Godechot says that 25 per cent of all *émigrés* were clergy, 20 per cent peasants, 17 per cent nobility, 14 per cent artisans, 11 per cent upper bourgeoisie, and 6 per cent petty bourgeoisie.[103] Bosher contends that most *émigrés* were 'ordinary' members of the Third Estate, yet the most 'famous' were invariably nobles or clerics – those who put themselves at the forefront of the counter-revolutionary effort.[104] This is significant, for we must not think that the emigration was somehow a purely aristocratic phenomenon.[105]

Furthermore, individuals were provoked by different emotions, as Pasquier explains:

> In '89, '90 and '91 there were a few who were compelled to fly from actual danger; a small number were led away by a genuine feeling of enthusiasm; many felt themselves bound to leave, owing to a point of honour which they obeyed without reasoning it out; the mass thought it was the fashion, and that it looked well; all, or almost all, were carried away by expectations... and the plotting of a few ambitious folk.[106]

At the same time there were definite landmarks in the course of the emigration.[107] Winock tells us that Artois gave the initial signal for the 'royal and military emigration' the day after the Bastille fell,[108] and thereafter the 'triggers' are obvious: the Civil Constitution of the Clergy (Spring 1791), the Flight to Varennes (June 1791), the King's endorsement of the Constitution (September 1791) and, finally, the execution of the King (January 1793). Different groups of people were provoked at different junctures: the clergy after the Civil Constitution, the military in late 1789, and so on. Greer says: 'This flight from France is best envisaged not as a series of waves but as a stream rising as a rivulet in midsummer, 1789, gathering volume as the Monarchy weakened and toppled, swelling to a torrent in the climactic violence of 1793, and subsiding to a trickle after Thermidor.' It is in this sense that he talks about the emigration being 'in synchrony' with the Revolution.[109]

The most 'famous' *émigrés* were Artois (the King's younger brother), Calonne (the King's ex-finance minister), the Duc de Condé and the Comte d'Antraigues. Although the exiles were scattered all over Europe, and kept on moving and circulating, there were a few main centres: Koblenz, Turin, Venice, Vienna and London.[110]

According to one view, 'there were men of Coblenz at the Tuileries, and there were men of the Tuileries at Coblenz'.[111] All the time there was talk of the possibility and potential of an *émigré*-led invasion of France. Hibbert talks about one programme of action:

> Plans had been laid for a royalist restoration by force. It was intended that the Prince de Condé, father of the Duc de Bourbon, who had fought against the Revolution in conjunction with the Austrians, should advance with a royalist army from the east; that an insurrection should be simultaneously provoked in the south; that the extravagant and pleasure-

loving General, Charles Pichegru, commander of the Rhine Army, should be suborned by huge bribes, by the promise of his promotion to marshal and the offer of the château and park of Chambord; and that an expeditionary force of *émigrés*, for which the English government were to provide money, naval support and uniforms, should be landed in the north-west to link up with the Chouans. But, as with so many other royalist plots, the execution bore little relation to the planning.[112]

This seemed to be representative.

We have talked about the 'triggers' of emigration, but it would be painting only half the picture if we thought about the question of motivation solely in these terms. Rather, we have to go further and get inside the mindset of the *émigrés* and ask whether it was ideology or just self-preservation that provoked them. Greer and Roberts conclude that there were both '*émigrés* of fear' (those who were provoked into political escape by the 'events' or 'triggers' just discussed) and '*émigrés* of disdain' (those whose motivation was ideological). Greer talks about 'pressure and propaganda' as two factors that affected individuals' decision to leave France.[113]

Roberts divides the 'ideological' *émigrés* into two groups: 'pures' and *monarchiens*.[114] He describes the 'pures' as those *émigrés* who wanted the *ancien régime* to be restored in its entirety, those who recognised the failings of the old system but did not believe in any kind of compromise. *Monarchiens*, by contrast, was a term of abuse used by the more extreme *émigrés* to describe the more moderate and less intransigent *émigrés*.[115] Bosher highlights the gulf separating the two factions, arguing that whereas the 'pures' wanted the restoration of the king, 'the constitutional monarchists were readier for practical compromises'.[116] Godechot suggests that the Koblenz exiles were anything but united.[117]

This 'division', however, should not blind us to the fact that most *émigrés* – whatever their exact political orientation – did have significant things in common. They all believed in aristocratic rights and privileges and in the role of the *parlements*, and in the 'external' sphere they condemned the Franco-Austrian alliance – and the personification of this alliance, Marie-Antoinette. Furthermore, they put their faith in an attack on Paris and the Revolution from outside.

On balance the emigration is a curious phenomenon, but not, perhaps, a hugely important one. The *émigrés* lived the high life while they were at large, and were only really taken seriously by themselves. Their plots were unsuccessful and their expeditionary plans half-baked. Even the monarchs of Europe got tired of them; the King of Sardinia, for example, announced that the *émigré* court was unwelcome in Turin.

It would be wrong to depict all *émigrés* as 'ideological' or 'of the right'. Of course, they were conservative and, to an extent, reactionary, but it should be remembered that most too were just ordinary people: members of the Third Estate and completely unpoliticised. That said, a small minority of *émigrés* were powerfully driven by doctrine and ideology and it was these people who re-emerged as the Ultras under the Restoration.

It is interesting to consider the main loyalties of the *émigrés*. In later chapters we will see how, for the most part, individuals and movements on the far right after 1880 owed their absolute allegiance to the nation, to an almost spiritual or mystical entity called 'France'. In the era of the Revolution, however, it was the left that identified itself with the (newly formed) nation. The right and the extreme right, on the other hand, still conceived of 'France' as a kingdom and displayed loyalty to notions of 'monarchy' and 'aristocracy'. Pasquier explains the thinking of the *émigrés*:

> It occurred to the minds of a few men in the entourage of the Comte d'Artois, and whose moving spirit was M. de Calonne, that it would be an easy matter for them to create a kingdom for their sovereign outside of France, and that if they could not in this fashion succeed in giving him provinces to reign over, he would at least reign over subjects, and that this would serve to give him standing in the eyes of foreign powers, and determine them to espouse his cause.[118]

Thus, for d'Artois and his soulmates, *la patrie* was not, strictly, a geographical term. They were loyal to an idea and an institution and they were prepared to 'do their time'. Thompson says they suffered as a result:

> That he [the *émigré*] should flee the country hardly seemed unpatriotic to an age which remembered the Huguenots and the Pilgrim Fathers... Yet the *émigrés* of the revolutionary period were rightly reproached for their association with the enemies of their country. They were justly blamed for deserting not only their country, but also their king. No theory of class excused them for treating their fellow-countrymen as revolted vassals. No theory of patriotism excused them for preparing armed vengeance upon the state they should have defended against foreign attack.[119]

As the anti-*émigré* decrees make clear, it was this 'anti-national' dimension to the emigration that most offended Paris.[120]

The reality of the emigration was nothing to write home about, but this did not stop Artois scribbling a letter to his confidant, Vaudreuil, from Liege on 19 November 1792. Out of money and luck, he wrote:

> One would need the pen of a Jeremiah, my dear Vaudreuil, to give you a true picture of our position since you left us. I had hoped to be able to keep up my spirits, but I must admit that I feel terribly distressed about everything... Everything is falling to pieces insensibly and we are all starving to death... Ah! My dear friend, what a multitude of misfortunes! I assure you that I constantly feel myself on the verge of losing my

reason... Give my love to all good friends. The life I lead is becoming unbearable as time goes on.[121]

This extract is full of poignancy. In Thompson's words, 'the capital mistake of the *émigrés* was to emigrate'.[122]

Action II: the Vendée revolt

Historians differ in the way in which they characterise the Vendée revolt. For Furet, it was part of 'the merciless conflict between revolution and counter-revolution'; in the view of Hibbert, it was merely a 'conservative uprising'.[123] According to Hampson, it was 'no flash in the pan, but a major civil war'; and to Winock, it stood as one of the 'most important counter-revolutionary symbols'.[124]

Earlier we talked about a Counter-Revolution 'at the top' and we equated this to the activities of the Court and the *émigrés*. It is now tempting to talk about a Counter-Revolution 'at the bottom', and to equate this to the rebellion in the Vendée.[125] In one sense this would be accurate, but in another this would be missing the point, for just as the emigration involved many members of the Third Estate, so the revolt in the West involved a small number of aristocrats and clergy – the ring-leaders in fact.

As Hampson suggests, the Vendée episode had all the hallmarks of a civil war. In comparison with the other counter-revolutionary revolts – in Brittany, the Midi, the south-west and the south-east[126] – it was the most threatening and violent. The region rose in March 1793 in protest at the Republic's wish to impose conscription (Paris had declared that it needed 300,000 men for the European war). Violent rebel bands emerged, composed mainly of peasants but led by nobles, and by the middle of 1793 the rebels had captured most of the region and besieged the city of Nantes. The new Paris authorities had serious problems to contend with. Raising an army was not easy, and neither was the management of the war – Furet and Richet talk of 'conflicts' and 'speculation' in Paris, while Bouloiseau speaks of 'lasting jealousies and irresponsibility' among commanders.[127] However, by December 1793 the rebel army had been destroyed, and by 1795–6 most of the region had been pacified and a peace treaty signed.[128] However, when one of the rebels, Cormatin, declared, 'we shall never surrender', he was not joking.[129] The Vendée would continue to erupt into anti-regime protests – in 1796, 1799, 1815 and 1832.

Why was the revolt so important? In military terms it was not the scale or outcome of the warfare that was unusual, but the type. The primitive gang warfare practised by the Chouans was unique.[130] Bosher talks about 'guerilla' tactics and 'counterrevolutionary vengeance', while Godechot has likened the Chouans' underground operations to those of the Maquis resistance during the Second World War.[131] Bouloiseau talks about the Vendéans in more general terms: 'Taking advantage of natural shelters and of the undergrowth [they] conducted night-time raids on outposts and convoys... They were excellent marksmen and sturdy walkers, marching tirelessly and causing panic by their elusiveness.'[132] Hugo depicts a revolt based on ambush, poaching and bush fighting.[133] Turreau, a republican general, is most descriptive of all:

> The Vendéans possessed a hitherto unknown style of fighting and an inimitable one, in that it was solely appropriate to the country and to the genius of the inhabitants... Their skill in the use of fire-arms is such, that no known people, however warlike, however skilled in manoeuvring make better use of their muskets... When they attack, their onslaught is terrible, sudden and almost always unforeseen.[134]

Sometimes the rebels' tactics were just eccentric: for example, cutting off opponents' hair and tearing up their uniforms.

Overall, the Vendée army comprised approximately 10,000 men in March 1793. It has been described as a 'permanent menace', but the fact of the matter is that Paris was able to put out a military force three times the size.[135] Paret puts things in perspective: 'The civil wars of the Vendée during the 1790s possess an interest that transcends the place they occupy in the history of the French Revolution, an interest arising from the specific military and political methods with which the opposing sides translated their beliefs into action.'[136]

Whatever the true importance of the Vendée, the authorities in Paris perceived it to be the most dangerous threat to the future of the Revolution. On 19 March 1793 they responded to the outbreak of revolt:

> Article 1 – All persons who are convicted of having taken part in the rebellion, or in the counter-Revolutionary riots, or of having worn the white cockade, or any other sign of revolt, shall be outlawed.
> Article 2 – If they are taken or arrested armed, they shall be handed over to the executioner and put to death within twenty-four hours after such fact has been attested before a military Commission formed of the officers of each division employed in quelling the disturbances.[137]

Just as the revolutionaries exaggerated the threat posed by the *émigrés*, so they exhibited paranoia about the Vendée. However, in the West their anxieties were better founded. There were genuine fears that the rebels might march on Paris and topple the government, so in revolutionary discourse the Vendée was depicted as a conflict between 'good' and 'evil', a 'fearful struggle between crime and virtue'. The rebels became known as 'brigands', or even 'wretches'. The new vocabulary was understandable – the revolt was draining the Republic economically as well as politically.[138]

In the Vendée, more than elsewhere, landlords and peasants put to one side their mutual hostility and lined up on the same side.[139] They were certainly not natural allies but, with a traditional way of life at stake, they were forced into each other's arms. Cobban says that the people handed over leadership of the revolt to the nobles, and thereafter the aristocrats relied on the 'born fighters' to engage in combat and bear the brunt of the hostilities.[140] And because of the number of peasants that took part in the revolt, the Vendée is now seen as a 'peasant insurrection', not just a 'counter-revolutionary insurrection'. In this respect Godechot says the revolt has a 'dual aspect'.[141]

The Vendée revolt also gave rise to grave fears about 'federalism', the gradual breakup of the organic nation state. This was viewed as a scourge, a prelude to national dismemberment, a 'crime'.[142] In the light of revolts in Lyons, Marseilles and Toulon, the revolutionaries were petrified that the Vendée would 'break off' from Paris and plunge France into the 'ravages of federalism'.[143] They had condemned the King for lacking 'national' legitimacy and now the revolt in the west gave them problems of their own.

The Vendée rebels had the opportunity not only to ignite other areas of France into anti-Paris violence, but also to join forces with the *émigrés* and the foreign powers in some kind of 'umbrella' attack on the revolutionary authorities. On 1 October 1795, Artois arrived on the Île d'Yeu but soon demonstrated his lack of interest in 'waging guerilla warfare' and 'departed for England, abandoning the Vendéans to their fate'.[144] This indicates the fatal lack of real coordination on the counter-revolutionary right.[145]

Finally, the conflict in the West has left a massive legacy. Nowhere else, argues Tackett, did opposition to the Revolution 'produce such a lasting collective memory'.[146] The revolt did not derail political change, but it certainly left an imprint on French political life. It gave rise to a fear of 'new Vendées', and was also instrumental in the configuration of the nineteenth- and twentieth-century right.[147] In addition, for 200 years and more the region has traded on its unique heritage. Tourists now encounter museums, memorials and even picture postcards devoted to the 'epic' counter-revolutionary history of the Vendée.[148] On a different plane, novelists have drawn great inspiration from the conflict. Godechot says: 'The war of the Vendée has a very particular character in the history of the Revolution... Balzac, Victor Hugo, Alexandre Dumas and Michelet all devoted books or short stories to the wars of the Vendée and to the *chouannerie*.'[149]

In recent times historians have used the word 'genocide' to describe the treatment handed out to the Vendée by the Paris authorities.[150] Winock, for example, talks about a state of 'total war' and cites Barère's advice to the Convention – 'Destroy the Vendée' – as important evidence.[151] Legislation passed by the Paris authorities did nothing to dispel the image of a deliberate pogrom. Take this extract:

Article 6 – The Minister of War shall send combustibles of all kinds to be used in the destruction of the woods and forests.
Article 7 – The dwellings of the rebels shall be destroyed, their crops cut

by companies of workmen, and their herds seized.

Article 14 – The goods and chattels of the rebels in the Vendée are hereby declared to be the property of the Republic.[152]

The revolutionaries' position was unequivocal. The Vendée was a gangrenous sore that needed amputating. Bire tells us a little more about the rhetoric of the revolutionaries:

> It was at the Jacobin Club that the evil was pointed out, and at the Grey Friars that the remedy was suggested. 'Let us', said one of the speakers, 'adopt vigorous measures to exterminate the villains in the Vendée and in other parts of the country. Let us prepare red-hot shot and set fire to some forty or fifty villages in the affected departments. Such rigorous measures would only be an act of justice, for though there may be some innocent men in the midst of these insurgents, they are, nevertheless, cowards whom we ought not to spare.'

The best part of two centuries later, the Vendée authorities announced that they were not going to 'celebrate' the 200th anniversary of the Revolution – an event that, in their view, was synonymous with genocide. This declaration would have been viewed as 'eccentric' by some, but the attitude of the revolutionaries in the 1790s confirms that the revolt was an event of great significance. And, as we have seen, Paris did not balk at taking extreme measures to combat it.

Origins and causation of the revolt

For historians the Vendée's main fascination lies in the issue of causation. How do we explain this 'unexpected' reaction in the West?[153] The discourse is long-running, complex and infected by 'partisanship'.[154] Even on the issue of 'triggers' there is much debate. Most commentators, however, point to the *levée en masse* of March 1793 as the spark that lit the fuse of rebellion. The authorities in Paris declared that they needed 300,000 soldiers for the European war, but did not take account of the hostile reaction that this announcement would provoke. The peasantry was especially tired of the war, and in the Vendée this fatigue was highly apparent. Jones says conscription was a 'powder keg' and states: 'Nowhere did recruitment provoke quite so much fury as in the West.'[155]

The rural nature of the Vendée is also an important factor in explaining why the area was so immediately hostile to the Revolution. Many peasants came to the conclusion that the Revolution was made by and for townspeople and, whether this conclusion was based on reality or perception, it provoked concerted anti-Paris agitation in the region. In addition, the establishment of the Terror in late 1792 had profound consequences in the West.[156]

For his part, Godechot points to the small-scale rebellions in the West in

1790, 1791 and 1792 as key 'triggers' of the large-scale revolt. He contends that by 1793 there was a culture of conspiracy and revolt in the region and that arms had already been transported there.[157] Tilly agrees with this view, and talks about 'the importance of essentially local conflicts, beginning long before March, 1793, in the development of the terrible counter-revolution'.[158] There may or may not have been 'triggers', but what is certain is that, for a fuller and deeper explanation of how and why the revolt occurred, we need to look elsewhere.

What we find is a wide-ranging historiographical debate: in essence, was it a plot or popular rebellion?[159] On the one hand we have the 'republican' or 'anti-clerical' interpretation. This emphasises the way in which the people of the Vendée were 'led astray' by a combination of nobles and priests – an alliance supported by the *émigrés* and the foreign powers. This explanation obviously demonises the forces that made up the Counter-Revolution and depicts 'the people' in a positive and wholly innocent light. Furet says that republicans have an 'obsession' with this line of thinking.[160] On the other hand, we have the view put forward by counter-revolutionary historians which stresses the Revolution's uniqueness and in particular the way it 'broke' with all of France's traditions. In this sense the Revolution is viewed as 'unnatural': its atheism, reformism and alignment with the urban bourgeoisie are particularly unappealing for right-wing historians, who cling to the notion that the Republic was guilty of upsetting 'the golden age of rustic harmony' and going against 'the natural order of things'. Reflecting on this dichotomy, Mitchell speaks of the 'ancient quarrel between the pro-Revolutionary historians who cannot conceive of popular opposition to the Revolution... and the anti-Revolutionary historians who nostalgically romanticise the revolt and accept without question the effectiveness of the ties binding elites and led.'[161] Tackett just refers to 'sterile jousts between left and right'.[162]

Cobban says the main problem is the 'superfluity of explanations'[163] – but four specific theories of causation are worthy of detailed attention. The 'Noble' thesis is one of the oldest and postulates that the Vendée revolt was the product almost exclusively of aristocratic pressure. The event is viewed as a general rising of the nobles with the intention of restoring the monarchy and the other component institutions of the *ancien régime*. In very general terms, this theory holds water but it does tend to ignore the fact that many of the rebels were ordinary peasants and that many nobles joined the revolt in the later stages. It also lumps all nobles into one bloc, as if each and every aristocrat had exactly the same political inclinations. This, of course, was not the case; some, for example, were reformers who had actually embraced the Revolution at first. So, to characterise the Vendée revolt as an aristocratic revolt, purely and simply, is a misnomer. It was far more complex than that and, as such, the 'Noble' thesis is now viewed as a slightly outdated interpretation.

The 'Clerical' thesis is another long-standing would-be explanation. It concentrates on the spiritual dimension to the Vendée episode and implies that the rebels in the West put a higher premium on the preservation of religion than on the preservation of the monarchy. Contemporary evidence supports this argument. The Vendéan fighters wore the Sacred Heart of Jesus with pride, and one revolutionary officer talked about the rebels as 'men who fight with their scapularies and rosaries in their hands... [they] do not fight for the nobles, whom they detest, but for those whom they call their good priests.'[164] (Balzac was also convinced that the rebels had a powerful religious motivation. 'Sent by God and the King!', announces one Vendéan in *The Chouans*.)[165] It is also interesting that the rebels' fighting force was known as the 'Catholic and Royal Army' (the ordering of the words is particularly significant). On balance, Aston says, religion gave 'purpose and justification' to the Vendée revolt.[166]

Other evidence is brought in to support the 'Clerical' thesis, chiefly the widespread opposition in the Vendée to the Civil Constitution of the Clergy, which demanded that all priests swear an oath of allegiance to the Revolution. Predictably, this piece of revolutionary legislation was vehemently disliked in the West.[167] Godechot says that the clergy in France displayed more and more displeasure towards the Revolution as it progressed, and it is a fact that most priests in the Vendée were 'refractories'.[168] It is probably very significant that, in the end, the region was only pacified by concessions granted to the Catholic Church by Napoleon's Concordat.

Religion was clearly a live issue. Sceptics have argued that the time-lag between the Civil Constitution (1791) and the outbreak of the revolt (1793) demonstrates that the religious factor was not fundamental, but it would be foolish not to accept the 'Clerical' thesis to some degree. Tackett observes that 'we must seriously entertain the possibility that it was this very religious confrontation which served as a key catalyst in the relative cohesion and unity of so much of the rural west', and also says, crucially, that 'none of the newer accounts neglects the religious issue'.[169]

The Marxist line stresses the economic dimension to the revolt and portrays the rebellion as a response to authoritarian legislation being passed in Paris – the Maximum and the *levée en masse* especially. What Marxists do not explain, however, is why other areas of France – also affected by the price ceiling and conscription, both imposed by the Jacobins – did not react in the same manner as the Vendée. In recent times, the Marxist thesis has lost ground and more sociological interpretations have gained currency. Le Goff and Sutherland point to the system of land tenure and the role of leaseholding as important factors in the West's rejection of the Revolution,[170] but it is the works of Tilly and Bois that have been especially influential.[171] These two writers are more interested in the 'effect of modernisation on rural areas' than the 'conscious motives' of historical actors.[172] They divide the Vendée into two segments. In the first, a north-eastern zone around Val-Saumurois, the Revolution was welcomed, mainly because bourgeois values had been penetrating this area throughout the nineteenth century; thus, the value-system associated with 1789 was not too much of a departure. The second area, in the west of the Vendée around Les Mauges, had only recently in 1789 been penetrated by commercial influence; thus, this zone was at the forefront of reaction.

In short, Tilly depicts a 'rebel *bocage* and a Republican plain and valley'.[173] He states that the western zone was still in the process of modernisation, still anxious about the future, and thus home to significant counter-revolutionary tendencies. Tilly and Bois depict this area as backward, isolated and insular and the people who lived there are portrayed as conservative, traditionalist and extremely sensitive to the impact of modernisation and the arrival of pro-Revolution merchants and traders. In Tilly's view, the level of urbanisation is the key variable.[174] This thesis obviously has much to commend it, but the fact of the matter is that it remains fairly simplistic and mechanical. It takes very little account of the 'raw history' of the period – the events, ideologies and personalities that made up the revolutionary decade – and is not able to explain why other areas of *bocage*, in other parts of France, did not also erupt into violence.

So, do any of these interpretations convince as stand-alone explanations of the Vendée rebellion? Not really – for each has its flaws and drawbacks. But what we can say is that a plausible synthesis can be established. Let us start with Mitchell and McManners, who both talk about the intense poverty of the region.[175] On to this base, we can graft the thoughts of Tackett, who emphasises that even the most recent historical interpretations – those stressing the sociological dimension to the revolt – do not forget the religious factor.[175] In this sense we are moving towards a fusion of 'new' and 'old'. There are other views as well. Cobban describes the revolt as the 'climax' of town-versus-country tension, but it is clear that in the final analysis it was a complex juxtaposition of economic, social and religious factors that provoked full-scale revolt.[177] Summing up, Godechot talks about 'geographic determinism'[178] and Jordan, in the same vein, refers to 'regional dislocations and antagonisms'.[179] Perhaps the truth lies here.

Thus, we have an almost complete picture of the Counter-Revolution in the decade 1789–99. There were several prongs to this offensive: the doctrine of de Maistre, the high-level plotting of the Court and the *émigrés*, and the anti-Paris rebellion in the Vendée. When Napoleon succeeded the Directors in 1799 the forces of Revolution and Counter-Revolution were still at loggerheads, even though the intensity of the conflict had diminished. During the period of Empire the Counter-Revolution went temporarily into abeyance, but with the defeat of Napoleon in 1814 and the Allies' insistence that in order to safeguard European peace the Bourbons should be returned to power, a new phase of counter-revolutionary activity was unleashed.

The Ultras and the Restoration

The Restoration – the name given to the period 1814–30 – witnessed a royalist renaissance and intense counter-revolutionary activity. In many ways it was the moment that de Maistre, the *émigrés* and even the Vendée rebels had been waiting for. Magraw talks about the 'Indian Summer of the Aristocracy' and McPhee identifies a 'clerico-noble resurgence'.[180] Providence had delivered – at last.

The Charter of 1814 was designed to foster a new moderate consensus, and the first Restoration monarch, Louis XVIII, did all he could to make things work. However, the arrival of Charles X on the throne in 1824 – 'the most fervid reactionary of them all'[181] – and the ascendancy of the 'Ultra-Royalist' faction (or the 'Ultras') marked a watershed in right-wing politics. Weiss states that with the Ultras, 'the history of the radical right had begun'. And, without qualification, Weber, Artz, Hudson and Phillips all pin the 'extreme right' label on the Ultras.[182]

The story of the Restoration can be summed up in the chapter titles chosen by Jardin and Tudesq: 'The Government of Constitutional Monarchists', followed by 'The Royalist Reaction'. Magraw puts it slightly differently, referring to 'alternative periods of moderation and ultra-royalist reaction.'[183] The era began amid the hopes raised by the Charter – the nearest thing there was to a 'constitution' of the Restoration – and ended with the attempted *coup d'état* of Charles in 1830. In between times, there was almost constant political infighting between the Ultras on the right and the liberals and constitutionalists who occupied what passed for the centre ground in early nineteenth-century France.[184] Hugo describes the Restoration as 'one of those intermediate phases, difficult of definition, in which there are fatigue, buzzings, murmurs, slumber, tumult, and which are nothing more or less than the arrival of a great nation at a halting-place.'[185]

The Charter was granted by Louis and designed to forestall extremism. Although its opening line bore all the hallmarks of the past – 'Divine Providence, in bringing us back to our realm after a long absence, has imposed great obligations upon us'[186] – the document tended to avoid the vocabulary of the *ancien régime*. Instead, it stated that the Restoration would guarantee personal liberties and that the monarch and his ministers would govern in association with parliament. Whereas the Chamber of Peers was appointed, the Chamber of Deputies was elected. Restoration democracy, however, was fairly superficial: prospective deputies had to be aged over forty and had to pay over 1,000 francs in taxes, and voters had to be over the age of thirty and pay over 300 francs in taxes.[187] Most historians have interpreted the Charter as a compromise. Artz goes further and points to the 'contradictions' contained within it. Phillips probably sums things up best, describing it as a 'regrettable necessity'.[188]

After the hullabaloo of Napoleon's 'Hundred Days', the elections of August 1815 returned a huge Ultra majority and the resulting parliament came to be known as 'The Incredible Chamber' (*Le Chambre Incroyable*).[189] It was so reactionary that the Allies – who had been instrumental in restoring the monarchy in 1814 – suggested dissolution. Rémond is in no doubt that the amazing election results of 1815 marked the birth of Ultra-royalism as a political force.

Hudson labels the era 1820–8 as 'Ultra-royalism in power', but the fact of the matter is that the Ultras were influencing government policy well before 1820.[190] That said, Louis' death in 1824 was a landmark, for it unleashed a fresh wave of right-wing extremism. Price says that the new king was 'hardly compatible' with constitutional monarchy and Charle talks about a new era of 'favouritism and unfair promotion'.[191] Charles' over-the-top coronation ceremony in 1825 confirmed the new political climate. De Sauvigny argues that the occasion was bathed in the 'greatest possible splendour'[192] but Béranger, a contemporary critic, had a different perspective:

> At feet of prelates stiff with gold,
> Charles's *Confiteor*;
> He's robed, and kissed, and oiled; and next,
> With hand upon the Holy Text,
> Whilst sacred anthems fill the air,
> Hears his Confessor whisper, 'Swear!
> Rome here concerned, is nothing loath
> To grant release from such an oath.'
>
> In belt of Charlemagne arrayed,
> As though just such a roystering blade,
> Charles in the dust now prostrate lies;
> 'Rise up, Sir King,' a soldier cries.
> 'No,' quoth the Bishop, 'and by Saint Peter,
> The Church crowns you; with bounty treat her!
> Heaven *sends*, but 'tis the priests who *give*;
> Long may legitimacy live!'[193]

The poem sent out a clear message: in trying to close up the 'wounds' of the Revolution, Charles was committing himself to *ancien régime* values. Phillips regards the ceremony as the 'high-water mark of Legitimate Monarchy under the Restoration' and talks about 'the triumph of reaction'.[194]

It was the Ultras who personified the extremism of the Restoration. Artois (brother of Louis XVI and the future Charles X) was their de facto leader and his closest colleagues were Chateaubriand, Bonald, La Bourdonnaye, Villèle and Polignac. Weber depicts them as extreme, romantic and intransigent. Artz says they stood for 'violent Royalism and reactionary views'. Rémond argues that they looked to the Middle Ages for their 'ideal society'.[195] Poumiès de la Siboutie, a writer of the time, summarises the situation:

> Members of the old aristocracy, who had emigrated, and those who had belonged to the former Court of Versailles, crowded back to Paris. They were furious with Louis XVIII for having granted a Charter. They called him Jacobin... They had fondly imagined that there would be no

difficulty whatever in restoring the *ancien régime* in its entirety ... It was said of them that 'they had forgotten nothing and learnt nothing.'[196]

This last tag said so much about the Ultras and was to haunt them indefinitely. They were not a political faction in the modern sense, even though Wright says the group was almost homogeneous.[197] 'Ultras' was a nickname pinned on the group by its enemies – and it stuck. They championed a particularly virulent form of right-wing Catholicism and, as such, talk of 'less extreme Ultras' is a contradiction in terms. According to Rémond, they represented an important staging-post in the history of the far right.[198]

The vast majority of Ultras were nobles and clerics. Some had stayed in France during the Revolution and fought their corner (many of these people had been involved in the formation of the Chevalliers of Faith, an overtly political Ultra organisation), but on the whole the Ultras comprised the 'returning elites'.[199] Once in power, they 'failed to see the constructive side of the Revolution' and wished to right the wrongs of 1789.[200]

They started close to home with the indemnification of the *émigrés*. In 1824 Martignac, an Ultra minister, declared:

> The *émigrés* lost everything all at once. All the evils which befell France struck them, and in addition they suffered still graver misfortunes which were reserved for them alone... The laws against the *émigrés* took everything – their shares, their goods, their income; and in addition these cruel laws deprived them, and them alone, of their fields, of their houses, of that part of their native soil for the preservation of which the owner has the right to demand protection and security from society. It is for this latter misfortune that reparation is demanded. It is a misfortune quite out of the common run; nothing else can be compared with it.[201]

This was not just a practical policy proposition but a statement of intent and ideology. Jardin and Tudesq call it an 'appeasement measure' and Hudson says it 'crowned the efforts' of Restoration statesmen, but de Sauvigny endeavours to show that the commitment to compensation had been shared earlier in the decade by the moderate Louis XVIII. This decree, he argues, was not the product of the 'blind spirit of reaction', as many now believe.[202] Either way, the far-right faction wanted to roll back time.

On one level the Ultras were the epitome of intransigence but on another they were thoroughly pragmatic. They formed a significant parliamentary force, engaged in violence when they saw fit, and even allied with the extreme left when it was *politique*.[203] They were 'more royalist than the king', but this did not stop them from disliking Louis or going against monarchical authority when they felt they needed to.[204]

Doctrine and belief

For most of the time the Ultras gave the impression of being totally out of touch with reality, not entirely surprising given their self-imposed exile during the Revolution. When *Ultracisme* gained a foothold in government, it showed itself to be an illiberal and near-totalitarian creed. Bourgeois claims that the nation was 'excluded from the discussion and terrorised'.[205]

In June 1820 the Law of the Double Vote altered the electoral system in favour of the wealthy – those most likely to have pro-Ultra convictions.[206] Two years later Villèle passed the Law of Tendency, a piece of legislation that epitomised Ultra attitudes to society:

> Article 1 – No newspaper or periodical, devoted wholly or partly to news or political matter, and appearing either regularly on certain days or in separate numbers at irregular intervals, shall be founded and published without the king's consent.
>
> Article 2 – The first copy of each paper or the first number of each periodical or magazine shall be deposited as soon as it is printed at the local office of the public prosecutor.
>
> Article 3 – If the character of a newspaper or periodical, emerging from a series of articles, shall have a tendency to endanger law and order, or the respect due to the state religion... or the authority of the king... the royal courts shall... pronounce suspension of the newspaper or political journal for a period not exceeding one month for the first offence and three months for the second.[207]

A Royal Ordinance announcing the appointment of more censors followed in June 1827 – a development that provoked a new wave of opposition to the King.[208] More broadly, the conception of society embraced by the Ultras rested on 'Throne and Altar' and, in power, Charles announced that he wanted to seal a 'pact' between the two notions.[209]

The Ultras believed in a particular brand of monarchy. They reminisced about medieval France – the 'ideal' society that should be revived – and took Henri IV rather than Louis XIV as their role-model. Their royalist views were grounded on 'blood' and 'instinct', not 'rationality'. They did not believe that monarchy was necessarily the best system of government for France, but just felt a strong sense of personal loyalty to the idea.

However, it was religion that was the pre-eminent issue of the Restoration. Here the two monarchs held contrasting attitudes: Louis championed moderation while Charles stood for an 'austere and bigoted pietism'.[210] Much of the Ultras' thinking on religion came straight from de Maistre – especially their loyalty to Ultramontanism over Gallicanism. Although they went well beyond de Maistre's teachings, his name is now inextricably linked with the excesses of the Bourbons. At the core of *Ultracisme* was the belief that 1789 had been an atheistic revolution and that the Restoration must act as a retort. So, instead of dechristianisation, the Ultras demanded re-christianisation – in effect, the restitution of the privileges, wealth and influence of the Catholic Church.

On a broader level the Ultras operated through the Congregation – a devotional Catholic movement[211] – and encouraged a major religious revival across France.[212] Phillips highlights the zeal of the *missionnaires* during the Restoration and Hudson talks about the 'proselytising zeal of the orders'.[213] But, naturally, the Ultra agenda did not go down well with everybody. Stendhal, for instance, was worried by what he saw: 'All the present French priests are young peasants, all more or less imbued, unfortunately, with a spirit of fanaticism.'[214]

In essence, the Ultras wanted to change the nature of French society. They announced that Catholicism was the sole religion of the state and, moreover, that the Church was 'above' the state. The Sacrilege Law, passed in April 1825, vividly illuminates this element of Ultra thinking:

1 The profanation of consecrated vessels and of the consecrated wafers constitutes the crime of sacrilege.
2 Every attack... whether committed voluntarily or out of hatred of or contempt for religion, constitutes profanation...
4 Death shall be the penalty for the profanation of consecrated vessels...
6 Public profanation of consecrated wafers shall be punished with death. The execution shall be preceded by the public penance of the condemned criminal, in front of the principal church of the place where the crime was committed, or of the place where the court of assizes is held.[215]

For various reasons this 'amazing proposal' was never enacted, but even so it is a crucial testament to the Ultras' religious extremism and marked the dawn of theocracy.[216] Roberts states: 'The Sacrilege Law, the coronation, the indemnity of the *émigrés* gave impetus therefore to the unease which was never far below the surface of Restoration politics.'[217]

Underpinning all aspects of Ultra doctrine was an intense hostility to the 1814 Charter – merely a 'temporary concession' in the words of Charles X.[218] There was something hugely paradoxical about a group of ultra-royalists objecting to a 'divine' royalist decree, but this did not seem to worry anyone.[219] As it was, the Ultras condemned the Charter unreservedly. They attacked the notion of compromise – any compromise – and, on a deeper level, claimed that the Charter contained too many limitations on the 'divine right' of the King.

There were other planks to Ultracism, including a strong commitment to decentralisation. The Ultras did not support absolutism or despotism, campaigning instead for an end to administrative centralisation in Paris and for the restoration of provincial liberties. They defined 'liberty' and 'liberties' in a totally different way to those on the left: 'liberty' was not an abstract ideal but, rather, a product of tradition and history. Thus, the power of the provinces had to be enhanced to guard against over-zealous Parisian control. They saw the *départements* brought in by the Revolution as artificial and meaningless.[220]

And just as the provinces would act as 'intermediate bodies' in society, so too would the family. The Ultras, like many right-wing movements before and after them, argued that the family was a vital institution and should be honoured and respected as such, especially *vis-à-vis* the individual. In an attempt to emphasise this, the Ultras passed a law abolishing divorce,[221] and always conceived of the monarchy in paternalistic terms (for example, the King as the 'father' and his subjects as his 'sons'). They were just as vociferous in the things they did not approve of. Equality, for example, was viewed as something totally alien. Leaders of the faction believed that individuals were all different and also that human societies should be based on hierarchy and harmony rather then on spurious notions of equality.[222] This enabled the Ultras to argue that the aristocrats were the natural leaders of society.

All in all, the Ultras were the 'living antithesis of revolutionary style and principles'.[223] In 1830, wary of growing opposition to his rule, Charles issued four ordinances that amounted, in effect, to a pre-emptive *coup d'état*. The Chamber of Deputies was dissolved, freedom of the press suspended, and the King subsumed all executive power in his person.[224] Phillips says that the 1830 Revolution 'sent the flimsy structure of absolutism crashing to the ground'.[225] So why did reaction fail? Goubert offers this explanation:

> The majority of Frenchmen were not at first hostile to them, at least not in 1814. But the Bourbons tried to restore the white flag and divine-right monarchy at one fell swoop. They brought back the exiled nobles and priests with their antiquated costumes and ideas. Many of them thought of nothing but exacting vengeance for themselves… The whole situation was not well suited to a joyous return to power.[226]

The demise of the Ultras was not altogether unexpected. Weiss states that after the 1830 Revolution they 'retreated to their castles to brood'.[227]

Overall, the Counter-Revolution achieved little. Roberts summarises neatly: 'Counter-Revolution was to fail not just because of its ideology but because it was never the single great bloc in which revolutionaries in their more lurid moments affected to believe, or, for that matter, counter-revolutionaries also considered.'[228] The Court and the *émigrés* floundered from one failed venture to the next, while the Vendée rebels achieved only partial and localised success. Steiner believes the Counter-Revolution crumbled because 'moderates' inside France outwitted pro-monarchy activists and the Revolution always had the nation, or 'imaginings of nationhood', on its side.[229] Ironically, the main achievement of the Counter-Revolution may have been a negative one. It focused the minds of its enemies to such an extent that it 'saved the revolution from the decay into which it was in danger of falling'.[230]

However, as an 'idea' as much as an 'era', the Counter-Revolution is of profound significance. Hudson says the ascendancy of the ultra-right in the 1820s widened the breach between the 'old' and the 'new' France,[231] and since then successive groups have carried the torch for the counter-revolutionary right: the Anti-Dreyfusards of the 1890s, Action Française in the inter-war years and the *Pétainistes* during the Vichy interlude. In the words of Steiner, modern French history has witnessed 'an essential continuity of conflict between revolution and counter-revolution'.[232] The idea has lived on, even though the era was arguably a damp squib.

In essence, the Counter-Revolution was an exercise in self-interest and self-preservation that, at certain key junctures, evolved into an extreme ideological position. Tannenbaum says the Counter-Revolution developed into an enduring 'myth' and Rémond asserts that the right-wing 'Ultra' tradition would out-live the Restoration era.[233] Of even more significance, Roberts claims that the Counter-Revolution shaped French politics 'for another century and more'.[234]

3 1870–1918 – anti-Third Republic protest

Revanche and the new nationalism

The doctrine of nationalism present in extreme-right discourse is exclusive... and the definition of a 'true Frenchman' is determined biologically and racially... From Boulangism onwards, this form of nationalism became the doctrine of a new counter-revolutionary and populist extreme right which differed from the classic proponents of nineteenth-century counter-revolution by not necessarily advocating the restoration of the monarchy.[1]

1871 September: German occupation ends
1875 Proclamation of Republic
1877 16 May: MacMahon's royalist coup
1882 Déroulède founds Ligue des Patriotes
1886 January: Boulanger becomes Minister of War
      Publication of Drumont's *La France juive*
1887 May: Boulanger leaves government
      November: Wilson Scandal
1888 Boulangist campaign
1889 January: Boulanger elected in Paris
      April: Boulanger flees
1892 November: Panama Scandal
1893 Dreyfus condemned
1897 Publication of Barrès' *Les Déracinés*
1898 Barrès stands for election as a Boulangist in Nancy
1899 Attempted anti-Dreyfusard coup
      Action Française founded
      September: Dreyfus found guilty of high treason
1908 Founding of *L'Action Française* daily newspaper
1914 Papal condemnation of Action Française

Far-right politics in France underwent a sea-change in the last third of the nineteenth century, what Jenkins calls a 'remarkable political and ideological realignment'.[2] The 'old right' of the Counter-Revolution had gradually extinguished itself, and after 1880 a 'new right' appeared, nationalist and overtly revolutionary.[3] This evolution, based on the experience and legacy of the Franco-Prussian War of 1870–1, paved the way for a century and more of populist right-wing politics. According to McMillan, the 'traditional', 'Legitimist' right was dead and a new 'integral nationalism' had been born.[4]

This new 'radical right'[5] was never a totally coherent force but came to be embodied by a variety of movements and individuals. In the early 1880s the Ligue des Patriotes, led by Paul Déroulède, epitomised the new nationalism, and during the same decade General Boulanger launched his own political movement. 'Boulangism' shared many of the values trumpeted by Déroulède and attracted heavyweight backing in the shape of Maurice Barrès, a poet, politician and novelist. Barrès was to give the new right some much needed intellectual respectability, and the same could also be said of Charles Maurras, the founder of Action Française in 1899.[6]

We will focus on all these movements and thinkers and also consider the ideological cross-currents of the period: protest, xenophobia, anti-Semitism, anti-republicanism, anti-parliamentarianism and the demand for strong executive government. Some historians argue that the phenomenon we are dealing with here is akin to a 'pre-' or 'proto-' fascism, while others stress the 'socialist' dimension to this new right. We will explore a range of opinions on this matter, but one thing is for sure: the nationalist right of the 1880s and 1890s is a phenomenon of profound importance. The crucial question, of course, is: Why did the 1870s give birth to a new type of right?

The Franco-Prussian War and the birth of the new nationalist right

In the history of far-right politics, 1871 is a crucial turning-point, for it was in this year that France was ravaged by Prussian military forces. Napoleon III's defeat bred not just a feeling of humiliation but a demand for revenge (*revanche*). Buthman employs a range of powerful words to describe the emotions of the nation after 1871: 'mutilation', 'disenchantment', 'diminution'.[7] The new Germany – unified in the aftermath of victory – had subsumed both Alsace and Lorraine and, as a consequence, domestic politics in France came to be dominated by the 'sacred flame' or 'sovereign ideal' of revenge.[8] This was a crucial development because it affected all politicians, not just those on the radical right.[9] But of course, it was those individuals who came to be viewed as part of the 'new right' who let themselves be influenced most by the defeat. It bred a vehement anti-Germanism, a new nation-based discourse and a feeling that France had been raped. Sternhell has written:

> From September 1870 until the outbreak of the Great War the shadow of the disastrous defeat at Sedan hung over the French Republic, and the Alsace–Lorraine question constituted one of the constants of its political life. Indeed the years following the loss of the two provinces form an exceptional period in which the essential themes of a particular

nationalism aroused broad and fervent support, and in which the very expression of this nationalism tended, in the massive shock of defeat, almost to become confused with that of the national consciousness as a whole... At the same time the shock of the disaster, the territorial amputation, and the ensuing humiliation received their true dimension from the fact that the internal crisis came riding on the incoming wave of a new intellectual climate.[10]

It is this 'new intellectual climate' that we are interested in. Weiss adds substance on the matter, arguing that Darwinian ideas were surfacing in this period and that nations, just like human organisms, were beginning to view the world in terms of struggle and survival:

The Franco-Prussian War of 1870 was the first conflict to be interpreted in Darwinian terms. Both Prussians and Frenchmen drew appropriate conclusions. Had not Prussia prevailed because she knew the value of patriotic collectivism, class unity and authoritarian guidance from above? After the Dreyfus affair and until the Republic proved its capabilities in the First World War, the French right insisted that republican democracy and left-wing theories of class reinforced those weaknesses which ultimately caused nations and races to succumb in the struggle for survival.[11]

On one level, therefore, the emergence of 'another right'[12] was linked directly to nationalist resentments, but on another it was all about political context.

In the immediate aftermath of defeat, Emperor Napoleon III fled the country and by 1875 a republic had been proclaimed.[13] Ironically, though, the early years of the Republic were dominated by monarchism, and, as if to illustrate this, there was an attempted monarchist seizure of power in 1877.[14] Bourgin talks about the 'uncertainties' (*incertitudes*) of the early 1870s.[15] A saying of the time portrayed France as 'a monarchy without a king... a republic without republicans'.[16]

However, by the early 1880s the forces of French monarchism were internally divided and squabbling among themselves, and thus 'lost the capacity for political mobilisation'.[17] Anderson comments:

The confused period of the Republic of 'the Dukes' and of the *grands Notables* presided over by the ineffectual Marshal MacMahon disappeared, never to be restored. Agonising division over the form of the regime and inability to adapt to the realities of universal suffrage conducted the 'reactionaries' – the Legitimists, Orleanists and Bonapartists – into total and irrevocable eclipse.[18]

The post-1871 political climate was particularly conducive to the rise of new political ideas.[19] In choosing the republican option – that 'Jacobin–

republican dream'[20] – France had committed herself to change, but the consensus is that the Third Republic failed to measure up to expectations. As Jenkins says: 'Potential opposition focused on three main grievances – the regime's *parliamentary* character, its neglect of social issues, its failure to harness nationalist aspirations.'[21]

The new political system also meant democracy and more elections. This was the key turning-point because, henceforth, politicians, if they wanted to gain any kind of influence, would be forced to appeal to the masses, to the 'lowest common denominator'. This helps explain why the post-1871 right turned into the type of right it did. (Le Béguec and Prévotat describe this process in terms of the right embracing *la modernité politique*. They say the main changes came after 1898 but, as we will discover, the transformation was in motion well before this.)[22]

This, then, was the background to the emergence of the new right. But what did it stand for? If we were to create a 'model', we would have to say that it was urban rather than rural, centred on the nation rather than on traditional religion, revolutionary rather than conservative, orientated towards the masses rather than the aristocracy, and forward-looking rather than nostalgic about the past. And, as Sternhell argues, it was very different from Bonapartism, which, in his view, was 'pure authoritarianism' and lacked the 'radicalism' and 'organic nationalism' of the post-1880 right.[23]

In essence, new-right ideology was based upon twin pillars: a reawakened sense of national pride and (relatively speaking) an ultra-modern brand of populism. As we have seen, the desire for revenge was at the core of the new creed. In time, this would evolve into xenophobia, deep paranoia about a range of would-be 'threats', and belief that the nation had to be insulated and immunised. By the late 1880s and 1890s, the nationalist right had been infiltrated by a number of influential anti-Semites – convincing proof, if any was needed, that this was a new and radical doctrine.

At the same time, the nationalist right launched a scathing attack on the Third Republic and its institutions. Parliament and parliamentarians were ridiculed, the policies of successive governments were undermined, and the demand for a strong executive government was clearly articulated. For the most part, however, this rhetoric was nebulous. It was easy for the forces of the new right to offer a critique but not so easy for them to present an alternative. Boulanger gave the impression that he was a dictator figure in waiting, Barrès proposed a vague form of 'executive government', and Maurras wanted a king. There was no overall unity.

Grafted on to this critique of the Republic was an authentic 'socialist' agenda. This was part principle and part pragmatism, for, as has just been said, in the context of post-1871 France the right had to adapt and had to advance a political programme that could appeal to French workers. As if to emphasise the point, Boulanger portrayed himself as a late-nineteenth-century 'Jacobin' and Barrès campaigned under the banner of 'national socialism' in 1888–9.[24] Consequently, some historians have wondered out loud whether the new right was a 'rightist' phenomenon at all. On this matter Jenkins offers a balanced view:

> The emergence in the 1880s of an urban populist right was a complex process, not least because it drew on an ideological legacy and a social constituency that in the past had often been identified with the left... [The] combination of anti-parliamentarism, egalitarianism and nationalism was to undergo an ideological metamorphosis which produced a distinctly right-wing critique of the Republic.[25]

Thus, patriotic and populist strains coalesced in the individuals and movements of the new right, and it is for this reason that many commentators have detected the roots of fascist ideology in *fin-de-siècle* France. In Sternhell's words:

> The nationalism of the end of the nineteenth century presents features which can be defined as proto-fascist or as harbingers of fascism. It is very close to the emotional and sentimental fascist ethos; it had the same cult of youth, adventure, and heroism, the same hatred of bourgeois values, and the same faith in the power of the unconscious. It also exhibits that romanticisation of action, the activist mystique and spirit of negation which were to reappear in fascism.[26]

This is a contentious line of thinking that we will encounter again. For the moment, the words of McMillan will suffice. He argues that the dominant traits of the new right were 'aggressive nationalism, racialism and anti-parliamentarism'.[27] So, let us now turn our attention to the individuals and movements that best embodied the protest-centred thinking of the new right.

Déroulède and the Ligue des Patriotes

In 1888 Paul Déroulède wrote the following words:

> For seventeen years I have been watchful and I have looked out:
> Who will repatriate these exiled people?
> When will the hefty conquest be secured?
> When will we avenge the violated law?
> For seventeen years I have been watchful and I have looked out:
> And I have seen nothing to console me.
>
> For seventeen years I have talked and declared:
> Where is your force: where, then, your virtue?
> These are your children, O *Mère Patrie*,
> You owe them your heart, your blood is their due.
> For seventeen years I have talked and I have asked,
> And I have not heard anything in reply.

For seventeen years I have ceaselessly fought,
Always fearlessly attacking our leaders,
For the conflict is wisdom,
When the true peril is cowardice.
For seventeen years I have fought ceaselessly
I have attempted all and obtained nothing.

For seventeen years I have hoped all the same
That the people achieve their dues, grasp power!
For me, before everything, it is the people that I love!
For seventeen years I have hoped in vain
Strong in my love
In my hope.[28]

As a poet turned political agitator, it was natural for Déroulède to express himself in verse and *Depuis dix-sept ans* (*For Seventeen Years*) serves as a powerful introduction to his main political ideas.

The date of publication indicates that *For Seventeen Years* was aimed directly at those who held power in France between 1871 and 1888, with Déroulède bemoaning the inertia, impotence and 'cowardice' of France's leaders in all spheres. He was disappointed by the inaction of the 'Opportunists'[29] and, overall, the poem stands as a damning indictment of the Republic and republicanism. The verses are dominated by emotive language. The author talks about 'blood', 'love', 'hope', 'the true peril', 'the violated law', and addresses France as *Mère Patrie*. This kind of vocabulary is indicative of the way in which 1871 – and its aftermath – was dramatised by new-right spokesmen and acquired almost mythical status in the discourse of nationalists.

In a more specific sense, Déroulède was angry that the Third Republic had not responded to popular pressure and had not even attempted to claim back the annexed territories of Alsace and Lorraine. His allusions to this matter are pointed, referring as he does to 'exiled people' and 'conquest'. This nation-centred discourse is complemented by an embryonic populism. The word 'people' is used three times in quick succession and the transparent hope of Déroulède was that they would 'achieve their dues, grasp power!'. The poem also says much about Déroulède himself. He had – in his own words – spent the period 1871–88 working 'fearlessly' and 'ceaselessly', and had 'obtained nothing'.

For Déroulède *revanche* was a patriotic duty and, not surprisingly, Rutkoff identifies 'something more than a physical, geographical and economic loss'.[30] In his public pronouncements on the subject, Déroulède was high-sounding and emotive. Addressing members of the Ligue, he declared:

Some people have thought the wound in our side which the loss of Alsace–Lorraine has created has healed. You have continually reopened it. You have enlarged it. You have poured molten iron into it. You have let it bleed anew and have prevented the healing. The operation should not be without success. The result is surprising and has exceeded your fondest expectations.[31]

On the subject of revenge the republican Gambetta had stated, 'Think of it always, speak of it never'.[32] Déroulède might have said, 'Think of it always, speak of it always'.

As the poem suggests, the origins of the Ligue des Patriotes are bound up implicitly with 1871 and its aftermath, and it would not be taking things too far to suggest that the Franco-Prussian War was the 'cause' and Déroulède's movement was the 'effect' – the relationship was that fundamental. But we still have to explain away the eleven-year period between the end of the conflict and the beginning of the group's political activity. Again, the poem can help us; after a decade and more of governmental inaction, the poet-nationalist felt the time was right to take things into his own hands.

Déroulède founded the Ligue in May 1882.[33] Prochasson says the infant movement boasted the support of numerous VIPs – including Victor Hugo – and was strongest in urban areas (especially Paris, Lyon and Marseilles).[34] It came to boast around 300,000 members and fifty-two regional committees,[35] and was eventually banned. Milza claims that it was born of the left, but had a middle-class clientele.[36]

The movement – in Magraw's words, 'a noisy, vulgar, violent pressure group'[37] – was set up to campaign on the revenge issue and aimed to 'bully' the Republic's leaders into action. Rutkoff believes that Déroulède was never regarded as an ideologue of stature, but that he had what many other political activists lacked: an organisation.[38] He eventually resigned from the Ligue in 1887, but the influence of the man and his movement was to endure well into the twentieth century. Historians differ in the way they evaluate his significance. Winock says he was dominated by the need to create the 'moral and physical' preconditions for revenge, Sternhell argues that his brand of nationalism 'strangely prefigures fascism', and McMillan offers the ultimate in back-handed compliments when he says that Déroulède is 'not to be dismissed as an eccentric crank who struck no chords with sections of French public opinion'.[39]

What was to be the political strategy of the movement? By instinct Déroulède was a rabble-rouser – Irvine talks about the 'ridiculous blustery' of his organisation[40] – but this approach soon got him into trouble. Tint argues that Déroulède wanted to present the crusade for revenge as a 'holy war' but that he regularly had to tone down his language and instead talk in terms merely of 'national self-defence'. It is argued that the history of the movement 'evolved between these two extremes'.[41]

On a broader level, Mazgaj refers to the way in which the organisation's strategy evolved away from legality and towards direct action.[42] This was a slow process but a profound one, for, as Sternhell notes: 'Déroulède was the first in the republican camp to call publicly into question the old revolutionary heritage; it was in the name of patriotic feeling that the Ligue des Patriotes was gradually transformed into a weapon for use against the Republic.'[43] We can put this another way: at the end of his journey Déroulède was 'more nationalist than republican'.[44] The movement also had to think seriously about its focus. Was it *just* a single-issue pressure group, or was it going to have a concrete position on all political matters, domestic affairs in particular? Tint suggests that Déroulède and company did eventually 'abandon their early political neutrality'.[45]

A number of distinct themes emerge from the Ligue's discourse but, in one way or another, they all connect to *revanche*. First, Déroulède put a high premium on national unity and believed that patriotism should be 'taught' in the classroom, but his approach was hardly conventional. He had a fetish about flags – unsurprisingly his movement's newspaper was christened *Drapeau* – and he even told stories about the 'conversion' experience in 1870 that turned him into a zealous patriot.[46] Sternhell says the Ligue was the first mass movement in France to base itself around nationalist and authoritarian ideology.[47]

Second, beyond the mystical nationalism was a powerful militarism. Déroulède had fought for his country in 1870–1 and had almost lost an arm in combat. He had been surrounded by the military and military values since his youth, and in this sense it was natural for the Ligue to be infected likewise.[48] Young men were exhorted to serve their country in uniform, rifle-shooting competitions were sponsored by the organisation, and military cemeteries were glorified in a distinctly Barrèsian manner.[49] In addition, Déroulède appeared to condone individual acts of violence committed against German nationals in France and campaigned forcefully for a Franco-Russian alliance (clearly seeing the military advantages to such an *entente*).

There was, third, a curious obsession with gymnasia and physical fitness. Quite simplistically, Déroulède equated the strength of a nation to the physical fitness of its people and this assumption came to underpin the entirety of his socio-political thinking. Tint states: 'It was felt that… investment in lithe bodies and keen eyes would stand France in good stead when the moment of reckoning came.'[50] Déroulède's excessive interest in athleticism can be traced back to his association with Léon Gambetta, a man who, in one sense, was a close political ally but also a political foe. During the 1880s Gambetta was the arch-republican nationalist and Déroulède the most high-profile anti-republican nationalist. In the years prior to the formation of the Ligue, Gambetta had appointed Déroulède to a special commission of 'patriotic instruction' and, as a representative of this body, Déroulède had been involved in an in-depth 'study' of physical training societies. In this respect his fascination with gyms and their galvanising effect on individual people – and on the nation – was reflective of more general trends in French society.[51]

If we are to assess the long-term significance and legacy of Déroulède's movement, we must look in two main directions. As many historians have confirmed, the value-system of Déroulède fed through into Boulangism, the nationalist thinking of Barrès and the Action Française of Maurras. Not only did Déroulède view Boulanger as a would-be national saviour, but there were important connections between the Ligue and Boulangism. For a start, as Jenkins explains, Boulanger benefited from the organisational support of Déroulède's group – it gave him 'the nucleus of a political movement'.[52] For his part, Déroulède was to bestride Boulangism and came to personify, quite graphically, the populist, anti-parliamentary creed known as *le révisionnisme* (which acquired real political kudos in the period 1888–9 and was actually synonymous with *Boulangisme*).[53] Sternhell says, 'Déroulède's political ideas received their final shape through Boulangism'.[54]

We could go further and postulate that the Ligue was a harbinger of fascism. Payne states that 'pre-fascist ingredients' can be located in Déroulède's movement,[55] while Levillain claims that it is the best example of an early mass movement in France.[56] Griffin, however, argues that the Ligue should be pigeon-holed on the 'non-fascist radical right' on account of its single-issue focus.[57] Historians are thus divided on this issue.

In more general terms, the least that can be said is that there are interesting continuities at play – most notably the movement's extreme nationalism and obsession with physical fitness. However, it must be pointed out that, even though Déroulède was happy to talk in terms of 'race', he never incorporated any element of anti-Semitism into his political programme.[58] Perhaps we should leave the final word to Sternhell, who argues that Déroulède and his organisation were the embodiment of that process whereby French nationalism evolved from 'official republican and Jacobin ideology' to 'the common ideology of the right-wing opposition'.[59]

Boulanger and Boulangism

According to Dansette, there were four distinct 'Boulangisms': *le boulangisme jacobin*, *le boulangisme revanchard*, *le boulangisme antiparlementaire* and *le boulangisme des royalistes*. Each, in his view, can be linked to a specific phase of the late 1880s.[60] This schema demonstrates the heterogeneity of the creed.[61]

Boulangism has already been identified as one of the core components of the post-1880 new right. Now we can assess it more thoroughly. Why is it important? How did it develop? What did it stand for? What legacy did it leave? And, in fundamental terms, was it a movement of the far right or the revolutionary left? The first thing to be said is that Boulangism was of more substance than Boulanger. Whereas the political doctrine influenced and mobilised people, the General – even though he rose to the heights of Minister of War in 1886 – was a weak-willed and shallow individual who fled to Belgium when power was within his grasp.[62] And therein lies the main significance of the whole episode. Boulangism – an amalgam of 'apparently incompatible' forces[63] – had the potential to topple the Republic, but this went unrealised. Boulanger saw himself as 'the providential man',[64] but in the end it was more like Caesarism without the Caesar.[65]

Nevertheless, the Revisionist movement (so-called because it aimed to 'revise' the constitutional arrangements heralded by 1875) still holds its historical importance. It was taken extremely seriously by the authorities and by established politicians like Jules Ferry,[66] and for its time it boasted two novel, almost revolutionary, characteristics – a cult of personality and a desire to engage in mass politics and adapt its political programme accordingly. For this reason Irvine sees the Boulangist episode as a 'critical turning point in the history of French nationalism and French royalism'.[67]

The emergence of Boulangism is intimately connected with 1871 and its aftermath. Just like Déroulède, Boulanger was personally affected by the defeat, and in his political statements the General hit the same raw nerve as his poet friend. However, with his impressive quotient of charisma and mass appeal, Boulanger was able to establish a powerful, nationwide movement on a different plane from mere 'pressure group' agitation; so much so that Déroulède was happy to trade in his loyalty to the Ligue for Boulangism.[68] The General was aided by additional factors: his widely acknowledged military prowess, the vagaries of the electoral system under the new Republic, and the prevailing political context.[69] Levillain talks about a background of social unease, growing anti-parliamentary feeling and an emerging nationalism.[70] Mayeur goes further and suggests that the 1882 economic crisis was of crucial significance in stoking the fires of protest politics and unleashing both nationalist and socialist ideas.[71]

There is much irony in the fact that Boulanger, the man assigned to 'republicanise' the army as Minister of War,[72] eventually came to personify a political movement that aimed to undermine and destroy the Third Republic. In the light of this, some historians have pointed to the Bonapartist influence at the heart of Boulangism. Rémond says Boulangism inherited from Bonapartism its 'verbal violence, the excesses of language, and the oratorical demagoguery', while Rothney concludes that Boulangism was the last desperate 'fling' for a Bonapartism that had failed to adapt to the new political context.[73] On the same theme, Berstein and Milza point to the fact that whether Boulanger was a 'new Bonaparte' or not, he was certainly perceived as such.[74]

However, on the whole, historians are now inclined to view Boulangism as an innately modern political phenomenon, having more in common with mass organisations of the twentieth century than anything else. Jenkins is representative: 'The movement was above all urban rather than rural, *petit bourgeois* rather than peasant, and it was Catholic reactionaries rather than capitalists who opportunistically exploited it.'[75] Boulangism was also about propaganda. It gained the backing of newspapers such as *L'Intransigent, La Croix, Le Soleil, La Lanterne, L'Autorité, La Nation, L'Événement* and *La*

France, and it set great store by posters, badges, songs, games and other commercial gimmicks.[76] In this sense as well, Boulanger's movement embraced the modern age.

There is no doubt that *Boulangisme* was a coalition. Tombs argues that the left provided it with 'brains and brawn' and the right offered votes and money.[77] As 'General of the Discontented', Boulanger was a catalyst, a natural reference point. Jenkins says Boulangism, 'temporarily brought together widely different sources of hostility to the regime under the banner of authoritarian populism, nationalism and anti-parliamentarism'.[78]

On the left, Blanquists were seduced by the 'legend' of Boulanger. Although Hutton claims that Boulangism was a 'lost cause', he is still able to rationalise its appeal for Blanquists, pointing, in particular, to the common enemy ('Opportunist' politics), the shared outlook (the hostility to parliament and republic and the belief in constitutional revision) and the 'populist affinities'.[79] He contends that in practical terms the two factions could offer each other much and that, when push came to shove, they were both movements of 'radical republican protest'.[80] For his part, Sternhell says that it was *Blanquisme* that supplied Boulangism with its non-Marxist socialist vision and its 'patriotic and revolutionary fervour'.[81]

On the right, Boulanger struck up a pragmatic alliance with the Royalists in the late 1880s.[82] In essence, this was the coming together of old and new forces for purposes of political expediency. On one level it is easy to understand the alliance – Boulanger wanted additional support, royalists wanted to resurrect their political fortunes – but on another it is less so. For royalists, Boulanger, on the surface, personified alien political forces and ideas. He was a demagogue, an individual who had embraced democracy and egalitarianism, and someone who stood for revenge, nationalism and war. Predictably therefore, Levillain argues that it was an 'error' for the right to trust in Boulanger.[83]

Nevertheless, whatever their intrinsic misgivings, royalists in France knew that Boulanger had 'utility'.[84] He could be used to drive a wedge between 'the opportunists and the radicals' and at the same time could inject the royalist right with a much-needed dose of 'popular dynamism'.[85] As Irvine states: 'The urban masses clamouring after the latest Boulanger song... were what stood between the royalists and any hopes of regaining power. By themselves, royalists could never hope to appeal to those segments of the population; allied with Boulangism they might.'[86]

Thus, in the hope of gaining additional support Boulanger posed as the man who might restore the monarchy. But there were dissident voices within his own movement. Mermeix, for one, believed that the General had 'sold out', announcing that 'in associating with the Royalists, the Boulangist leader lost the true ideal of Boulangism which at the outset was a great popular and democratic movement'.[87] In addition Déroulède and Rochefort talked about 'treachery'[88] and the Blanquists felt they had been tainted by association.[89] In retrospect the royalist alliance can be seen as probably the most controversial aspect of Boulanger's brief political fling.

A new revolutionary right?

In Boulangism one can detect the same doctrinal strands that one can see in the Ligue des Patriotes: the unending search for revenge, the desire for firm executive government, contempt for parliament, belief in 'direct democracy', and a desire to tap into the social and economic aspirations of ordinary people – though whether this was more myth than reality is open to question (as it is with Déroulède and his movement).

As a proud soldier Boulanger understood more than most the agony of 1871 and, as such, 'Revenge' dominated his rhetoric. In time he acquired the nicknames 'General *Revanche*' and 'Minister of *Revanche*',[90] and he was to square up to Bismarck in a rhetorical sense on more than one occasion.[91]

Nationalism coalesced with anti-parliamentarianism. Boulanger's contempt for the legislative body was intense. He campaigned under the slogan A BAS LA CHAMBRE! (DOWN WITH PARLIAMENT!), and a cartoon of the time showed him 'slapping the bottom' of parliament – represented as a 'naughty schoolboy'. The General announced that France was 'ill and decadent',[92] elaborating on this theme in an 1889 election address:

> The parliamentarians, who have done all they could to prevent my standing for election, are panic-stricken today at the idea of seeing me elected. My sword upset them. They took it away from me. And now they are more anxious than when I was still wearing it. In reality it is not me they are frightened of, but universal suffrage, whose repeated decisions testify to the disgust the country feels at the state of degeneracy to which their incapacity, low intrigues, and tedious debates have brought the Republic. It is in fact more convenient to make me responsible for the discredit into which they have fallen than to attribute it to their egoism and their indifference to the interest and sufferings of the people... I want, and France wants, a Republic composed of something other than a collection of ambitions and greed.[93]

There are key words in this passage: 'degeneracy', 'incapacity', 'discredit', 'indifference'. Mermeix explained the problem further: 'It is the omnipotence of legislative power and the annihilation of executive power that characterises the regime of... 1875. Parliament is everything... Executive power was nothing but a decorative factor; the Boulangists considered restoring it, giving it back authority for the good of the public.'[94]

The corollary of this critique was a passionate call for 'firm government'. Jenkins sums up Boulanger's manifesto as 'revision of the constitution, the dissolution of the Chamber and the setting-up of an authoritarian presidential Republic'.[95] Hence the campaign slogan: DISSOLUTION, CONSTITUANTE, RÉVISION.[96] Boulangists proposed a system of 'popular', 'plebiscitary' democracy whereby France would be governed via referenda,[97] and the General played up the uniqueness of his blueprint. He wanted 'a new, national Republic, open to all honest men and to every progress made by the people, for the people, and in which the people would have not only the too illusory right to express their wishes, but the power to realise them'.[98] This all sounded good in theory but it was never tested in practice. The suspicion is that Boulanger stood for a form of executive government that could easily have evolved into dictatorship, whatever his personal protestations.[99]

In the long term Boulangism revolutionised the nature of the French right. The key point was that Boulanger, a convinced nationalist, was also able to pose as an authentic man of the left, as a Jacobin, and an heir to 1789 rather than 1851.[100] Indeed, there was such a discernible 'socialist' drift to much of the General's rhetoric that it would not be exaggerating matters to describe Boulangism as a socialist movement with an intense nationalist outlook.[101] It is in this sense that the General has been portrayed as the 'catalyst' in the creation of a 'revolutionary process'.[102]

So was Boulanger 'a comic-opera Bonaparte' and Boulangism 'a disappointing tragicomedy', as Nord argues?[103] It is easy to belittle the Boulangist movement,[104] but in reality it carried real weight. It stood as the 'union of the discontented' (*le syndicat des mécontents*)[105] and, in the view of some historians, was able to appeal to both town and country.[106] More importantly, it changed the very nature of politics, for recent interpretations emphasise the ability of Boulanger to engage working people, to identify, as early as the late nineteenth century, the 'great mobilising issues' of the twentieth century (like anti-Semitism and social discontent), and to exploit universal suffrage effectively.[107] As such, Winock describes Boulangism as a kind of national-populism[108] and Levillain says it put France on the path to mass democracy (*une dèmocratie de masses*).[109]

But perhaps the most significant verdict comes courtesy of Sternhell who says that Boulangism in the 1880s and 1890s plays the role 'later played by socialism'.[110] This was what was revolutionary about the new right.

Barrès and the cult of rootedness

Over time it was Maurice Barrès – novelist, politician and intellectual – who was to give Boulangism a dose of intellectual respectability. He argued that the Achilles heel of the movement had been its lack of real doctrine,[111] and his achievement, if that is the right word, was to supply it with one. Barrès shared many of the convictions expounded by Déroulède and the General. He criticised the Third Republic, mistrusted parliament, and poured scorn on episodes like the Panama Scandal,[112] but he articulated his ideas in a vastly different manner.

In the history of far-right politics in France, Barrès is a pivotal figure and *Barrèsisme* is a value-system of central importance.[113] It was not just that Barrès was a man of letters but that he had connections and influence. To begin with, he was an accomplice of Déroulède and a supporter of Boulanger;

and by the late 1890s he was a keynote figure in the Anti-Dreyfusard Movement, and thereafter played a formative role in the politics of Action Française. In the twentieth century both Vichy politicians and FN (Front National) activists have utilised political ideas first espoused by Barrès.

Historians weigh Barrès up differently. Milza says that in many ways he was a conservative – he was deeply attached to the traditions and institutions of France – but that he also exhibited a range of 'pre-fascist' traits, most notably the belief in 'revolt' and mystical nationalism.[114] It is no surprise, therefore, that Soucy has labelled him 'the first French fascist'[115] and that many modern historians view him as the founding father of the far right.[116] In the view of Magraw he 'personifies' the values of the new right, while Jenkins argues that he stands for race and the ethnic tradition.[117]

Barrès operated on two different planes. On one level he was just an ordinary politician who stood for election in Nancy, sat in parliament as a Boulangist *député* between 1889 and 1893, and concerned himself throughout this period with day-to-day matters.[118] On another level, however, Barrès was anything but a run-of-the-mill politician. As a prolific writer and novelist he brought a highly vivid sense of 'emotionalism' into politics,[119] and his depiction of the graveyards and cemeteries of Lorraine, and their significance for nationalists, is wonderfully prosaic. In this sphere of his political life he put immense emphasis on the spiritual and the mystical, and argued that the nation is an entity to be worshipped and that nationalism was the new religion. Brogan sums up neatly, saying that Barrès was both 'preacher and practitioner of the nationalist doctrine'.[120]

More specifically, Barrès stands for a very distinct form of closed nationalism. *Barrèsisme* was a fusion of political ideas and at its heart was the insistence that France must gain back the 'lost territories' of Alsace and Lorraine. This, of course, was an omnipresent theme on the new right but Barrès injected it with a new passion and a new thirst. Boulanger's crude rhetoric was replaced by a sophisticated and almost lyrical approach, and pro-revenge, anti-German discourse was taken to a new plane.

Barrès was born in Lorraine and felt Germany's territorial annexation particularly badly. It is this deep longing for revenge – a desire to get 'even' with the Germans – that makes him such a key patriotic figure in the late nineteenth and early twentieth centuries,[121] but in elevating the nation above everything else, he advanced a creed that was overtly anti-individual and anti-individualistic. Putnam explains that in *Barrèsisme*: 'The nation... is an organism *distinct from* and *superior to* the individuals who compose it.'[122]

Moving on, Barrès held that the nation is determined by *la terre et les morts* ('the earth and the dead'). This was an exclusive vision of nationhood that would mean some people, or rather some groups of people, being left outside. In *Scènes et doctrines du nationalisme*, he sets out his thinking:

> The problem for the individual and the nation is not to make themselves

into what they want to be… but to preserve in themselves what the centuries have predestined for them… Nationalism is the acceptance of a particular kind of determinism… My *intelligence* is tempted on all sides; everything interests me, stimulates me and amuses me. But there is, at the very bottom of our souls, a fixed point, a delicate nerve; if it is probed the result is a total reaction which I cannot mistrust, a movement of my whole being. It is not the awakening of the sensibilities of a mere individual; what frightens me is the awakening of my whole race.[123]

It is around this 'fixed point' that Barrèsian ideology revolves.

Barrès' obsession with *la terre et les morts* stems from his fascination with cemeteries and graveyards. When he was not in Paris, or writing, or engaging in more conventional political activity, he spent a huge amount of time wandering the burial grounds of his native Lorraine. It was in the graves of French soldiers that he located the key to identity. They were symbols – of memory, ancestry, martyrdom and the soul of the nation. In 1902 he visited the military cemetery at Chambières and spoke in mystical terms about 'the piles of corpses' located there.[124] On another pilgrimage Barrès surveyed the battlefields of La Mortagne and later reflected on his visit: 'Our brothers have died, and they lie in these mounds; our houses are shattered and burnt, and our fellow-citizens have been shot or taken away into captivity. But you have not suffered in vain, and your terrible sacrifices have ensured the salvation of France.'[125]

There was a strong neo-religious dimension to Barrèsian nationalism; people had died, martyrs had emerged, and resurrection would follow. In 1917, in an article entitled 'Young Soldiers of France', Barrès focuses on the death of an army lieutenant: 'Only the dead have spoken to us here. This is seemly; we need put no curb on our praise. The living, however, are in every way their peers. Though they have not received the supreme consecration, theirs is the compensating glory of continuous service.'[126] Here it is as if the dead are actually more important than the living. Barrès relished the opportunity to discover more about the 'heroes of France' and felt that people had a duty to explore their nation. Putnam writes:

> Young Frenchmen, then, should study the conditions, material and spirtual, which had made them what they are. They must leave Paris and return to their native provinces, there to roam about the cemeteries and fields, absorbing the aura of *La Terre et les Morts*. In silent meditation they must engender in themselves the sense of power and purpose which arises when they grasp in their inner beings a feeling of oneness with their illustrious dead and the soil which had spawned them.[127]

This firm, unconditional belief in the nation and national spirit belies the fact that Barrès had commenced his political life as a committed individualist.

But, from a position where 'ego worship' and 'self-glorification' was central, he ended up convinced that the individual needs roots, and that the self (*le moi*) can only develop as part of a community. In this regard Soucy locates a 'conversion to rootedness',[128] and Tint talks about Barrès' new belief 'in a kind of national collective unconscious'.[129]

'Rootedness' (*enracinement*) is a key term in Barrèsian vocabulary and implies stability and loyalty and is viewed as the key to a happy and prosperous nation; this is contrasted with 'unrootedness' (*déracinement*). Barrès was contemptuous of the 'unrooted' (*les déracinés*) and portrayed the Jews as a particularly non-rooted people (his first novel was actually titled *Les Déracinés*). This led on to a discourse of anti-Semitism that presaged his involvement in the Anti-Dreyfusard Movement.[130]

Implicit in Barrès' brand of closed nationalism is the delineation of outsiders or 'barbarians'. In his mature doctrine the *moi* is no longer the individual but the nation, and so the *non-moi* is the foreigner or – as he prefers to put it – the 'barbarian'. He views the 'barbarian' as a threat to national integrity, national purity and national stability and it is for this reason that 'walls' are an important concept in Barrèsian thought. It is 'walls' that will keep the 'barbarians' out and keep the nation intact.

The Lorrainer's political creed set great store by emotion, irrationalism and the power of 'unconscious forces'[131] and it was a doctrine that was opposed to Enlightenment thinking before almost anything else.[132] This is illustrated in the way that 'truth' is defined. Barrès was very flexible: there was 'a French truth and a German truth' (*une vérité française et une vérité allemande*)[133] and in his mind 'truth' equated to whatever was good for France, whatever was in the general interest of the nation. Weiss says: 'There could be no international standards of abstract truth. For the French there could only be French truth, French reason and French justice... Truth was always relative to a situation and forged by emotional needs.'[134] The gross subjectivity of this definition is almost the epitome of irrationalism.

Barrès' irrationalism is also illustrated in the way that he encourages 'hate' and 'hatreds'. His argument is that within human beings, emotion should be sovereign. So in the same way that he was powerful in his loves (France, Lorraine, *la terre et les morts*), he was graphic in his hatreds (Germans, Jews, other 'barbarians', parliament, the Third Republic, reason, rationality). This, for Putnam, emphasises the 'sickness and evil' within his doctrine.[135]

In a distinctly Sorelian manner, Barrès was also happy to create and then manipulate 'myths' for political ends. He was in favour of leaders embroidering their rhetoric to unify opinion and during his political career he used Lorraine and the Dreyfus Affair as useful myths.[136] Naturally, the 'truth' of these myths is unimportant; that, after all, is why they are myths.[137] Putnam says, 'His experience, especially his experience in the Boulanger Affair, had taught him that the action of most people was... based on emotional rather than rational factors.'[138]

Xenophobia and insularity

Barrès' hostility to threatening 'outsiders' was taken on to the plane of practical politics. As a Boulangist deputy in the 1880s and 1890s, Barrès was forced to grapple with the major social and economic issues of the day. In this period we can see how Barrès applied his nationalist philosophy to the demands of practical politics. His aim throughout was the material and moral improvement of French citizens and he was particularly strident on the question of immigrant workers. When he stood for election in Nancy under Boulangist colours in 1898, his manifesto was unequivocal:

> In the top ranks of society, in the heart of the provinces, in the moral and in the material sphere, in commerce, industry, and agriculture, even in the shipyards where they are competing with French workers, foreigners are poisoning us like parasites. One vital principle that should underlie the new French policy is to protect all its nationals against this invasion, and to beware of that brand of socialism that is so cosmopolitan, or rather so German, that it would weaken the country's defences.[139]

Barrès goes on to pillory the Jewish community and concludes by stating: 'We should insist that military service is a condition of nationality.'[140] This is a significant statement because it emphasises the Barrèsian notion of sacrifice. He is suggesting that foreigners need to actively 'prove' their national loyalty because, in his view, France's naturalisation laws were too lax.

The organisation that backed Barrès' candidature in Nancy was the 'Nationalist Socialist Republican Committee of Meurthe-et-Moselle'.[141] The title of this body is significant, for it demonstrates the coming together of socialism and nationalism on the new right in a natural and almost spontaneous fashion.[142] On balance, Barrès would argue that his manifesto was as much about protecting French workers as about singling out foreigners, and he always felt that socialism as a political doctrine was doomed if it did not embrace nationalism.[143] McClelland puts it succinctly: 'For him, the important thing was that if a man was to be a socialist, he ought to be a French socialist if he is French, a national socialist in a specific sense.'[144]

In the economic sphere it was logical that Barrès would believe in protectionism. His 1898 manifesto is full of references to this:

> It has taken some centuries for the French nation to give political security to its members. It must now protect them against that economic insecurity that prevails at all levels... They have begun to remedy this situation, which is basically a socialist measure, intervention by the State in the natural course of events... We are in full agreement with the major aspects of protection. It aims at guaranteeing a minimum price to the producer...[145]

It is interesting that Barrès actually points out that protectionism 'is basically a socialist measure'. He is comfortable with this and goes on to delineate a range of other left-wing policy proposals, including 'a superannuation fund for workers', 'freedom of association' and 'development of public education'.[146] Mazgaj talks about Barrès' 'Proudhonian-style socialism – with its populist anti-Semitism, its concern for social justice, and its rejection of collectivism'.[147] It is no surprise at all that Barrès went on to stand for parliament as a socialist candidate in the mid-1890s.[148]

It is easy to criticise Barrès and cast aspersions on *Barrèsisme* as a political creed. For a start, there is a narrowness and insularity about Barrès that is difficult to countenance. The erection of 'walls' to protect the *moi* from the *non-moi* is rationalised in a step-by-step fashion, but in the modern world is this kind of approach possible or desirable? What are the humanitarian implications of such an attitude? Lynch, a contemporary of the Lorrainer, was one of his biggest critics. In 1900 she said: 'The national instinct M. Barrès refers to seems to consist in a liberal abuse of all foreigners.'[149]

Moreover, Barrès was very ambiguous on the subject of his ideal regime. He demonstrates loyalty to the 1875 constitution via the title of his political movement,[150] but at the same time he undermined the Third Republic at every possible opportunity. The suspicion is that Barrès – a man with Bonapartist affections[151] – harboured anti-democratic dreams. McMillan states: 'Though claiming to be a republican, he stipulated that he wanted a certain kind of Republic. "I love the Republic," he said, "but armed, glorious, organised". Like Déroulède, Barrès was at heart an authoritarian with a complete contempt for parliament.'[152]

Likewise, there seems to be an element of ambiguity in the way that Barrès viewed regionalism and regional identity. As we have seen, he treads a philosophical path away from individualism and towards national rootedness, but at all points along this journey he still glorifies provincialism and, in particular, his home province of Lorraine. Is this possible to do? Or is it just over-sentimental posturing? Furthermore, is 'France' or 'Lorraine' the ultimate loyalty? And what happens when 'healthy regionalism' turns into the desire for autonomy or secession?[153] In fundamental terms, how can we take him seriously when he moves from a philosophy of individualism to collectivism in the blink of an eyelid? There is also severe irony in the fact that Barrès, the ultimate in cosmopolitan intellectuals, spent most of his time deriding cosmopolitan intellectuals.[154] Overall, the suspicion is that he was wrapping a cloak of intellectualism around a set of very unpleasant ideas.

Perhaps the most measured conclusion we can reach is that in the history of right-wing ideas, *Barrèsisme* is an important landmark.[155] Moreover, as many scholarly studies confirm, Barrès is now viewed as a central figure in the origins of generic fascism. For instance, Soucy and Sternhell paint a picture of Barrès the 'proto-fascist', even though the former acknowledges the problems inherent in such a portrayal.[156] But, however we choose to assess Barrès, we must acknowledge that his realism was commendable. He accepted that 1789 had happened in a way that Maurras did not, and he adapted to the context of late nineteenth-century and early twentieth-century politics in a way that Maurras was incapable of.[157] As Brogan puts it: 'He had too much wisdom, too much human sympathy, not to notice that it was impossible to build a system of political architecture on a tradition that was not generally accepted; without the people, no political renaissance was possible.'[158]

One is left with the feeling that Barrès had, in a sense, outgrown the 'old' politics, revolving as it did around aristocracy, church and royalty, and in consequence it may be appropriate to describe him as a 'new conservative'[159] – a man of the right, but a figure who had substituted socialist instincts for 'old right' loyalties. It is here that he emerges as a representative of the 'new' or 'radical' or 'revolutionary' right. The new idol for Barrès was the nation and a new determinism, based on roots, is located at the very heart of his writings. Guérard talks about 'subconscious influences, ancestral and local, which create in men's souls a sense of their nationality'.[160] Putnam puts it another way: '*Barrèsisme* envisages a France in which the weight of *la terre et les morts* will rest so heavily on the soul of every Frenchman that, when the interests of France are brought into any question, thought and rational discussion will give way to blind, unreasoning emotional exhilaration.'[161]

Edouard Drumont and the Anti-Dreyfusard Movement

In the second half of the 1890s Barrès was a central figure in the Anti-Dreyfusard Movement, a right-wing coalition in which 'nationalism joined hands with conservatism and became the defender of ancient institutions'.[162]

Alfred Dreyfus was a captain in the French army and a Jew.[163] He had been accused of spying for the Germans and his case became the ultimate *cause célèbre* in 1890s France. It is a gross simplification to say that the forces of the left lined up to defend him and the forces of the right stood opposed to him, but this was the nub of the situation. 'Dreyfusards' squared up to 'Anti-Dreyfusards' and in the words of Joll there was 'bloodless civil war'.[164] According to Kedward, the case encompassed 'nationalist tensions', 'racial tensions', 'religious tensions' and 'political tensions',[165] while Miquel claims that, above all, the Dreyfus Affair was about 'opinion'.[166] In the fullness of time Dreyfus was shown to be innocent and the army deemed to be guilty of a horribly cynical cover-up designed to frame him.

Barrès, together with political soulmate Maurras, was at the forefront of the Anti-Dreyfusard Movement. There was emotive rhetoric and public protest but ultimately the alliance was unsuccessful and the new right-wing threat to the regime evaporated. Dreyfus was pardoned, the army lost credibility, an attempted right-wing coup in 1899 ended in farce, and the institutions of the Republic gained in stature.[167] Notwithstanding this, or perhaps even because of this, *antidreyfusisme* is of profound significance as regards the evolution of the extreme right in France.

Although anti-Semitism 'may not have been at the root of the affair',[168] the episode does mark the full-scale, almost permanent, coming together of right-wing politics and anti-Semitic agitation. McMillan states: 'The Dreyfus Affair seemed to offer just the right opportunity for the creation of a new mass-based movement of the Right, held together by anti-Semitism.'[169] Of course, hostility to the Jews has a long history in France[170] but, as Sternhell notes, it was only with Boulanger and Barrès, and then the Anti-Dreyfusard Movement, that anti-Semitism became a political force.[171]

In this regard Edouard Drumont's book, *La France juive*, is a landmark and a harbinger of further anti-Semitic activity.[172] Drumont, a failed journalist, had always wanted to make his name in the publishing world, and what he produced in 1886 was a vicious and unpleasant anti-Semitic tract. Part of its potency was its appeal, if that is the right word. In the words of Bredin, 'it was intent on addressing the working class and the petite bourgeoisie, the victims of international capitalism and large industry'.[173] The book ran to two volumes and 1,200 pages. It is difficult to measure its impact, but over 100,000 copies were sold in the first six months and 200 different editions were published, including an illustrated version. Hot on the heals of the book came Drumont's anti-Jewish newspaper *La Libre parole* (1892), the emergence of the Jeunesse Antisémite et Nationaliste (1894) and Guérin's Ligue Antisémitique (1897), full-scale riots (1898), and an anti-Semitic 'group' in parliament.[174] Milza says Drumont played an 'immense' role in spreading prejudice.[175] Wistrich labels him 'the high priest of French anti-semitism'.[176]

Drumont's work was quite transparently of new-rightist character. In a calculated way he was appealing to the lowest common denominator, to 'the newly literate masses by using a crude Darwinian racism and claiming for it the prestige of science'.[177] This passage from *La France juive* is representative:

> The two races are doomed to come into conflict, because of both their qualities and their shortcomings. The Semite is mercantile, covetous, scheming, subtle and cunning. The Aryan is enthusiastic, heroic, chivalrous, disinterested, frank and trusting to the point of naïvety. The Semite is earth-bound with scarcely any concern for the life hereafter; the Aryan is a child of heaven who is constantly preoccupied by higher aspirations... The Semite is a businessman by instinct; he is a born trader, dealing in everything imaginable, seizing every opportunity to get the better of the next man. The Aryan on the other hand is a peasant, a poet, a monk and, above all, a soldier... The Semite has no creative ability, whereas the Aryan is an inventor. Not a single invention has ever been the work of a Semite. He exploits, organises and produces

whatever the creative Aryan has invented, and, needless to say, retains the profits for himself.[178]

And he goes on:

> It is a fact, the Jew smells bad. Even the smartest of them give off an odour, *fetor judaïca*, or as Zola would say, a whiff, which reveals the race and helps them to recognise one another... The question of understanding why the Jews stink has long preoccupied a number of well-intentioned people... In Prussia, the proportion of lunatics is much higher among Israelites than among Christians. Whereas there are 24.1 per 10,000 Protestants, and 23.7 for the same number of Catholics, per 10,000 Jews there are 38.9. In Italy the ratio is one lunatic per 384 Jews and one per 778 Catholics.[179]

As we can see, *Drumontisme* was an unpleasant mix of political, economic, religious and racial anti-Semitism, combined with prejudice, gross stereotyping and pseudo-science. His 'biological and psychological determinism'[180] offered people an 'ideological cement'.[181]

Like other radical agitators of the 1880s, Drumont was hostile to various aspects of the Third Republic, most notably the 'anti-clerical' legislation it had enacted and the endless political scandal involving top-ranking Jews. The subtitle of his newspaper, *La Libre parole*, was *'La France pour les Français'*, which suggests a nationalist agenda,[182] but he was never very concerned about *revanche*, mainly because in his mind there was always something more important than nation-based conflicts: race.[183]

We should not just assume that Drumont was, *ipso facto*, a man of the right. Of course he was a racist – an individual who believed in inequality and superiority – but we should not ignore the fact that he was also a populist, a man who wanted to ingratiate himself to the masses and someone whose mistrust of Jews was based primarily on their 'money-making' ethic and their involvement in 'international finance'.[184] Sternhell, for one, is happy to locate anti-Semitism on the left: '[It] was a progressive and non-conformist ideology, an ingredient in the revolt against the established order, in short, one of the facets of Socialism.'[185] We should certainly bear this point in mind as our discussion progresses.

For Bredin, a variety of reasons can be put forward to explain the 'anti-Semitic fever' of the late nineteenth century,[186] but the fanatical scribblings of Drumont must be given their due. It has been argued that Drumont's main 'achievement' was to synthesise political, economic and racial anti-Semitism and to create an atmosphere in which anti-Semitic attitudes and anti-Semitic activity were somehow 'normalised'.[187] It is in light of this that we should think about the origins of the Dreyfus Affair, in general, and the Anti-Dreyfusard Movement, in particular.

Conservative reaction

The Anti-Dreyfusard Movement is interesting and important for a number of reasons, most obviously its coalition nature. Curtis talks about a combination of:

> Old Boulangists, the army, the professional anti-Semites, the Church and some intellectuals... The antirevisionist belief, partly the crystallization of anti-intellectual reaction to the excessive faith in science of the nineteenth century, was in large measure a desire to maintain the order of traditional authorities... The antirevisionists were largely Parisian and upper middle class, including Royalists and most of the French Academy...[188]

Thus, we are talking about an unusual alliance and one that briefly united 'new right' and 'old right' loyalists. At the heart of the coalition were a variety of individuals who in the 1890s would still have described themselves as 'counter-revolutionaries'. Maurras, in particular, had not given up hope of a 'conservative revolution' and was still railing about the 'evil' of 1789. In the specific context of the Dreyfus Affair, he and like-minded thinkers argued that the concept of the 'rights of man' was null and void, preferring to view Dreyfus as an individual whose rights could be sacrificed in the 'national interest' – a cynical tactic that owed much to Barrès' thinking on 'truth'.[189] The fact that Dreyfus was a Jew made him an ideal target and gave the forces of conservatism extra elbow room. Brogan states: 'Not only the Army but the Frenchness of France seemed to be under attack.'[190] It was predictable that the anti-Dreyfusards thought little of the Dreyfusards; one senior military figure spoke of 'the horrible campaign by those vile people'.[191]

The value-system of the typical anti-Dreyfusard was conservative and reactionary and, in due course, the nature of the coalition meant it emerged as a bastion of militarism and clericalism. Déroulède, the man responsible for the shambolic attempted coup of 1899, expounded the movement's attitude to the army in a speech of the same year:

> *Vive l'armée!*... Long live the army that sacrifices itself! The army that suffers and ages! Long live... the spirit of obedience, the spirit of discipline, the spirit of *la patrie!* What is the good of crying: Down with the Ministers! Down with the Presidents! Down with the Panamaists, the Dreyfusards, the Parliamentarians, Parliamentarianism! The Corrupters and the Corrupted! Do not these two words say all that needs to be said: *Vive l'armée!* Yes, long live the army, that is our last honour, our last recourse, our supreme safeguard.[192]

As this passage indicates, the army was regarded by the right as 'the true repository of the interests of the nation'.[193] As an institution it was viewed not only as infallible but as 'above' normal processes of law – hence its strategy of attempting to pervert the course of justice during the Dreyfus Affair. The army interpreted the Dreyfusard offensive as an attack on the French military and this is why 'the extreme right were soon trying to use the case to overturn the Republic'.[194] Charle puts it another way: 'The cadres of the armies of the Republic were increasingly linked to an older France, even if they did not all originate from it socially. This France found a substitute for its nostalgia for the monarchy and State Catholicism in *revanchiste* nationalism and the cult of the army.'[195] The fact that Dreyfus was from Alsace and that, in the light of 1871, a climate of 'spymania' was enveloping the country just added to the poignancy of the situation.[196] As in many other periods, far-right thinking was the product of paranoia.

In its time of trouble, the army found a loyal ally in the church.[197] The two institutions had two important things in common: both were dominated by conservatives and both were highly suspicious of 'liberal' republicanism. But for the church there was an added piquancy to the Dreyfus Affair – the Jewish question.

In this period of French history the church was strongly anti-Semitic. In 1890 *La Croix* – the Assumptionist newspaper – described itself as 'the most anti-Jewish newspaper in France, the one that bears Christ, the sign of horror for all Jews'.[198] Moreover the Assumptionists framed the Dreyfus Affair as 'a duel between the army and *le syndicat juif*',[199] and even co-opted the language of the left, announcing that, 'without doubt, *c'est la patrie en danger*'.[200] It was as if a religious war had broken out. Weiss states:

> In the spirit of de Maistre and Bonald, the editors of the Assumptionist paper, La Croix, called for a restoration of the old unity of throne and altar. They also insisted that Dreyfus was part of an international conspiracy bent upon weakening the French army and seizing France's territories. The Jesuit Order called for political and economic sanctions against Jews and publicly expressed hope for the day when they might be banished from Europe altogether.[201]

Here we touch on another significant aspect of the Anti-Dreyfusard Movement: its 'irrational, intransigent stance'[202] and its terribly pragmatic conception of politics. Barrès was the epitome:

> The campaign mounted by a certain group of people which is called 'the Dreyfus Affair' is an example of the disassociation and decerebralisation of France. At the same time it widens the division amongst us and troubles the spirit of the nation. Déroulède's formula is really striking. He states: 'It is highly improbable that Dreyfus is innocent, but it is absolutely certain that France herself is innocent.'[203]

Barrès and Déroulède did not care about the guilt or innocence of the individual, only the credibility of the army and the 'grandeur' of the nation.[204]

The legacy of anti-Dreyfusardism was immeasurable. In the words of Goguel there was a 'psychological aspect and political consequences'.[205] On one level the Republic had survived and grown stronger. (One indicator of this was the series of anti-clerical decrees passed in the immediate aftermath of the Dreyfus Affair).[206] On another level, however, the forces of conservatism and nationalism had undergone a renaissance. Milza says the Dreyfus Affair gave French nationalism a range of unique traits: a defensive mentality, a close alignment with the military, verbal violence and 'anchorage on the extreme right'.[207] In terms of practicalities the main outcome was the birth of Action Française in 1899.

The new right was a complex phenomenon. Bourgin says the nationalism of the Dreyfus era was as heterogeneous as the Boulanger-style creed,[208] while Mayer claims it is impossible to understand either episode without recognising the significance of Barrès.[209]

The fact of the matter is that by 1918 the extreme right had changed dramatically. Of course, aspects of the old right were still on display, for there remained a Catholic undercurrent to much of what the new right said and stood for, but it was only an undercurrent and certainly not pre-eminent. Things had changed. The Franco-Prussian War and the birth of the Third Republic had brought a political realignment, and nationalism 'transferred from left to right a whole combination of ideas, sentiments and values'.[210]

In fundamental terms, the nation had replaced traditional religion as the focal-point of far-right discourse. Irvine says the new right was 'new' in the sense that 'it became identified with doctrines of the revolutionary left', which traditionally had been 'anathema' to conservatives.[211] In more specific terms, the 'virus'[212] of anti-Semitism had emerged – a 'vehicle for anti-establishment protest'.[213] However, we should guard against over-simplification. Most certainly, a 'new right' had been born, but not everyone fitted neatly into this category. Drumont, for example, is described by Bredin as representative of 'counter-revolutionary thought, the Catholic tradition, and a populist anticapitalism of socialistic tendency'.[214] This was the essence of the new right: it was reactionary and revolutionary at the same time. It also anticipated the rise of fascism.

4   1919–39 – inter-war fascism

The *ligues* and 6 February

One of the main problems confronting the historian of French fascism is to decide whether or not it even existed.[1]

1919 June: Signing of Treaty of Versailles
1924 May: Cartel des Gauches government formed
1925 Papal condemnation of Maurras and Action Française (AF)
1933 Stavisky Affair
1934 January: AF demonstrations in Paris
      6 February: *Ligues* riot in Paris
      7 February: Daladier's cabinet resigns
      9 February: Doumergue forms new 'National Union' government; Communist protests
      12 February: Socialists and Communists launch general strike; Doriot leaves Communist Party
      16 February: Government launches official enquiry into the Stavisky Affair
      May: Socialist Section Française de l'Internationale Ouvrière (SFIO) launches 'battle against fascism'; Laval becomes Foreign Minister
1936 13 February: Socialist Léon Blum attacked by Camelots du Roi; Front Populaire issues decree against the *ligues*
      16 February: Maurras accused of inciting murder of Blum in newspaper article; Action Française activists arrested
      21 March: Maurras sent to prison for four months
      April: Electoral victory of the Front Populaire
      18 June: *Ligues* officially banned
      31 October: The Croix de Feu becomes the Parti Social Français (PSF)
1937 Disturbances involving the PSF and the Communists – seven dead
1939 Arrest of journalists on *Je suis partout*

In retrospect, the period 1919–39 can be seen to have witnessed an intersection of right-wing currents. The 'pre-fascism' we identified in Chapter 3 evolved into something more substantive in the inter-war years, and we are able to understand Vichy in deeper terms if we take account of the themes at play on the far right in the 1920s and 1930s. Not only this, but in the way he argues for monarchy, Charles Maurras, the leader of the AF, is arguably heir to de Maistre. His nationalist thinking has also impacted on the far right for the rest of the century and beyond.

We called Chapter 3 'Anti-Third Republic Protest' and this section could easily have been entitled 'Anti-Third Republic Protest Part 2'. But the inter-war years were distinctive in the sense that they witnessed the emergence of French fascism in mature form, or so some historians would have us believe. This debate – about the nature and character of *fascisme français* – will underpin Chapter 4.

The story of the inter-war period can be divided into three parts: the rise and growth of the AF, the emergence of the *ligues*, and the threat to the Republic symbolised by the 'events' of 6 February 1934. The obvious question to ask is: was there such a thing as French fascism? Clearly there was 'something' happening in inter-war France, something that embraced fascist-style discourse and fascist-style ritual. Because of this we will use the word 'fascism', in its broader generic sense, so frequently over the course of the following pages in connection with the French experience that it may be more realistic to construct another question. What form did fascism take in France and what characteristics did it possess? However, by assuming that something along the lines of a French fascism did exist, we are not implying that it in any way resembled German or Italian 'fascism'; only that it was part of the same extended 'family'.

L'Action Française

In the history of the extreme right, the AF holds central importance. This is not because it gained power or had any significant electoral success, but for other reasons. For a start it is, in McClelland's view, the perfect embodiment of the reactionary right and, furthermore, it boasts unusual longevity. It has exerted a considerable impact on French political life but in no way is it a conventional political movement. In the inter-war period it sought intellectual influence rather than votes and wanted to create a 'state of mind', a 'Conservative Revolution'.[2] To some onlookers it was, in addition, both monarchist and fascist.

The AF is important also on account of its leader. Charles Maurras was one of France's leading thinkers and from the late nineteenth century through to the middle of the twentieth century he wielded a profound influence on intellectual life. He was a member of the Académie Française and an unpredictable, eccentric man. As the Pope of the day commented, he was 'a very fine brain, but alas, only a brain.'[3] Soltau argues that Maurras and the AF were synonymous.[4]

In one way or another, the AF has been a constant on the political scene for over a century. It emerged amid the Dreyfus Affair at the end of the nineteenth century, was a favoured political grouping during the Vichy period and, quite remarkably in many respects, it has survived into the twenty-first century – a home to die-hard royalists yet to come to terms with France's republican history. In 1979 Pierre Pujo, a stalwart of the reactionary right, stated that 'three-quarters of a century after its foundation, the principles and objectives of the AF had not changed... It is counter-revolutionary... It is nationalist... It is decentralising... It is social... It is royalist'.[5] Twelve years later, Guardian journalist Bell painted a picture of the AF in the 1990s:

> Politicians are not well-known for giving straight answers to straight questions, but the man from the Action Française... proved to be an exception. When asked 'What is your political goal?' he replied 'To seize power through a coup d'etat...' [Today] Action Française has a membership of only a few thousand but it makes up for its lack of numbers through noisy provocation... The official who politely replied to my questions, however, could not have been more removed from the boots and crewcuts normally visible at AF meetings. Sylvain Roussillon, the joint general secretary, was immaculately turned out, his hair was long and almost foppish at the front. He could have been a junior employee in a publishing house, until he began expounding his ideas.[6]

It is clear that Maurras, long dead, is still the man who guides AF thinking.[7] In recent years the organisation has published four different periodicals – *Aspects de la France*, *Le Feu follet*, *Insurrection* and *L'Action Française* – and in 1991 the AF ran two speech lecture sessions entitled *Louis XV, cet inconnu* and *Burke, un conservateur ambigu*.[8] It is clear, therefore, that the central thrust of AF thinking has remained unchanged.

Where Maurras' movement is concerned, there is a range of historical issues to consider. How did the movement originate? What exactly did it stand for? What kind of impact did it have? And, perhaps fundamentally and controversially, was it fascist?

The AF was formed in 1899, a successor to the uninspiring Ligue de la Patrie Française;[9] by 1905 it had developed into a full-scale 'activist league' and in 1908 it launched its own newspaper, *L'Action Française*.[10] Mazgaj identifies this as the turning-point in AF fortunes. The movement started to attract 'national attention' and by the mid-1930s its flagship publication had a circulation of well over 30,000.[11] As if to emphasise its intellectual pretensions, the movement also established its own academy, L'Institut d'Action Française.[12]

It was probably in the period immediately before 1914 and immediately after 1918 that the AF reached the peak of its influence. Even so, there was still something quite incongruous about the movement. In one sense it saw itself as 'above' normal party politics; in another, however, it was happy to engage in raw, low-level combat. Here the focus shifts to the Camelots du Roi, 'strongarm squads' reminiscent of the *squadrista* employed in Italy by Mussolini.[13] The combination of brain and brawn was effective, and by the early 1920s the AF was, to all intents and purposes, France's most famous and influential *ligue*.

It is not insignificant that Maurras was almost deaf. Some historians have discerned something quite symbolic in his hearing problem: namely, a tunnel-vision approach to politics and a reluctance to engage with other views.[14] Much is also made of Maurras' flying visit to the Athens Olympics in 1896, where he was not only impressed by the classical grandeur of the host city and the 'patriotic fervour' on display, but also by the above-average showing of British and German athletes.[15] He concluded that this was linked to the fact that both countries had a monarch as Head of State, and this finding would influence his political beliefs in later life.[16] Maurras was, first and foremost, a student of literature, but by the late 1890s he was reaching political maturity. As a young thinking person he had been conditioned by a series of political events: the 'horror' of the Franco-Prussian War, the Wilson Scandal – which had revealed the extent of republican corruption – and the Dreyfus Affair.[17]

The AF has very definite origins in the Affair.[18] As we noted in the last chapter, Maurras was a leading anti-Dreyfusard spokesman, and when he founded the movement in 1899 it was as a direct response to issues raised in the case. Nolte says that a 'mutual cause-and-effect relationship' existed between the Affair and the AF.[19] If the episode was a turning-point for France, it was a watershed for Maurras because, for him, it crystallised a collection of truths. First, that the army was synonymous with the nation and could not be questioned. Second, that the Republic was inept and inadequate. And third, that lies were justifiable if they helped to protect the nation. In time, Maurras was able to utilise the Dreyfus Affair as a political myth – one that he could exploit for the rest of his life. Nolte reflects on the importance of the Affair:

> It cannot be denied that the young men of the Action Française brilliantly discharged their duty of digesting, justifying, and radicalising the experiences of the Dreyfus Affair and thus creating for the Right a coherent ideology adapted to modern requirements. They invented nothing, but they analysed the system of 'counterrevolutionary' doctrines and frequently combined its elements in new syntheses of far-reaching consequences.[20]

Monarchism and nationalism

So what were these 'counterrevolutionary doctrines' and 'new syntheses'? The best clue comes from the membership oath that, after 1905, all AF loyalists had to affirm:

French by birth, heart, reason and will, I shall fulfil the duties of a conscious patriot. I pledge myself to fight against every republican regime. The republican spirit disorganises national defence and favours religious influences directly hostile to traditional Catholicism. A regime which is French must be restored to France. Our only future lies, therefore, in the Monarchy, as it is personified in the heir of the forty kings who, for a thousand years, made France. Only the Monarchy ensures public safety and, in its responsibility for order, prevents the public evils which anti-Semitism and nationalism denounce. The necessary organ of all general interests, the Monarchy revives authority, liberty, prosperity and honour. I associate myself with the work for restoration of the Monarchy. I pledge myself to serve it by all the means in my power.[21]

Thus, the main themes in AF discourse are clear: monarchism, anti-republicanism, traditionalism, patriotism, nationalism, anti-Semitism.[22]

It was the monarchism of the movement that stood out. Eatwell describes the AF as 'highly anti-republican'[23] and McClelland expands on this theme:

The centrepiece of Maurras's political thought is his account of royal authority in the very modern sense of political leadership. He believes that the republic has consistently failed to produce dynamic leaders of its own, and he sees in this a failure of political legitimacy. It is as if republican leaders do not themselves believe in their own right to govern. Maurrassian monarchy is about highly visible authority embodied in one man.[24]

The last French king had been overthrown in 1848, but this did not stop the AF leader from trumpeting the merits of monarchism as a concept and a reality. Curtis says that 'monarchy was the pole around which he spun his theories, and which he defended in the name of science and history.'[25]

However, what distinguished the AF from monarchist groups in the past – like the Ultras, for example – was the way in which they rationalised their royalism. Whereas the Ultras were 'born' royalists, and had never questioned the notion of monarchy, the AF was a movement that had used logic to deduce what type of regime would be best for France. For Maurras, monarchy was the solution to a problem – as simple as that. In 1899 he argued that the return of the kings would bring 'the rule of order' and he went on: 'We see that order conforming to the nature of the French nation and to the rules of universal reason. In other words, we see a regime which is exactly the opposite of the one now inflicted upon us.'[26]

In general terms, it was the institution that was important for Maurras, not the person, and it is because of this 'rational' position that AF doctrine has acquired the label 'neo-royalism'.[27] There was, in fact, much intra-movement discussion on the issue. In 1899 the AF was not monarchist but by 1903 it was, and Maurras was fundamental to this conversion. Tannenbaum says that the movement had found a 'formula'[28] – one that, in the end, alienated Barrès (an early member of the movement).[29]

For the AF, nationalism went hand in hand with monarchism. In 1901 the *Revue d'Action Francaise* announced:

> The idea of the nation is not nebulous. It is the representation, in abstract terms, of a strong reality. The nation is the biggest solid and complete circle of community on earth. Break it and you will break the individual. He will lose all his defence, all his force, all his sense of competition... All that he is, all that he has, all that he loves, is conditioned by the existence of the nation.[30]

So, AF nationalism was not mystical and neo-religious like the Barrèsian variety, but at its heart there was a powerful xenophobia. Maurras depicted Jews, Protestants, Freemasons and *métèques* as the 'four confederated states' (*les quatre états confédérés*), and in his imagination these groups combined to form 'Anti-France'.[31]

Maurras was quite specific in the way he described and explained the phenomenon of 'Anti-France'. He questioned the loyalty of the four groups he identified and said they embraced what he called 'conditional patriotism', an attitude that could be summarised in the phrase *la France, mais* ('France, but').[32] Wistrich states:

> Maurras's *antisémitisme d'État* was above all political – aimed at eradicating the influence of the four *'états confédérés'* within the state whom he believed to have seized the levers of command... The purging of alien elements would involve sweeping away the satanic Republic and the evil work of the Revolution in order to restore the strong, homogeneous state of the ancient régime – based on the Roman virtues of order, hierarchy and authority.[33]

This then paved the way for 'integral nationalism' or what Winock calls 'integral xenophobia' (*la xénophobie intégrale*).[34]

Maurras defined this creed as 'the exclusive pursuit of national policies'.[35] *La patrie,* or the Fatherland, was the Goddess. France had to be first.[36] Sovereignty had to be absolute. Love of France had to be unconditional, not conditional. And, in Maurras' view, the King had to be integral to the nation. In 1900 he wrote:

> In France hereditary monarchy is the natural and rational constitution, the only possible constitution of the central power. Without a king, all that nationalists want to conserve will weaken and soon perish. Without a king, all that needs reform will linger and worsen or, if destroyed, reappear in a different form. The monarchy is a condition of reform – it

is also the norm and indispensable. Essentially, royalism corresponds to the many assumptions of nationalism. It is an integral part. Thus, I will say to Royalists that all that is done for the national is done for the royal. Hence Royalists must apply themselves to the success of nationalism. They must act as if the enemy was at the border; they have to help in the defence of the nation. In the past, to serve the king they had to render themselves useful to *la patrie*; today, reversing things, to make themselves useful to *la patrie*, they must serve the King.[37]

This equation of the monarch with the nation was new and unique. Previously, 'King' and 'Kingdom' had been synonymous but Maurras had updated this. In the era of the Third Republic, the King had to take account of the nation and the people; hence the notion of a 'new right' and hence the description of Maurras as a 'neo-royalist'.

One of the many interesting features of Maurrasian nationalism was its parameters. The AF leader was as pro-revenge and as anti-German as anyone else on the far right but, nevertheless, he did not feel the need to resort to notions of 'blood' or 'race'.[38] For him, nationalism was primarily about loyalty and protecting France from cosmopolitanism. He did not approve of foreign culture 'invading' France, arguing that French should be the only language taught in schools and belittling non-French intellectuals like Kant and Tolstoy. He also took a dislike to foreigners' names because many featured the letters 'K', 'W' and 'Z' – letters that were extremely rare in French names.[39] In the light of this it is no surprise that Brogan has described the discourse of Maurras as 'The Politics of Hate'.[40]

Implicit in both the monarchism and nationalism of the AF was a fundamental belief in hierarchy and inequality. Maurras was caustic about any notion of equality or egalitarianism. In *The Politics of Nature* he sets out his convictions from first principles:

A tiny chick breaks from its shell and at once begins to run about. It has virtually all it needs to claim 'I am free'... But the infant man? The infant man has nothing. Long before being able to run he has to be extracted from his mother's womb, washed, wrapped up, fed. Before being taught his first steps, his first words, he has to be protected from danger. What little instinct he does possess is incapable of providing for his needs; he has to get them from someone else, who has carefully made the necessary preparations. He is born – but not his independent will, nor an individual basis for action. He will not for a long time be able to say 'I' or 'me', and yet already a circle of protection and care is drawn around him... From the first moment of his first day... he attracts and concentrates upon himself the effort of a whole group upon whom he depends as he depended upon his mother when he was imprisoned inside her womb.

He goes on:

> The first characteristic, then, of his social activity is to comprise no
> degree of reciprocity whatsoever. It is an activity which proceeds from
> one point only and which operates only in one direction... The group
> to which he belongs is totally innocent of any notion of equality: no
> pact is possible, nothing which remotely resembles a contract... No
> description could be too explicit, no admiration too great, for this
> spectacle of pure authority, this image of hierarchy so perfectly defined...
> Total inequality, unqualified necessity, these are the two inexorable laws
> of guardianship to the genius of which, to the power of which, he must,
> for his salvation, submit. It is only within the framework of this order
> (graded and stratified like all hierarchical orders) that the infant man
> can achieve the stature of the one ideal type of progress; by the growth
> of his body and of his spirit. He will grow by virtue of these same
> necessary inequalities.[41]

This belief in inequality leads Maurras to ridicule France's revolutionary
heritage and is the basis upon which he argues against democracy and
pacifism and in favour of monarchy, nationalism and war.[42]

In addition, we should note the AF's commitment to regional 'liberties'.[43]
This does not compromise the movement's belief in a centralised monarchy
nor its passionate nationalism, for regions, like families, are viewed as
essential intermediary bodies – a kind of safeguard or 'check' on centralising
tendencies.[44] The belief in regionalism also goes to illustrate the Barrèsian
influence at the heart of the movement. Maurras, like Barrès, put a premium
on roots and rootedness, hence his attachment to the provinces and to the
concept of decentralisation.[45]

AF doctrine was clearly the product of a range of influences. On one
level it was a response to landmark events in France's history: Maurras
produced in-depth critiques of 1789, 1848 and 1871, and was also at the
cutting-edge of anti-Dreyfusard politics. On another level, however,
Maurrasian doctrine was an unusual synthesis: of de Maistre's conservatism,
Barrès' nationalism and *fin-de-siècle* revolutionary syndicalism.[46] It is this
juxtaposition of ideas that marks out the AF as such an interesting
phenomenon.[47]

Beyond the fusion of ideas there were weaknesses and flaws. How could
Maurras be so out of touch as to think that a monarchical restoration was
possible in the twentieth century? Equally, how can we take seriously a man
who paid such scant attention to economics and the impact on politics of
economic factors? Furthermore, Maurras exhibited an ambiguous attitude
towards the masses. In one sense he appeared to view himself as 'above' the
people; in another he seemed to tailor policy positions towards their needs.
And likewise, how was it possible for the AF leader to embrace so many of
the social teachings of the church – and to incorporate them into his political

philosophy – when, at the same time, he was such a vociferous critic of the Rome authorities? What this does demonstrate perhaps is Maurras' style and approach. He was, as Nolte suggests, 'a servant of expediency'.[48] But it was still a crazy irony when Maurras' works were placed on the Index and the man himself was ex-communicated.[49]

Winock says the influence of the AF 'was not negligible', but it is a tricky task to weigh up its exact significance.[50] In conventional terms – votes won, seats gained – it was innocuous in the extreme, but in its role as high-powered 'think-tank' – a kind of laboratory of ideas – and in the way it impacted upon the psyche of the nation, it was of profound importance. Maurras was a man of substance and his movement gradually came to reflect this.

Was the AF fascist? This, for historians, has been the main debate. It is true that Maurras and Mussolini were mutual admirers – Milza talks about 'numerous and warm' contacts[51] – and that, in the shape of the Camelots du Roi, the AF possessed a genuine fascist street gang.[52] Maurras also espoused a vicious xenophobia that bore the hallmarks of crude fascist-style thinking. Nolte is therefore happy to describe the movement as one of the 'three faces' of inter-war fascism, but Eatwell is sceptical, implying that it was just the left that branded the AF fascist.[53]

There are other reasons to doubt the AF's fascist credentials. On 6 February 1934, when the paramilitary *ligues* were flexing their muscles on the streets of Paris, Maurras was nowhere to be seen – hardly the behaviour of a would-be fascist leader.[54] Not surprisingly, he was deemed by some to lack the temperament of a revolutionary. Georges Valois defected from the movement to found Le Faisceau in the early years of the twentieth century;[55] and Robert Brasillach, who went on to collaborate with the Nazis, also burnt his bridges with the royalist group. Both men argued that Maurras lacked the necessary fascist zeal and Tannenbaum validates this view, claiming that, 'unlike the French fascists, the Action Française leaders were neither open apologists for the Nazis nor traitors.' For his part, Winock states:

> The Action Française is not specifically fascist but for a long time it constituted a school of extremist thought that, through its contempt for liberal institutions and republican traditions, the exaltation of *coup de force* and authoritarian governments, and perhaps more through its style, invective, excess, slander and attacks, contributed significantly to the emergence of fascism.[56]

In a sense, it is extremely difficult to see how Maurras' monarchical dreams could be reconciled with the fascist dreams of others. Of course, he wanted a dictator – a xenophobic dictator at that – but, on the whole, his neo-royalism had little in common with the type of fascism preached by Hitler and Mussolini. What we can say is that in 1940 the political ideas of Maurras acted as a guiding force for Pétain, and it is also true that many activists in the modern-day Front National (FN) look upon the founder of the AF as a prophet.[57] Here the notion of 'Anti-France' has been especially important, informing and impacting upon nationalist movements for almost a century.

More than anything perhaps, the AF held curiosity value. It was a political movement that was content to play around with ideas and appeared not to want power, but if we are to understand the psyche and lineage of the extreme right, we must give Maurras his due weighting. Tannenbaum says that throughout the inter-war period he was 'the best known publicist of the Extreme Right'.[58] McClelland follows this up by saying: 'It is easy to say that Maurrassism is now of the past, but that would be a mistake. What Maurras left in place was a radically intelligent critique of French republicanism.'[59]

The *ligues*

There is no doubt that the AF was the most famous *ligue*. Although its elitism, intellectualism and monarchism meant that it was not typical, its nationalist, xenophobic and anti-democratic discourse does enable us to categorise it with the other *ligues*. But what, in fundamental terms, was a *ligue*? And why were the *ligues* of such profound importance in the inter-war period?

A *ligue*, by definition, was an extra-parliamentary organisation, but this only tells half the story. On the whole, the *ligues* were also characterised by their anti-Semitism, paramilitarism and powerful anti-communism. They believed in direct action and – perhaps strangely, given their strident nationalism – showered adulation on Mussolini and Hitler. Weiss explains:

> All hoped for a strong leader to repress the Republic through coup or revolution. Each expressed with variations ideals roughly similar to those of the Action Française and Mussolini's Fascists: the warrior ethic, ultra-nationalism, the cult of virility, ruralism, patriarchy, imperialism and anti-communism.[60]

Bernard and Dubief shed further light on the *ligues*, telling us that they were an urban phenomenon and had the support of many top-ranking VIPs.[61]

So, this was a new era and the *ligues* ushered in a new type of politics. Winock talks about the emergence of the 'ultra-right' (*l'ultra-droite*).[62] Of course, there had been *ligues* before – Ligue des Patriotes, Ligue Antisémitique, Ligue de la Patrie Française – but they had always been fairly marginal to the main action. Now they sprang up like 'mushrooms after a storm'.[63]

By the mid-1930s French politics were bi-polar. The left was strong and the extreme right was resurgent. McMillan talks about a period of 'crisis politics'.[64] Apart from the AF, which were the most important *ligues*? And how have historians interpreted them? We also need to address more fundamental issues: Did the *ligues*, together, constitute an indigenous French fascism? If they did, what were the main characteristics of *fascisme à la français*? And, in general terms, would it be true to say that France possessed the right kind of 'preconditions' for the growth of fascism? Soucy asks another important question:

> Was French fascism an ideology at all? Was it, as some scholars have concluded, primarily a 'fever', a movement lacking clear-cut goals and doctrinal seriousness, a movement, to quote Professor Weber, in which 'the ends of action count less than action itself', a movement lacking 'an anterior plan or series of plans inspired by the original doctrine'? Was it, as these scholars suggest, essentially a romantic adventure, a kind of sentimental emotional fling whose participants were 'more interested in gestures than in doctrine', more concerned with style than substance, more apt to be irrational, subjective, and aesthetic in their approach to politics than realistic, objective and tough-minded?[65]

These matters are vital, but there is one overriding fact: fascism never gained power in France in the inter-war period and never came close to doing so. This is significant and says a lot about the *ligues* and the nature of French political culture. The issue is blurred further by problems of definition. Only a minority of movements on the right 'openly admitted to being fascist' and on the left, meanwhile, fascism was a 'fantasy'.[66] There was permanent propaganda value in exaggerating the strength of the *ligues* and the temptation was to brand any right-wing organisation 'fascist'.[67] This does not help us in our investigations.

It is not exaggerating the situation to say that hundreds of paramilitary *ligues* emerged in the 1920s and 1930s. Most were 'restricted and ultimately unimportant little groups',[68] but some were high-profile and of major relevance. Taittinger's Jeunesses Patriotes (JP) was part of the first 'wave' of French fascism.[69] This movement was founded in 1924 and, in many ways, was heir to the Ligue des Patriotes. Anderson claims that Taittinger dallied between anti-regime and pro-regime stances but, even so, his movement claimed to have over 100,000 members.[70] In the view of Bernard and Dubief, the JP stood for a Bonapartist-style nationalism – a creed that involved the staunch idolisation of Joan of Arc.[71] The Croix de Feu (CF), formed in 1927 and led by Colonel de la Rocque, was the biggest *ligue* and, in Warner's view, probably the most imposing.[72] Estimates put its membership at anywhere between 50,000 and 500,000. Most CF loyalists were ex-servicemen – individuals who had fought in the First World War and who felt let down by the reality of civilian life. The CF had all the characteristics of a trained military force: uniforms, regular marches, and a culture of combat. According to Eatwell, it was more interested in 'symbolic acts such as giant motorcades rather than systematic attacks on opponents or the state'.[73] In 1936 it evolved into a more orthodox political party, the Parti Social Français (PSF), and gradually lost its radical edge.

The key movement of the 1930s was the Parti Populaire Français (PPF), established by Jacques Doriot in 1936. It was relatively small in terms of membership but made up for this in its rhetoric and style. Doriot posed as the 'French Führer' and aped many aspects of Nazism. His movement also boasted incredible levels of support among the masses, with Woolf claiming that 57 per cent of delegates to the first PPF national congress had a working-class background.[74] Doriot was an ex-communist and, as a direct consequence, the PPF exhibited a powerful anti-communism. Anderson depicts it as an 'intimidating force'.[75] Some of the smaller *ligues* are also worthy of note: Solidarité Française (SF), Renaud's Nazi-style movement; Bucard's Francisme, an organisation that was influenced and sponsored by Mussolini; the Faisceau, a prototype fascist group, led by AF dissident Georges Valois and heavily shaped by syndicalist ideas; Rédier's passionately anti-communist Légion; and three rurally based factions: Défense Paysanne, Parti Agraire and Front Paysan.[76] McMillan, the master of understatement, says that 'France was not without its share of fascists'.[77]

Each individual *ligue* had its own character and its own constituency. The CF spoke for veterans, the JP saw itself as the voice of agricultural workers, and Doriot, at least in his own view, was the idol of the masses. The *ligues* had an interesting overall effect – they were loud, boisterous and impossible to ignore – but in no way was it a united or unified impact. Tint says everyone agreed on the need for strong government and an end to parliamentary weakness, but that was about it.[78] Soucy talks about 'variety, contradiction, and sheer ideological confusion'.[79] This, in time, was to prove a fatal flaw.

Historiography and debate

French, British and American historians have studied the inter-war period with rigour. Payne argues that France 'generated more small fascist, semi-fascist, or pseudo-fascist movements of radical nationalism than any other country'.[80] This is a verdict that Milza would not disagree with. He identifies a strong and complex fascist tradition, characterised ultimately by its lack of success.[81] Griffin argues that the far right was never close to seizing power, but that France gave birth to a rich 'variety of permutations of fascist thought'.[82] For his part, Soucy asserts that French fascism was not just 'imitation' and not just 'ideas'.[83] And it would be fair to say that, in general, there was a real flamboyance about the *ligues* – hence Kitchen's reference to 'the spirit of the thirties' (*l'esprit des années trente*)[84]. Most historians, in fact, are happy to conceive of a 'French fascism' in some shape or form.

And yet, at the same time, it is difficult not to be scathing about the *ligues*. They made a lot of noise and struck a range of provocative poses but, for the most part, there was little of substance to them. Bernard and Dubief put the case against them: 'Some historians have simply ignored the existence of the *Ligues* on the grounds that they were an old phenomenon only serving to prolong anti-Dreyfusard nationalism, offering no threat to capitalism and the liberal economy, and having no support from the working class.'[85] The accusation that the *ligues* were unoriginal – old wine in new bottles, if you like – is a common one. Many commentators have put forward the view that the *ligues* were primarily Bonapartist and Boulangist in character, and they have done so in a pejorative kind of way. It is as if the *ligues* had no real identity of their own and were just a regurgitation of the past.[86]

There are other criticisms too. Larkin says the *ligues* did not know whether to play on nostalgia or embrace new, modern political methods.[87] Anderson puts it another way, claiming the *ligues* were torn between 'moderation and intransigence', between 'attachment to the existing social order and desire for change'. In the end, he argues, 'the Right alternately gave the impression of timid and defensive conservatism and of aggressive innovation, without the two strands being entirely separate.'[88] The verdict must be that there was a shallowness about the *ligues*. They were good at agitation, good at making public statements, but not very good at doing anything meaningful or substantive. Eatwell states: 'It is easy to see why French legend holds that fascism was a marginal movement in France during the inter-war years. It is far more difficult to understand the counter-claim that France was riddled with fascist ideology.'[89] This sums things up neatly.

If there was such an animal as 'French fascism' in the inter-war period – a big assumption to make, of course – did it constitute an indigenous force or was it, rather, a product of foreign influences?

In reality, the strategy of direct action favoured by the *ligues* was not unlike the rabble-rousing approach of Boulanger, and the ultra-nationalist outlook of groups such as the CF and the JP had a mystical, neo-religious flavour that was reminiscent of Barrès. Likewise, many fascists looked to syndicalist theory and Sorelian notions of 'myth' for inspiration. Soucy talks about the 'many intellectual antecedents which fascism had in French thought well before the 1920s' and concludes that 'there was little that was un-French about a great many of the ideas associated with fascism'.[90] In a similar vein Sternhell identifies a 'revolutionary' doctrine in early twentieth-century France that combined elements of both left and right:

> On the eve of the First World War the essentials of fascist ideology were already well defined. The word did not exist yet, but the phenomenon it would eventually designate had its own autonomous existence, and thenceforward awaited only a favourable combination of circumstances in which to hatch into a political force.[91]

This 'hatching' process did not go smoothly but, even so, it is noticeable how the 'national-socialism' of the 1880s and 1890s fed directly into inter-war manifestos.

Others argue, however, that what passed for French fascism was, to a significant extent, 'imported'. Rémond claims that Francisme, the SF and the PPF all tried to ape movements in either Italy or Germany.[92] There was not just admiration for Hitler and Nazism, but direct contact with Il Duce. Mussolini, it is alleged, helped to finance several French movements and, as a consequence, there was a natural flow of ideas between Rome and Paris. This could not help but affect the configuration of French fascism in the inter-war years. However, even if there was a modicum of outside influence, it is difficult to play down the combined impact of Barrès, Maurras, Sorel and others. Sternhell is convinced that French fascism was 'in every respect an indigenous school of thought; in no way can it be regarded as a foreign importation, or – from the 1920s onward – as a vague imitation of Italian fascism.'[93] For a more balanced view we should perhaps turn to Milza, who says that fascism 'was not necessarily born in France, but it did have some French roots'.[94]

With all this doubt and scepticism, maybe the best conclusion to draw is that, on the surface, France lacked the real preconditions for the growth of an authentic, indigenous fascism. There are no historical laws about when, why and how fascism emerges but, that said, patterns did emerge in Italy and Germany. It could be argued that in France, during the inter-war period, the circumstances were not conducive. As we have already seen, there was a real sense of disunity and in-house conflict on the far right. According to Soucy: 'Fascism in France was a movement of sects which never overcame their differences.'[95] In addition, the threat from the left – the 'Red Peril' – was a figment of the fascists' imagination. By Western European standards, the French Communist Party was small, with a membership of 55,000 in 1929, and the Socialist Party, it could be argued, was more interested in middle-class concerns than in radicalism.[96]

More significantly perhaps, France lacked the sense of grave national crisis that precipitated the rise of fascism in countries like Italy and Germany. Politically, France was acutely unstable – cabinets and governments came and went – but the Third Republic had survived and had put down roots. It was not popular and it probably existed by default, but it was the lowest common denominator, and by the 1920s and 1930s had become ingrained in French political culture.[97] At the same time, the strength of the democratic conservative right meant that the undemocratic ultra-right – however buoyant – stood little chance of making headway.[98] This relationship between the 'radical right and the establishment' was ultimately of crucial significance.[99]

In the economic sphere too, France was relatively stable. Like every other European nation she had suffered severe post-war dislocation, but as a predominantly agricultural country she was insulated from wholesale crisis, and in 1931 only 60,000 people were unemployed.[100] Economic growth was modest and social dislocation minimal, hence there was little future in extremist politics.[101] Sternhell argues that fascism in France flowered in spite of, rather than because of, the socio-economic backdrop:

The process of industrialisation, which proceeded at a much slower rate in France than in Germany and northern Italy, did not have the destabilising effect in France that it had in the neighbouring countries. French society was never as deeply affected by its economic growth and consequently never reacted with the same violence. France was able to modernise stage by stage, and its relatively slow rate of development enabled it to preserve a very great stability.[102]

He also writes:

More than anywhere else, every conceivable kind of fascist sect, clique and group flourished in France. This multiplication of schools and tendencies no doubt contributed a great deal to the political ineffectiveness of French fascism, but it also attests to its ideological richness and its potential. Fascist influence in France was much deeper and far more groups were affected than is generally believed or recognised.[103]

Soucy tends to agree, arguing that economic and social factors did not prevent French fascism from 'hatching', but did prevent it from gaining a 'wide public following'. France, he says, escaped 'the devastating inflation which plagued Germany in the early 1920s' and was also spared 'the political and social consequences' of this freak economic phenomenon.[104] France, if you like, was never desperate.[105] And in addition, Italy and Germany had both emerged as losers in 1918 whereas France had come out of the war on the winning side. This was a key conditioning factor.[106]

The era of the *ligues* is interesting, but not hugely impressive. One thing is clear. However we wish to characterise it, French fascism remained pure. It never gained power and so it never had to compromise and, in this sense, it has been argued that it stands as a prime example of the species.[107] But, in another sense, it is easy to ridicule the phenomenon of the *ligues*. There was a lot of bluster and a few ideas, but not much else. The events of 6 February 1934 tend to confirm this.

The 'events' of 6 February 1934

Depending on one's viewpoint, 1934 can be viewed as either the high point or the low point of French fascism. The 'events' of 6 February – as they are ubiquitously known – represent French fascism's one and only genuine assault on power, if this phrase does not flatter the whole episode. The bizarre Cagoulard conspiracy of 1937 is worthy of mention[108] but in terms of legacy and historiography 1934 is vastly more important. Over the years various epithets have been attached to the events – 'attempted coup', 'anti-parliamentary revolt', 'street riot', 'aborted revolution' – but none of these descriptions quite do justice to the wholly chaotic nature of the day.

The facts of the matter are these. After weeks of unrest the *ligues* made plans for a major demonstration in Paris on 6 February 1934. When the day eventually came, many *ligues* were involved in a largely uncoordinated revolt and, in geographical terms, the parliament building was the focus of attention. The rioters – one estimate puts their number at 100,000[109] – fought police on the streets of the capital but their tactics were amateurish: buses were burnt, stones were thrown and opponents were pushed into the Seine. There was no effort to capture the main centres of communication. Trotsky, who might have been expected to exaggerate the gravity of the episode, says that the rioters were armed only with 'revolvers, clubs and razors'.[110] According to Werth, fourteen rioters and one policeman were killed, and 1,326 people were injured, the majority of whom were guards or *gendarmes*.[111] The authorities had been rattled but parliament and the Republic remained intact. The following day Daladier, the prime minister, resigned, and later stated that he did so 'to avoid having scuffles every day whose result would be that misguided and anyhow innocent Frenchmen would fall in the streets of Paris'.[112] He was replaced by veteran right-winger Gaston Doumergue and that, so far as the basic detail is concerned, was that.[113]

However, what we are dealing with here is a day and a set of events that have become the centre of historical and polemical debate. The bare facts may not be impressive, but the myth making and politicking that have followed undoubtedly have significance. And for us, a number of key questions are raised: was 6 February an attempt at a full-scale fascist coup or merely an outpouring of latent political protest? Were the events of the day planned in an organised way or entirely spontaneous? Was parliament or the Republic the main 'enemy'? How have historians interpreted 6 February? And how have left and right sought to exploit the riot-cum-revolution? If we can come to some understanding about the origins of the event, we may be able to shed some light on these questions and others.

Causation can be investigated on two levels. In one sense the riots of 6 February, and the series of mini-demonstrations that preceded them, were a product of events. The backdrop was government instability. There had been a huge turnover of cabinets and prime ministers in the early 1930s and this, for the *ligues,* was a visible sign of the Republic's weakness and instability. Added to this, republican politicians had been implicated in the Stavisky Affair, a rather unpleasant financial scandal. Eatwell says the saga was 'perfectly designed to inflame the extreme right',[114] while Hamilton notes that, 'not until the... scandal did the French Nationalists appear to have a unity of purpose which might lead to unity of action'.[115] In January 1934 Chiappe, the Paris chief of police, was sacked for being 'soft' on the *ligues* and, in many ways, his dismissal 'precipitated the great riot of February 6th'.[116] This is the raw history of 6 February – the origins viewed in terms of immediate causation.

In another sense, however, the events of 6 February can be viewed in climactic terms. The left interprets the day, and the circumstances of the day, as symbolic of fascist adventurism, as a rigorously planned 'plot' or 'conspiracy' aimed at toppling the foundations of the Third Republic. Was it to be the next domino to fall? Italy – 1922; Germany – 1933; France – 1934?

Clearly, the left has exaggerated the episode for partisan purposes.[117] Most socialists and communists interpret it as a fascist-military conspiracy,[118] but in typically extravagant style, Trotsky sees in it the emergence of a 'fascist-Bonapartist-royalist bloc', the initial move of the 'united counterrevolution', and the 'first step of the passage from parliamentarism to Bonapartism'.[119] If this is not enough, he goes on:

> The present role of Doumergue... is nothing new. It is a role analogous to that played, in different circumstances, by Napoleon I and Napoleon III... In the person of Doumergue we meet the senile Bonapartism of capitalist decline... To keep his balance, Doumergue needs at his right hand the fascist and other bands which brought him to power. To demand of him that he dissolve the Jeunes Patriotes, the Croix de Feu, the Camelots du Roi, etc. – not on paper but in reality – is to demand that he cut off the branch upon which he rests.[120]

Leaving aside the gross exaggeration inherent in this passage, Trotsky's heavy demonisation of the whole episode is counter-productive, for he assigns it more credit and credibility than it is due.

In 1947 the Chamber of Deputies Commission of Enquiry on the Events of 6 February 1934 was established. It is noticeable how, in his evidence to the Commission, Léon Blum, Socialist premier in 1936, links 1934 to 1940:

> These same elements, conservative elements for whom the evils of dictatorship counted for little by the side of the benefits of national discipline, and elements of the Left, tempted by the idea of a dictatorial authority applied to the revolution – one finds them joined together and confused on the 6 February as at Vichy and under the Vichy regime.[121]

If we ignore Blum's dig at 'elements of the left', it is clear that from the perspective of 1947 he sees February 1934 as an important stepping stone on the road to June 1940. He has hindsight on his side, of course, but this kind of argumentation – stressing the Republic's innocence in the face of a concerted fascist 'plot' – is common on the left. McMillan states: 'The notion of a fascist plot became, if anything, even more credible in the light of events after 1940, when a good number of the activists of the 6 February proclaimed themselves Vichyites or collaborators with the Nazis.'[122]

The right, by contrast, views things differently. The riots, they argue, were about legitimate protest – against parliament, government and regime

– and no 'illegal' coup was intended. February 1934 was merely 'the first step in the regeneration of France' – the moment when the forces of the right fought back against the hated Republic.[123] The words of President Lebrun – Head of State in 1934 – offer us a synthesis. Reflecting on events thirteen years on, he said that France had witnessed both 'a revolt against the parliament, an attempt against the regime' and 'a genuine insurrection, minutely prepared'.[124] Unknowingly perhaps, his interpretation seems to capture the essence of both main theses.

Meaning and legacy

For the most part, historians have been disparaging about the events of 6 February. Tint is alone in assigning the episode any real credibility. He says that any occurrence that forces the resignation of the sitting prime minister – and rewards the protagonists with a new premier – has got to be taken seriously.[125] He ridicules the arguments of other historians:

> There is… a remarkable tendency to play down the importance of these events. Chastenet engagingly maintains that the rioters merely wanted to beat up the deputies to teach them a lesson, that they had no intention of promoting a revolution. His evidence is one statement by one member of the Jeunesses Patriotes at the official enquiry.[126]

But as we said, most historians choose to denigrate the 'events'. Rémond – notoriously sceptical about French fascism anyway – argues that it was 'not a putsch, not even a riot, only a street demonstration that history soon would have forgotten if it had not turned into tragedy';[127] Austin suggests that it was a 'Boulangist' demonstration rather than a fascist putsch;[128] and Kitchen makes reference to 'a mob without any common purpose or platform, a collection of aspiring intellectuals, small shopkeepers, artisans, professionals and students, whipped up by demagogic journalists and held together by a common anti-parliamentarianism and anti-Semitism'.[129]

Whatever its impotence and shallowness, February 1934 has always detained historians. It is almost as if its significance is conversely proportional to its success. First and foremost, the riots of 6 February 1934 are entirely indicative of inter-war French fascism and, in an acute way, highlighted the strengths and weaknesses of the whole phenomenon. There was flamboyant spirit, but organisation was tentative, coordination poor and leadership almost non-existent. Hamilton paints a wonderful picture of the events:

> The only true Fascist movement, Bucard's Francistes, took no part in them. The Jeunesses Patriotes, the Camelots du Roi and the Solidarité Française participated independently, while Colonel de la Rocque did his best to keep his Croix-de-Feu out of the actual fighting. Maurras, in the offices of the Action Française, did nothing whatsoever. Lucien

Rebatet relates how one young man appeared in Maurras' office on February 7, and shouted at him: 'Maître, Paris is in an uproar. There is no government, everybody is expecting something. What shall we do?' Maurras' reply was: 'I don't like people to lose their self-control.'[130]

At the time, the British press was full of informed guesswork about the participants. The talk was of 'Royalists', 'ex-soldiers', 'Nationalists' and 'ex-servicemen'.[131] Beloff's research and Werth's eyewitness account demonstrate that the following organisations were at the heart of the chaos: Solidarité Française, Jeunesses Patriotes, Croix de Feu, Union Nationale des Anciens Combattants, Front Universitaire and Action Française.[132]

These movements might have been united in spirit, but that was about it. Whatever Warner says about the 'scrupulous attention' paid by the *ligues* to their 'independence',[133] and whatever Werth says about the existence of a 'single plan',[134] the logistics of the day were plainly bizarre. Beloff indicates that each group had a different meeting point and a different start time and each marched in a different direction. As if this was not enough, many of the participating groups published details of their plans in advance – just so the police and the powers-that-be would know![135]

It is interesting, and slightly perplexing, that left-wing militants joined right-wing agitators on the streets of Paris. It is conceivable that the Association Républicaine des Anciens Combattants (ARAC) loyalists were acting out the role of *agents provocateurs*, but it is more likely that they were there to swell the ranks of protestors. Werth says that ARAC had major complaints to make about the 'thieves' in parliament and the ongoing 'pensions cuts'.[136] Communists hated fascists, and fascists hated communists, but they had some common enemies. Parliament was one, the Republic another. On balance, as Kitchen asserts, the communists' 'desire to destroy the bourgeois state' was greater than their 'aversion to fascists'.[137]

The fact that the various groups' marches centred on parliament was significant.[138] It showed that the February events were an explosion of anti-regime sentiment, rather than an organised attempt to overthrow the Republic and replace it with something else. In fact, the more one investigates the reality of 1934, the more one realises that it was an open-house for critics of the Republic. One newspaper report stated that 'taxi drivers with a grievance' were joining in the protests,[139] and this, more than anything, indicates that the February events were not exclusively fascist in character, but rather a watershed in 'anti-system' protest politics.

The events of 6 February also left an important political legacy. In the short term, the right lost face. Granted, their efforts had yielded a change at the top of the French government, but the Paris riots had shown up their subversive aims as well as their incompetence on a national stage. The *ligues* became *personae non gratae* under the Front Populaire government, but come the Occupation and the formation of the Vichy administration, the right was back in the limelight. Many of Pétain's associates in government viewed the experience of that February as a formative one. If 1936 was the revenge of the left, 1940 was the revenge of the right.

On the left, the February events gave rise to an outpouring of polemic and some key practical developments. A general strike was organised for 12 February and almost instantly socialists and communists buried the hatchet.[140] Larkin says that Moscow's contribution to this development cannot be ignored, nor can grass roots feeling,[141] but the coming together was primarily a response to the right-wing threat. As we know, the curiosity of the situation was that some communist elements had actually taken an active part in the February riots![142]

In 1936 socialists and communists united to form the Front Populaire government. Julien Brenda was a witness to the left-wing demonstration of 14 July 1936:

> This giant procession, the like of which had never yet been seen in Paris, was the direct outcome of the 6 February. So also were the formation of the Front Populaire and the last general election... In the last 60 years a sharp offensive from the reactionaries has been followed, with mathematical accuracy, by a sharp, inevitable reaction from the Left. The men who organised the 6 February riots could have been sure of it.[143]

In power, the Front Populaire was quick to put a ban on the 'combat groups and private militias'.[144] Thus, the ultimate legacy of 6 February was 'an increasingly bitter struggle between Left and Right, providing both sides with a highly-exploitable "myth" '.[145]

Finally, the events demonstrated that the right, just like the left, could take to the streets. It is argued that in 1934 France witnessed street-level bloodshed on a scale not seen since 1871. Fascists were now following in the footsteps of Communards, and in the aftermath of February the strategy of direct action helped to define French political culture. Austin notes the 'evident approval extended by some sections of the population towards the use of extra-parliamentary pressure to remove the government of the day, which greatly boosted the employment of organised violence as part of the political process'.[146] This was a not insignificant consequence of the 1934 episode.

So, what conclusions can we reach regarding French fascism in the 1920s and 1930s? Should we talk about inter-war fascism or inter-war 'fascism'? The fascist *ligues* or the 'fascist' *ligues*? Do we need to use quotation marks or are we sure we are dealing with the genuine article?

It is tempting to say that, at heart, French fascism was nothing more than agitation. There was no organisation or unity or common purpose. It appeared to be men in uniform playing at politics: acting, posing and making grandiose statements of intent. Not for nothing is Anderson's examination of inter-war fascism labelled 'Aspirations and Initiatives', and Eatwell's chapter on the same subject entitled 'From Failure to Firing Squad'.[147] The greatest indictment was the confusion, impotence and lack of action – hugely ironic given the essence of fascism as an ideology.

Despite all of this, French fascism had its attributes and uniqueness. It was underpinned by an impressive intellectual tradition and was at times flamboyant, passionate and wholehearted. Soucy and McMillan help us to understand the phenomenon. The former describes French fascism as 'a kind of sentimental, emotional fling',[148] while the latter says, 'Fascism, though certainly not "unFrench", was fragmented, incoherent and badly coordinated'.[149] These verdicts capture the spirit and unpredictability of the genre.

5 1940–4 – Vichy

The National Revolution, collaboration and collaborationism

It would be difficult to overstate just how deeply the years of the Vichy regime and the German Occupation scarred the history of France.[1]

1940 May: Germany invades Low Countries
18 May: Pétain enters government
14 June: German forces enter Paris
16 June: Pétain succeeds Reynaud as premier
22 June: Franco-German armistice
23 June: Laval becomes Pétain's deputy
1 July: Government moves to Vichy
10 July: End of Third Republic
11 July: Pétain becomes Head of State
18 July: Vichy law on nationality
3 August: Abetz appointed German Ambassador to France
27 September: Germany demands census of Jews in Occupied Zone
3 October: First Vichy laws on the Jews
24 October: Pétain and Hitler meet at Montoire and formally agree to collaborate
13 December: Fall of Laval
1941 Darlan takes charge of government
2 June: Vichy law on the Jews
4 October: Vichy Labour Charter issued
1942 18 April: Laval returns to government
22 June: Laval states publicly that he wants a German victory
11 November: Germany invades Southern Zone
1943 16 February: Service du Travail Obligatiare (STO) launched
1944 January: Collaborationists enter government
6 June: Allies land in Normandy
August: Pétain and Laval leave Vichy for Germany; de Gaulle enters Paris

In retrospect, Anderson argues that 'Vichy, Collaboration and the purge at the Liberation were disastrous episodes for the extreme Right'.[2] This may well be so but, from a different perspective, it could actually be argued that far-right politics in France reached their apogée during the Second World War.

In 1940, Marshal Pétain – the 'Victor of Verdun' – announced himself as his country's would-be saviour.[3] Following military defeat, he was asked to steer France to safety, and he exploited the situation to launch an ultra-traditionalist 'revolution' that owed much to the thinking of Barrès and Maurras.[4] But this was just one influence. Pétain, a man of the right, had sympathies with the extra-parliamentary agitation of the 1930s and obviously saw the Third Republic as doomed. Nazism was another conditioning factor, for when Pétain agreed to collaborate with Hitler he did so in the knowledge that France would have to toe the German line. Historians do not agree on the extent to which Petain's *Vichyiste* doctrine was influenced by Nazism, but there were certainly common traits. Suffice to say that in 1940, as a result of a disastrous turn of events, Pétain was given the opportunity to put his political ideas into practice and what emerged was a unique brand of right-wing extremism.

With Pétain in power, politics took on a new configuration. Laval – the Marshal's right-hand man for a large part of the wartime period – acted as the main Vichy–Berlin go-between and he would eventually make a name for himself as collaborator and arch-manipulator. In a sense, though, Pétain and Laval were outflanked by the hardcore fascists congregating in Paris. These individuals, totally convinced by the merits of German Nazism, viewed Vichy as 'soft'. Pétain did not feature in their plans for France, and instead they dreamt of a New European Order with Berlin pulling the strings. The 'collaborationists'[5] saw themselves as the ideal henchmen for Hitler in France.

So, one could easily argue that extreme-right politics dominated the period 1940–4, but the fallout of the wartime years was so catastrophic that Vichy and collaboration are now viewed by the majority of French people as taboo subjects. Several key questions will underpin this chapter: What were the origins of Vichy, collaboration and collaborationism? How did they interact? What were the main aims of Vichyites, collaborators and collaborationists? How did they relate to the Germans? And what was the legacy of their actions?

Vichy and the National Revolution

On 16 June 1940 Pétain succeeded Reynaud as French premier, and six days later he signed an armistice with Germany that split France into 'Occupied' and 'Unoccupied' zones, which meant effectively that Paris–Berlin collaboration was inevitable. On 10 July the National Assembly voted him full powers. France was not just split physically in two but, at home and abroad, resistance forces emerged to fight Pétain and the Germans. Thomson speaks of an 'open schism', while Novick talks about 'two Frances'.[6]

The town of Vichy had been chosen as the 'capital' of the southern zone on account of its central geographical location and its plentiful supply of hotel accommodation. It was, and still is, a beautiful, tranquil and unhurried place but, in time, this would sit very uncomfortably with its notoriety. The government it hosted was not a single homogeneous bloc, for there were not just Pétain and Laval factions but also 'modernisers' and 'traditionalists'. This has led Rémond to speak of 'basic antagonisms whose principles came from opposed ideological systems'.[7] In addition, there was the vexed question of Vichy–Paris and Vichy–Berlin relations and, in due course, this created new lines of division within the Pétain administration.

The terms of the armistice meant that the Marshal's 'independence' was limited. It would be true to say that Hitler did not want to bother himself with the job of governing France, but he still exerted a significant influence on Southern Zone politics. After the German invasion of the south, Vichy policy and Nazi policy became almost indistinguishable; however, up until 1942 Pétain had some notional autonomy. Within weeks – almost days – of coming to power, the octogenarian leader had launched his 'National Revolution'. This was a wholehearted effort to return France 'to her roots', and the rapidity with which he introduced his ideas makes one think he had a preconceived plan and a definite ideological agenda. This is important ammunition for those on the left who argue that Vichy was a 'conspiracy' or preordained right-wing 'coup' and that Pétain was a Machiavellian plotter, who in 1940 'seized the moment' for personal and political gain.

Baudoin's memoirs record that the Marshal, whatever his political motivation, was infirm and in need of assistance when it came to the preparation of speeches,[8] but he was still regarded by many people – including himself – as a national saviour. In no time a cult of personality developed. Propaganda posters featured his wise and wrinkled face and he was spoken of in mystical, semi-religious language. A court of sycophants emerged too. The poet Paul Claudel wrote:

> Marshal, this poem is about someone coming back to life. It is no small thing, coming back from the dead!... Marshal, here is that France in your arms, who has only you and who is coming slowly back to life, slowly and with a low voice... Marshal, the dead have a duty and that is to return to the living. Certainly we will all come back to life on the day of the Last Judgment. But it is now, even today, that we are needed, that there is something to be done! France, listen to him who, ripe in years, bends down to you and speaks to you as a father.[9]

Pétain was viewed as the new God and the Lord's Prayer was reworded as well. As Desquesnes says, 1940 was 'more than a change of government'.[10]

Vichy saw itself as a mirror image of the Third Republic, condemning the 'laxity', 'weakness' and 'decadence' of the former regime and blaming it unreservedly for military defeat. Its whole *raison d'être* was anti-republican and in October 1940 Pétain stated:

Four months ago, France suffered one of the most thorough defeats in her history. This defeat was caused by many factors, not all of which were of a technical nature. In truth, the disaster was simply the reflection, on a military plane, of the weaknesses and defects of the former regime.[11]

As a soldier, the Vichy leader was never going to blame the military for France's collapse, so in this passage he deftly shifts the emphasis on to the Republic. Laval had done just the same only weeks after the Germans had marched into Paris:

France was overly fat and happy. She used and abused her freedom. And it is precisely because there was an excess of freedom in all fields of endeavour that we find ourselves in the present straits. It is also a fact – I say this sadly because a great calamity has befallen us – that the existing institutions cannot be allowed to survive a disaster of this magnitude.[12]

Coming from the mouth of an archetypal Third Republic politician, these words are particularly interesting. Laval implies that the Third Republic was 'too democratic' and 'lacked discipline', and thus, in his mind at least, Vichy was given the green light to construct a new order and to 'clean up' the nation.[13] Pétain used the phrase 'National Revolution' to describe this project.

'National Revolution' meant in effect 'Conservative Revolution'. Pétain actually preferred the word 'Restoration' or 'Renovation' but, whatever its defects, the chosen phrase pointed clearly to the essence of what he was trying to do. This is how he heralded the project:

Today we must rebuild France on a heap of ruins. The new order can in no way whatsoever imply a return to the mistakes which have cost us so dearly. Nor should it take on the features of a kind of 'moral order', or of a revenge for the events of 1936. The new order cannot be a servile imitation of foreign experiments – though some of these experiments are not without sense and beauty. Each people, however, must conceive of a regime suitable to its temper and genius. A new order is an absolute necessity for France. Our tragedy is that we shall have to carry out in defeat the revolution which we were not even able to realise in victory, in peace, in an atmosphere of understanding among equal nations.[14]

Here Pétain makes a variety of points. The Third Republic is likened to a 'heap of ruins', and there is also some regret that in the end military defeat had to act as 'midwife' to change. But the most significant line comes when he says that, although other regimes have their merits, the new regime must be based on French tradition alone. In the Marshal's mind at least, the National Revolution was indigenous rather than imported.

The Fall of France had sounded the death-knell for the hated Third Republic, but in Pétain's mind the first year of a new epoch had dawned simultaneously. In this sense the Marshal saw himself as something of a radical but in reality he was an arch-conservative, inspired by the 'old France' and the *ancien régime*. Bouderon and Willard argue that in government, 'paternalism' became the order of the day, and in three main areas – 'Work', 'Family', 'Country' – the Marshal wanted the country to 'get back to basics', to reinvent itself around 'concrete' values.[15]

What were these concrete values? On this matter Vichy's propaganda posters can help us. One stated: MARSHAL PÉTAIN DECIDES: NO MORE SHADY INFLUENCES... AUTHORITY SHALL BE RESPECTED, THE PEOPLE SHALL BE DEFENDED... WITHIN TWO MONTHS JUSTICE SHALL BE DONE.[16] Another featured a soldierly looking Pétain gazing out over an idyllic village scene, complete with church, beautifully mown farmer's fields and a small cluster of houses. The poster said simply: PATRIE. FOLLOW ME! PUT YOUR CONFIDENCE IN ETERNAL FRANCE.[17] Several key themes emerge from these images: the value of hierarchy, the importance of tradition, and Pétain himself – the wise and trusted father figure.

The debate about Vichy and fascism continues,[18] but Farmer says the regime came to be dominated by conservatives and it is manifestly the case that in 1940 the French counter-revolutionary tradition was still alive.[19] Pétain was fighting the memory of 1789 and it was no surprise to anyone when, soon after arriving in power, he banned the *Declaration of the Rights of Man and the Citizen*.[20] He condemned the Revolution, its legacy and the 'abstract values' it championed, and this is why he coined the slogan *Travail, Famille, Patrie* – a direct retort to *Liberté, Égalité, Fraternité*. He was scathing about 'freedom' in particular:

> What does freedom, abstract freedom, mean in 1940 to the unemployed worker or the ruined small employer – except freedom to suffer helplessly in a vanquished nation? We are really losing only some deceptive illusions of freedom, in order to make sure of saving the substance.[21]

So, in Pétain's mind at least, Vichy was about 'substance'.

'Work, Family, Country'

The British press was particularly interested in France's wartime economy. The message in the headlines was blunt: RECONSTRUCTION FOR NAZI BENEFIT, GERMAN GRIP ON FRENCH INDUSTRY, FRENCH ECONOMY IN CHAINS, THE BRAND OF THE SWASTIKA ON INDUSTRY. Clearly collaboration came to have an enormous effect on French industry, but on the morrow of defeat Vichy sketched out its own blueprint for the economy and Pétain announced that the 'new France' would be founded on toil: 'It is the first duty of all Frenchmen –

workers, farmers, civil servants, technicians and employers – to work. Those who disregard this duty do not deserve to be called citizens.'[22]

In the economic sphere Pétain wanted France to be true to her roots. Rémond says Vichy 'exalted labour, but its spontaneous sympathy clearly extended more to work on the land and to artisanry than to industrial activity'.[23] Indeed, there was a variety of tendencies at play and not all were pushing in the same direction, as Anderson notes:

> Different ministries sometimes pursued opposed policies: for example, whilst the Secretariat of State for Labour was attempting to make the unions the basis of social organisation, a section of Pétain's personal staff was trying to reduce the *syndicats* to powerlessness and even to abolish them. Those responsible for the Peasant Corporation argued that the agricultural sector should be the basic element of the French economy but the *Comités d'Organisation* of commerce and industry resulted in a considerable increase in the political power of large industrial interests.[24]

However, over time 'attachment to the land' would prove to be one of the 'major themes in *Pétainiste* discourse'.[25] This reflex or instinct was illustrated in December 1940 when the administration published a Peasants' Charter and launched a 'back to the land' policy. Pierre Caziot, Minister of Agriculture, said after the war that the re-establishment of farm life had been one his main priorities: 'It was necessary to concentrate all my efforts on the task of giving the farm families of France a realisation of their strength, and new pride in their life, for they and they alone were to preserve France and to bring it to a re-birth whatever happened.'[26] Agricultural revival was seen as a key element of national revival and Caziot even implied that the Franco-German struggle could be viewed exclusively in agricultural terms.[27]

The 'back to the land' policy was a conspicuous failure because only 1,561 families applied for the 'bribes' on offer[28] but, even so, Pétain had made a definite statement about his alignment with 'peasantism' and 'traditionalist organicism'.[29] France, he argued, would always remain 'an essentially agricultural nation',[30] and in this respect he was heavily influenced by Barrèsian notions of 'roots', 'earth' and 'soil'. And it was entirely fitting that the regime utilised the *francisque* – an axe-like agricultural implement used by the ancient Gauls – as its main symbol.[31]

On the whole, Vichy 'distrusted the forms of a modern economy',[32] but by 1942 a progressive faction had gained the ascendancy. Kuisel says that, on the whole, members of this clique were 'young, in their early forties, and ... experienced in business or public administration. Aggressive and elitist by temperament, *dirigiste*, and modernising by conviction, they soon ran the administration of the economy'.[33] Hitler's increasing economic demands meant the French economy had to adapt and change and, thus, Pétain gradually gave way to the 'sharp young fellows'.[34] McMillan states:

> At least some of the patronat, supported by powerful civil servants, welcomed the defeat as the opportunity not so much for moral regeneration as for transforming France into a dynamic, modern, highly technological economy. These technocrats came into their own when Admiral Darlan became Petain's chief minister in February 1941.[35]

In line with other right-wing authoritarian leaders, Pétain put strong emphasis on corporatist ideas.[36] In 1940 he declared: 'Two essential principles will be our guides: the economy must be organised and controlled.' He went on to say that disharmony would be disastrous for France, so 'let the working classes and the bourgeoisie together make an immense effort to escape from idle routine and become aware of their common interest as citizens in a nation henceforth united'.[37] In the words of Ehrmann, the corporatist ethic had been 'officially enthroned'.[38]

Vichy brought together employers and employees in 'single and obligatory' occupational associations.[39] The Marshal said they would 'deal with everything concerning the trade... With the authority of the State they will ensure that labour agreements are carried out. They will guarantee the dignity of the individual worker, by improving his standard of living right into his old age.'[40] Each and every sector of the economy had one.[41] Trade unions were abolished and an anti-worker Labour Charter was issued instead. The aim was a stable, harmonious society – of obvious political advantage to Pétain. But the historical verdict is largely negative. McMillan argues that, whatever the rhetoric, Vichy policy still favoured 'large-scale producers' rather than 'the small peasant farmer', and Ousby states that none of Vichy's economic initiatives 'answered the urgent problems of the Occupation'.[42]

Rossignol claims that Vichy propaganda was 'resolutely *nataliste*' and that the discourse of the regime could be summed up in one phrase: 'The child is king' (*L'enfant est roi*).[43] The family, just like agriculture, was viewed as one of the bases of the nation and, drawing on Catholic teaching and traditional right-wing thinking, Pétain announced the start of a crusade. The first step was the creation of a Secretariat of State for the Family in November 1940. Implicit in Vichy's 'familial ideology'[44] was a very specific concern about the French birth-rate which quickly evolved into paranoia. As a soldier, Pétain had been enormously hurt by the collapse of 1940, and in his view France had been defeated because she did not have enough soldiers. Rather simplistically, he equated the size of the population to military strength and believed the onus was on France to rekindle national power by procreating.[45]

Thus, Vichy pursued a range of pro-*nataliste* policies. Abortion was outlawed, contraception forcibly discouraged, and a law introduced in April 1941 limited the grounds on which couples could divorce.[46] But in addition to wielding the stick, Pétain also dangled the carrot: in August 1940 a 'priority card' was introduced for women who were either pregnant or had a large family, and legislation passed in November 1940 and February 1941 increased family allowance rates. Pollard says, 'woman was defined by her function of wife, mother and guardian of private space... Reproduction and female sexuality were constantly identified so that the natural destiny of the woman was itself continuously constructed... Femininity and maternity were key attributes of this promotion of gender identity.'[47] The hope was that demographic rates would rise and make France stronger.

There were additional strings to Vichy's social policy. Pétain wished to establish a new, nation-centred education system, encourage sport and physical fitness, and rid France of the 'vice' of alcoholism,[48] and in this he was aided and abetted by the Catholic Church.[49] Pollard argues that 'the overlapping or inter-relatedness of ideologies of Church and State in 1940, no less than their formal relationship, was highly complex'.[50] Pétain was a Catholic and based much of his moral teaching on 'Christian values',[51] and thus for most of the time he sought the Church's support and actually helped to re-establish its influence in the sphere of education.[52] Rémond puts it this way: 'The regime gladly invoked the patronage of religious authorities and was not at all stingy in granting to the Church both attentions and honours.'[53]

Of course there were priests who did not like the de facto alliance between Church and State and rebelled against it, but the Catholic hierarchy generally backed the regime. It contributed to the 'cult of the Marshal' and, most controversially, condoned important elements of Vichy's anti-Semitic policy.[54] In the end, however, there was only failure and division, as Halls indicates:

> The high hopes with which ecclesiastical leaders had greeted the advent of the new regime, including a state agreement with the Vatican, the support they gave to Vichy, the benefits that accrued from it (most of which in fact did not survive the Liberation), finally achieved nothing. On the other hand Catholic thinkers, who had usually toed the official line, encouraged a ground swell of revolt and of rejection of Vichy; the passage from passive obedience to active resistance. For the first time the lower clergy and the Catholic laity disregarded the exhortations of their superiors.[55]

Whatever the contours of the relationship, Vichy was determined to establish a new 'moral order'[56] with Pétain believing that young people should be, and would be, in the vanguard of France's renaissance. The Secretariat General de la Jeunesse was established and it was no surprise that many Vichy propaganda posters featured images of blond, youthful people.[57] Pétain might make political capital out of his own personal seniority and wisdom, but he wanted his regime to give off a vibrant, dynamic effect.

A range of youth movements existed under Vichy. In addition to religious and student groups, there was Scoutisme Français, a national organisation that grouped together all Scouts and Guides, and also Chantiers de la Jeunesse and Compagnons de France. The last was a voluntary group and the nearest Vichy came to sponsoring an all-embracing youth movement.[58] Compagnons never evolved into a Hitler Youth-style organisation nor did it have a mass following (Halls estimates it had 33,000 members),[59] but it still worried Pierre Tissier, a fierce opponent of Vichy, who wrote:

> We are assured that the Companions have nothing in common with the Hitler and Falangist and Fascist youth movements. Nevertheless it is somewhat disturbing to find that the Companions are grouped in 'squads' (*équipes*) of ten – five 'squads' make a company – and that they are subject to strict discipline and wear a (blue) uniform.[60]

However, Tissier may have been exaggerating things, for in truth the Compagnons movement was nothing more than a symbol and a statement, reflecting Vichy's obsession with 'service' and 'obedience'[61] and its desire for 'moral reformation'.[62]

It might well be true that 90 per cent of Vichy's propaganda material was printed in red, white and blue, but when Pétain talked about 'country' he was on problematic territory.[63] As a man he had first-class patriotic credentials – a lifetime of military service – but his government had agreed to the geographical division of France. Was this the action of a patriot? In his public utterances Pétain tried to square the circle – and even invoked the memory of Joan of Arc – but for most of the time it was in vain. When he referred to 'France' he did so in the abstract because France was no longer a geographical entity. However, the regime's propagandists still challenged people to emulate their leader. Photographs of the Marshal were accompanied by the words ÊTES-VOUS PLUS FRANÇAIS QUE LUI? (ARE YOU MORE FRENCH THAN HIM?).[64] And obviously no-one was.

The National Revolution may well have run its course by 1942,[65] but while it lasted it was definitely Pétain's personal project. However, Laval had a different agenda and a different dream.

Collaboration

If France was 'no longer a geographical entity', it was because her leaders had agreed, or been forced, to collaborate. Pétain may have personified the National Revolution, but it was Laval who came to embody the new Franco-German relationship.

Pétain and Hitler met at Montoire to formalise the new relationship,[66] but the policy of collaboration had been preordained by the Franco-German armistice of June 1940, which historians have generally viewed as a diktat. Articles 2 and 3 stated:

> 2   In order to assure the protection of the interests of the German Reich,

French territory will be occupied by German troops to the north and to the west of a line drawn on the attached map. The occupation of the territories which are to be occupied and which are not yet in German hands will start as soon as the Convention has been signed.

3   In those regions of France occupied by the Germans, the Reich is to exercise all the rights of an occupying power. The French Government undertakes to assist in all ways the carrying-out of orders made for the execution of these rights and to have them put into force with the help of the French administration.[67]

Some looked upon the armistice as a 'temporary arrangement' – and imagined that occupation and collaboration would also be interim measures – but the reality was different. Germany had occupied the north and the coastal regions in the west, and the new Vichy administration had to deal with the situation. The new diplomatic relationship would have severe political and economic ramifications.

Several introductory points need to made about collaboration. First, the military defeat of 1940 provoked a range of responses and individuals were forced to make choices.[68] Pétain and de Gaulle took different paths – one the arch-collaborator, the other the Resistance hero – but both argued they were motivated by the 'national interest'.[69] This is important because, as the war went on, Pétain and Laval would use this argument to justify collaboration; they felt they were doing their patriotic 'duty', just like de Gaulle.[70] Likewise, they would also try to justify collaboration by recourse to the 'shield' metaphor,[71] arguing that by standing up for France and working with the Germans, they were protecting the nation and 'shielding' it from the worst excesses of Nazism. This is how they could claim that their patriotic credentials were still intact after the armistice and Montoire.[72]

Notwithstanding this it is clear that, second, Pétain and Laval had slightly different agendas.[73] The Marshal shook hands with Hitler in October 1940 but thereafter sought to gain enough space for himself to implement his National Revolution. Meanwhile, Laval was over-zealous in his first dealings with the Germans but soon started to procrastinate on certain key issues. In general terms, it would not be unfair to say that the two men conceptualised the Franco-German alliance in divergent terms and, quite predictably, tension and rivalry developed. Thomson talks about the 'recurrent storms and explosions on either side'.[74]

Third, we must be aware that collaboration was a 'triumph' for some sections of the French right.[75] The mentality of many right-wing politicians led them automatically in the direction of *rapprochement* with Germany (and Italy). There was much admiration for Hitler among *ligue* activists and, in this sense, collaboration felt almost natural to some. (It has been pointed out as a matter of fact that from mid-1942 onwards, 'Vichy's programme' and 'German priorities' were almost indistinguishable.[76]) Finally, it is difficult to understand collaboration without comprehending the personal relationship between Laval and the German Ambassador in France, Otto Abetz. The two men were to dictate the course of Franco-German relations during the Occupation and it is patently clear that this did not make Laval's relationship with Pétain any easier.

In no way could either Pétain or Laval be described as a hardcore Nazi. The former was a high-ranking soldier who had started to move in conservative and reactionary circles during the 1930s, and, as we have seen, when he arrived in power in 1940, his first instinct was to develop his own personal political agenda. Of course Pétain was influenced by Nazism, and some of his policy initiatives did bear unmistakably fascist traits, but the fact remains that collaboration was less of an ideological coming-together than a pragmatic liaison. In metaphorical terms, it was not love but a one-night stand.[77]

On an ideological plane, Laval had even less reason than Pétain to collaborate with Hitler. He was an individual of moderate views who held various ministerial posts – most notably, Foreign Affairs in the mid-1930s – and in 1931 had been voted 'Man of the Year' by *Time*.[78] Rémond notes that he had little concern for 'doctrinal fidelity' or 'ideological considerations',[79] and there was certainly very little in his pre-1940 career to suggest that he would 'sell out' to the Nazis.

At the governmental level, collaboration was remarkably pragmatic and yet, by association if nothing else, Pétain and Laval have been branded 'fascists' and 'Nazis'. Of course, in the current study we are examining collaboration as a phenomenon 'of the extreme right', but we must not fall into the trap of thinking that Pétain and Laval were motivated by any deep ideological attachment to the Nazis.

Collaboration d'état

In the economic sphere Germany mercilessly exploited France. The terms of the armistice stated that the 'Occupied Zone' was to include the main industrial areas and the vital ports in the west but this was just the beginning. By 1943, 15 per cent of French agricultural produce, 40 per cent of her industrial output and 85 per cent of her vehicle production was being taken by the Germans.[80] By 1944 Germany was overseeing 85 per cent of France's railway network.[81] Overall, France contributed 42 per cent of the Nazis' 'special income from abroad'[82] and, significantly, 58 per cent per cent of the Vichy government's income went on the 'upkeep' of the occupying forces[83]. It was not just a pillage but a rape.

The *relève* was a further sign of the Nazi stranglehold over France. Laval agreed to send skilled French workers to Germany and once more there was a 'plan': for every three workers sent, Hitler would release one prisoner of war. Warner states:

> The Germans were indeed short of labour and, on 21 March 1942, Hitler had appointed Fritz Sauckel as special plenipotentiary for labour

to fill the gaps. The Germans had recruited labour in France before March 1942, sometimes using force, but Sauckel's appointment gave the matter fresh impetus.[84]

The STO, introduced in February 1943, further cemented the Franco-German economic relationship. Laval agreed to despatch workers to Germany to oil Hitler's war machine and, although some individuals had exemptions and some fell through the net, three-quarters of a million crossed the border to work as 'industrial conscripts'.[85] That amounted to approximately 3.5 per cent of the total French population.[86] This was the kind of deal that Laval made his trademark. Ousby says that 'no concession Vichy ever made to the Reich was more publicly damaging'.[87]

The policy towards the Jews was even cruder, and many historians now put forward the view that Vichy's anti-Semitism was 'home-grown'. They point to the number of confirmed racists with which Pétain surrounded himself, the rapidity with which Vichy initiated anti-Jewish measures in June 1940, and the long-standing anti-Semitic tradition in France.[88] The post-Liberation comments of Vichy's Commissioner General for Jewish Affairs, Xavier Vallat, add credence to the 'indigenous' thesis:

> The government of Maréchal Pétain decided to restrain this influence [the Jews' influence] within proper limits by publishing on 30 October 1940 a law establishing the status of the Jews in France. There are those who believed that this law was the result of pressure by the occupation authorities on the French government. Some accept this belief as a reason for excusing Vichy while others see it as one more element in the indictment against the government. Both are wrong. The Alibert Law – it is more convenient to indicate it by the name of the Minister of Justice who took the initiative in the matter – owes nothing at all to Nazism. Proof of this is to be found… in the confidential statements made by M. Dumoulin de la Barthète, Director of the Civil Cabinet of the Maréchal, when he was interrogated on 26 October 1946 at the (police offices in the) rue des Saussaies by police commissioners Bugé and Collier. In this declaration, during which he rather smugly allowed it to be understood that he was personally hostile to all laws of exception for Freemasons and Jews, he declared definitely that 'Germany was not the cause of Vichy's anti-Jewish legislation. This legislation was, so to speak, spontaneous and indigenous'.[89]

This is significant evidence but, at the same time, Vichy had to fit in with Hitler's plans. McMillan argues that the Germans needed logistical help in rounding up Jews for the 'Final Solution' and Pétain's administration offered 'invaluable assistance'.[90]

The *Statut des Juifs*,[91] Drancy[92] and the *Grand Rafle*[93] were the most notorious landmarks in the history of French wartime anti-Semitism and the most graphic examples of Vichy policy in action. Historians quote various statistics: Defrasne says 76,000 Jews were deported, of whom only 3 per cent survived;[94] McMillan states that in 1942 France sent 42,500 Jews (including 6,000 children) to Auschwitz;[95] and Larkin claims that of the Jews deported by France, just 2,500 survived.[96] Whatever the exact figures, the reality of the situation was horrendous. In the period after 1942 Laval was effectively using the Jews as a bargaining chip in his political calculations – an attitude that Warner deems 'remarkably callous'.[97] Both he and the Vichy administration as a whole[98] were more than willing to sacrifice 'foreign Jews' if this meant that fewer 'French Jews' would perish. As Eatwell puts it, 'this was hardly a high moral position'.[99] It is true that countries such as Belgium and the Netherlands sent a higher percentage of Jews to their deaths than did France (55 per cent and 86 per cent respectively, set against 26 per cent), but 'what remains particularly shameful was the extent to which the French authorities colluded with the Occupier in rounding up victims among the foreign Jews who had fled to France as refugees.'[100]

On occasions the Vichy authorities allowed for 'exemptions', and this further indicates the outright cynicism of the regime. Reitlinger lists a number of Jews who were 'saved': a marquise, two countesses, the husband of the writer Collette, the widow of Professor Bergson, the wife of De Brinon, six officials of d'Arquier's anti-Jewish police and one person who worked for the secret police.[101] Hilberg tells us that 'front-line soldiers of 1914–18 and 1940' formed 'another exceptional group'.[102] The policy was nothing if not pragmatic. Eatwell understates the case when he says: 'Probably in no area has the record of Laval and Vichy been more attacked than in its dealings with the Jews.'[103]

It is also significant that the Catholic Church, or parts of it, condoned Vichy policy. Many individual priests joined in the Resistance effort and hid Jews from the Vichy authorities but, in general terms, the Catholic establishment acquiesced. Halls writes:

> It cannot be emphasised enough that attitudes among the lower clergy and the rank-and-file laity were vastly different from those of their leaders. By and large those of the latter failed to evolve because they were rooted in prejudices that harked back to the separation of Church and State and Dreyfus, and perhaps even to the great Revolution itself.[104]

Cohen argues that the Jews were naïve in the way they trusted the French authorities,[105] but they could never have expected the Catholic Church to turn a blind eye to Vichy's anti-Semitic offensive.

Origins of collaboration

But why did France collaborate in the first place? Historians have constantly debated this question. Was it on the insistence of Hitler? Or Pétain? Or Laval? Defrasne says it was a combination of factors: moves towards Franco-

German *rapprochement* in the period 1919–34, the totalitarian tendencies of the French right, the increase in pacifistic sentiment in the mid- and late-1930s, the growing attractiveness of fascism and, ultimately, the Munich crisis.[106] Paxton puts the issue into perspective:

> Collaboration was not a German demand to which some Frenchmen acceded, through sympathy or guile. Collaboration was a French proposal that Hitler ultimately rejected... [He] insisted upon a docile and amenable France... It was from the Pétain regime, however, that a stream of overtures came for a genuine working together: for a broad Franco-German settlement, for voluntary association... In the end, 'Kollaboration' meant only booty, a cheap way to get the French to keep their own people quiet, and an eventual peace of revenge.[107]

This may be so but, given the circumstances of 1940, there was no real alternative to collaboration. It was a necessity and an inevitability, and it was eventually sealed by the armistice of June but, that said, other issues do come into the equation.

During the 1930s Laval, as Foreign Minister, had already indicated that he wanted France to move into the orbit of the Axis powers, especially Italy. Conventional wisdom has it that this was an early signal of his pro-fascist intentions, but Werth – presenting the revisionist line – says, 'in Laval's case, what mattered perhaps more was a temperamental and sentimental attraction towards a Latin country'.[108] Whatever the exact reason, Pétain's right-hand man genuinely believed that France had a lot to gain through befriending Hitler and Mussolini.

Moreover, Johnson argues that Laval 'was convinced that there was a continuity in history [and] saw himself as the successor to Aristide Briand and the diplomacy of the 1920s which had sought to end the enmity between France and Germany'.[109] Here the argument is that pre-1940 and post-1940 attitudes were linked; that Laval's thinking in the 1920s and 1930s almost anticipated the policy of collaboration that was pursued after 1940. According to this view, the Fall of France should be seen merely as a staging-post on the road to full Franco-German collaboration. This line of thinking becomes even more compelling if we take account of Laval's obvious ambition. As we said at the outset, he was a man of few political ideals who had made a career out of ducking and diving. He evolved into the ultimate wheeler-dealer and even came to be known as 'the horse-trader'.[110] The fact that he began life as a socialist and gradually moved to the right adds to the image of a man who lacked genuine convictions.

In July 1940 Pétain appointed him deputy prime minister but sacked him in December 'mainly because he seemed too ready to collaborate with the Germans'.[111] Whatever Laval said at his trial, he invariably gave the impression that he was eager to please. On this matter historians seem to be agreed. Werth says much historiography has depicted Laval as 'morbidly ambitious',[112] while Eatwell claims he saw 1940 as an opportunity for 'personal advancement'.[113]

But the personal and the political were always intertwined, and after France's catastrophic defeat Laval made two calculations. First, he was convinced that a worldwide conflict between Nazism and communism was looming and that Hitler was bound to triumph. Of course many Vichy politicians shared the view that 'Germany had won the war',[114] but the fact is that Laval went further than this, and was pilloried as a result.[115] Second, he held that France could become a 'most favoured' state – and could avoid the dreaded scenario of 'polonisation'[116] – if she was especially enthusiastic and efficient in her dealings with Hitler. Laval soon put this theory into practice on the Jewish question. Ousby comments:

> It was not enough to talk vaguely, as Laval did, of the Reich's intention to establish a Jewish state somewhere in eastern Europe. But he chose not to enquire further because it was easier not to know. It was easier to go along with the general drift of what the occupiers were doing, and, by his enthusiasm in the matter of the children, score a few points which might be to his advantage in a future round of bargaining.[117]

Johnson agrees, stating that 'winning concessions' was Laval's primary *raison d'être*.[118] However, if Vichy leaders believed that the Nazis were going to offer them a 'good deal', they were kidding themselves. McMillan, for one, feels that Hitler had 'no intention' of making concessions on any of the major issues: prisoner release, occupation costs and north zone–south zone logistics.[119]

Nevertheless, it is clear that Laval harboured a dream: that after the war, in a new 'Nazi Europe', with Pétain either dead or dying, Hitler would ask him to take on the role of 'puppet' French leader. Eatwell says Laval 'believed that by accommodating German demands, France could become a major partner in the creation of a new Europe once communism had been eliminated'.[120] Maybe this is the real reason why France collaborated in 1940.

Azéma argues that Pétain 'chose political and economic collaboration',[121] but many including Cobban still place all the 'blame' for collaboration at Laval's door.[122] The case against him is a thorough one and is based on the fact that he was unwilling to make a 'distinction between bargaining about economic details… and bargaining about human lives'.[123] However, we must remember that Laval's protestations are both concerted and supported by others – allegedly.[124] He was not involved in the signing of the armistice – the one event that made collaboration almost inevitable – and commentators have also pointed to his anti-German tactics and efforts at procrastination. Werth says he always opposed the 'yellow star' rule and that, on the whole, his record in office after 1942 was 'a good deal more creditable than his record of 1940'.[125] This is how Laval defended himself:

I devoted every waking minute to saving France, to preserving its framework and its life. There was untold suffering and wounds which never will be healed but that I could not prevent. I say in modest humility that I preserved in the body of France that breath of life which permitted her to survive, to be liberated and to begin her renaissance. I did my best. That is all I claim. But who could have done better than I did when confronted by an enemy as harsh, as unprincipled, and as pitiless as the German was? Another man would have saved his honour, you may say. Yes, perhaps, if he had looked on things in a different light. And in doing so he surely would have crucified France. I have a different concept of honour. I subordinate my personal honour to the honour of my country. My ideal of honour was to make every sacrifice in order to spare our country the final indignity of being ruled by a Gauleiter or by a band of adventurers... For me the road of honour consisted in lightening the burden of suffering and sorrow for the whole French people. Tens of thousands of men and women, Frenchmen and Frenchwomen, owe me their lives. Hundreds of thousands more can thank me for their freedom.[126]

His protestations were in vain and he was executed in 1945 for his wartime role. Apologists might claim Laval's 'trial' was 'a legal monstrosity' (*une monstruosité juridique*), but this does not begin to address the core issues.[127]

McMillan says the Jews who died at Laval's hands 'were not being sacrificed on the altar of racist ideology'.[128] This is no compensation for the Jewish community in France or elsewhere, but it does tell us a lot about Laval the man. He initiated a range of shocking anti-Semitic policies, but was less 'ideological' and less 'of the right' than almost anyone else who is dealt with in this study. However, in the history of extreme-right politics, he cannot be ignored.

Collaborationism

Collaborationism was far more ideological than either the National Revolution or Laval-style collaboration. Pétain's project, it could be argued, was founded upon a 'common sense' and 'back to basics' philosophy; the policy of collaboration, however, was *realpolitik* in action and owed far more to Laval's political and diplomatic calculations than to any genuine belief in anything. Collaborationism, by contrast, was explicit about ideas and doctrine. Whereas collaboration implied a working relationship between victor and vanquished, collaborationism can be defined as an ideological 'alliance' or 'coming together'.

Individuals like Pétain and Laval were not 'in love' with Nazism but came to accept it and work with it. The political activists, literary fascists and far-right intellectuals who gathered in Paris during the Occupation were different. They not only aligned themselves with it, but glorified and mimicked it. The key figures were Robert Brasillach, Pierre Drieu La Rochelle, Jacques Doriot, Marcel Bucard, Marcel Déat, Fernand de Brinon, Joseph Darnand, Alphonse de Châteaubriant, Henri Béraud, Jean Luchaire, Horace de Carbuccia, and Louis-Ferdinand Céline.[129] Soucy asks, 'how could such sensitive, intelligent men, men steeped in the riches of European literature, become fascists?'[130] The simple answer is because they viewed Nazism with envy – as the ultimate political ideology and the force of the future.

The terminology used is slightly confusing. Werth talks about the 'French Nazis',[131] but other historians call them 'Paris Nazis' or 'pro-Nazis'. Commentators also speak of 'French fascists', 'literary fascists', 'fascist intellectuals' and 'quasi-fascist organisations'.[132] Ousby identifies *ultra-collabos* and 'quasi-Nazi *groupuscules*',[133] but some French people may just prefer the word 'traitors'. Give or take the odd ideological nuance, we are dealing here with one and the same political phenomenon.

Déat and Doriot were 'fugitives from the French Left',[134] but most collaborationists were literary figures and articulated their ideas in the pro-German Paris press. Drieu La Rochelle was editor of *Nouvelle revue française*, Céline and Brasillach worked on *Je suis partout*, Béraud was a propagandist on *Gringoire*, Luchaire edited *Nouveaux temps*, and de Brinon was also a writer.[135] Other collaborationists were associated with specific movements. Darnand's powerbase was the Milice;[136] Déat created the Rassemblement National Populaire (RNP) in 1941 in the hope that it would become 'a single party on the fascist model';[137] Bucard was in charge of the Francistes; de Châteaubriant coordinated the activities of Groupe Collaboration; and Doriot founded the Légion des Volontaires Français contre le Bolchevisme (LVF) – the anti-Bolshevik fighting-force – in 1941. *Doriot au pouvoir* ('Doriot in power') was the main aim of his PPF.[138]

These individuals had a double problem. They had little credibility with ordinary French people as 'they existed only because the Reich licensed or at least agreed to tolerate them',[139] and, at the same time, they were 'too divorced from the main currents of French opinion to be of more than limited interest to the Germans'.[140] This created an impossible situation, compounded by the fact that collaborationism was a minority pastime. Ousby suggests that the RNP boasted about 20,000 members and the PPF likewise.[141] These figures are not impressive and tell us much about the scale and overall influence of the pro-Nazi movement in wartime France.

In Werth's view, the French Nazis were a strange mixture of 'hooligans' and 'idealists', 'thugs' and 'intellectuals'.[142] McMillan says the collaborationists were 'a heterogeneous lot... mingling their romantic notions of the new heroic fascist man with vicious anti-Semitism and gutter journalism'.[143] Given their number and odd configuration, it is easy to belittle the French Nazis, but it is a fact that at the Liberation collaborationists were treated severely. Werth writes:

The most famous trials after the Liberation were not those of the economic profiteers of the Occupation, but of the men who supported the Germans on the political and ideological plane... it was a curiously French tribute to the power of the pen, to the prestige of the intellectual.[144]

Eatwell says that the arena of ideas was 'an important one in a country which takes intellectuals seriously'.[145] He goes on:

> Whereas few politicians were willing openly to proclaim themselves 'fascist', more intellectuals were willing to embrace the ideology – or to exhibit aspects of thought which had strong affinities with fascism, and which more generally contributed to the critique of parliamentary democracy. Whilst this may not have produced a fascist mass movement during the 1930s, it undoubtedly helped to condition attitudes after France's defeat in 1940.[146]

The Fall of France was undoubtedly a catalyst, for it brought into the open a range of anti-democratic, pro-German and pacifist positions.[147] McMillan says that 'France had spawned an impressive number of fascist organisations in the inter-war years and the defeat presented them with a further opportunity to demonstrate their commitment to building a new Europe along Nazi lines.'[148] But we should not assume that collaborationism was a product of 1940 and nothing else. Werth suggests that 6 February 1934 was a formative influence for many individuals who then went on to make their names as wartime 'traitors'.[149]

Doctrine and ideas

In the early years of the war the collaborationists' headquarters was Paris. However, when the Germans moved into the Southern Zone and Vichy lost its independence, the French Nazis started to infiltrate government. Their dream, it appeared, was about to take shape. Déat and Darnand were both appointed to office in December 1943.[150]

Their value-system was based on a 'fascination' with Germany and Italy and also a series of violent hatreds.[151] Communism was viewed as a threat to peace and European civilisation,[152] and the Jews were castigated as a 'fifth column' menace. Rebatet talked about 'a detestable race... trampling us to death' and was all in favour of the yellow star being introduced in France.[153] Meanwhile, Celine argued that 'Jews and freemasons were behind everything and the white race was threatened'.[154]

Underlying collaborationist doctrine was a paranoia about 'decadence' and the disease of 'rationalism'.[155] It was argued that France and Europe were on the verge of irreversible decline, and thus it was the task of a new fascist elite to stem the flow of history and help create a 'new civilisation' and a 'new man'. Larkin says that 'Brasillach saw the Occupation as an opportunity for national regeneration, while Drieu La Rochelle saw it as the beginnings of a united and renovated Europe.'[156] But there were serious tensions on the fascist right. One group of thinkers sought a 'solution' on the European level, while a second talked exclusively about 'France'.[157] Moreover, there was no single attitude to Nazism. Some collaborationists argued that France would have to swallow her pride and follow Germany's lead wherever it took her. Darnand, for example, swore an oath of loyalty to Hitler and was proud to wear a German uniform when he joined the LVF.[158] Others, though, perhaps conscious of their ultra-nationalist past, claimed that France should not just 'give way' to Nazism.

In all of this, the nuances were of less importance than the symbolism, for the Paris Nazis were showmen who put the drama and theatre back into politics. Eatwell talks of Brasillach:

> [He] was an aesthete more than a serious thinker, a man who sought an art which would fuse force and form. Details of programme mattered less than images. Symptomatically, he described fascism as 'poetry' rather than doctrine – it was about feeling, rhythm and spirit rather than rational thought.[159]

Graphic imagery also emerged, as Hamilton indicates:

> In all the articles of Châteaubriant, Drieu and Brasillach we find curious metaphors which present the relations between France and Germany as a sexual intercourse in which France plays the woman's part. And there is no doubt that the feudal relationship between the collaborator and his master has a sexual aspect.[160]

However, if the 'ultras of collaboration'[161] were drawn to Nazism, they were unimpressed by Vichy. Price says the 'traditional conservative values' (of Vichy) were as alien to the fascist intellectuals as the 'liberal democratic regime' (the former Republic).[162] The Paris fascists were scathing about Vichy's 'soft' politics and only really warmed to the regime when Pétain initiated a series of severe anti-Semitic measures.[163]

Overall, 'Vichy and Paris attracted markedly different types of clientele',[164] and it is a fact that the government and the 'government-in-waiting' were never reconciled in any meaningful sense. That said, there was the occasional sign of interplay. Déat hoped his RNP would be asked to enter government in the south and Doriot, on one famous occasion, declared his undying loyalty to the Marshal.[165] According to McMillan: 'The gap between Paris collaborators and Vichyites… narrowed considerably… as Vichy developed into a repressive police state, at one with the Nazis in persecuting Jews, Communists and all who refused to accommodate themselves to the new order.'[166] For the most part, however, there was a significant gulf in mentalities, one that could never be breached.

The consensus seems to be that the French Nazis were taken seriously by very few people. The Germans viewed them as 'tools' rather than 'partners', Vichy was happy to 'cold-shoulder' them, and ordinary French people had probably never even heard of people like Brasillach and Bucard.[167] Ousby is close to the mark when he says: 'Collaborationists were guaranteed their brief hour in the sun: access to print and the airwaves, the right to hold parades and wear uniforms apeing those of the occupiers.'[168] This comment indicates the shallowness and artificiality of their position.

For our purposes, the Paris Nazis are an interesting case study in far-right politics. During the later stages of the war there were Frenchmen in the Gestapo and Waffen SS and Germans congratulating Darnand on his role as head of the Milice. This, for McMillan, is 'part of the same story of perverted idealism'.[169] Overall, there was little of substance to the collaborationists. For the Germans they were 'a useful threat, the basis of a possible alternative government',[170] but that was about it. Their only real function was a negative one. For the decade following the Liberation, the extreme right was a spent force. After the imprisonment of Pétain on the Île d'Yeu, the execution of Laval, and the demise of the collaborationists, it had little credibility left.[171]

Pétain had been granted little time to push through his National Revolution and it did not help that his administration was deeply divided on the direction that policy should take. It is accurate to portray Vichy as a regressive, backward-looking and cynically anti-democratic regime, but we should not disregard the modern, welfarist nature of some measures it introduced, particularly in the area of social policy. It should also be noted that the drive to modernisation, masterminded by government technocrats, had a significant, positive legacy in the post-war era.

Collaboration and collaborationism were related concepts. They were hugely different in form and effect,[172] but both left an indelible stain on the history of the far right and the history of the nation. Webster, writing in 1990, is clear about their legacy:

> The spirit of Vichy's unrepentant anti-Semites is still alive, nurtured by politicians like the National Front leader, Jean-Marie Le Pen, who has twice been charged with making anti-Semitic remarks and by the anonymous Jew-haters who dug up the body of an eighty-year-old man in the Jewish cemetery at Carpentras in 1990 and tried to impale the corpse.[173]

On a different level, Conan and Rousso talk about Vichy as an 'obsession' for post-war France.[174] Rousso identifies a neurosis:

> In the late 1970s I began research on the history of the Vichy regime, obviously still a subject of heated controversy. Nevertheless, in all innocence, I thought sufficient time had elapsed to allow me to wield my scalpel. But the corpse was still warm. It was too soon for the

pathologist to begin an autopsy; what the case called for was a doctor qualified to treat the living, not the dead – perhaps even a psychoanalyst. What surprised me most was not the passionate reactions – even among historians – to everything written about the 'dark years' of the war but the *immediacy* of the period, its astonishing presentness... witness the constant scandals, the endless invective and insult, the libel suits, and the many affairs that attracted the attention of all of France.

And, clearly, there is much evidence of this 'Vichy syndrome'[175] in action: the Klaus Barbie affair, the Touvier, Bousquet and Papon war trials, and the Mitterrand revelations.[176] Not for nothing has Rousso equated Vichy to 'The New Dreyfus Affair'.[177]

6 1945–present day – ultra-nationalism and neo-fascism

Algérie Française, Poujadism and the Front National

The National Front represents a natural continuation of an omnipresent political tradition in French society.[1]

1953   Formation of UDCA (Union de Défense des Commerçants et Artisans) (the Poujadist movement)

1954   Fall of Diên Biên Phu (Indo-China)
1 November: Algerian insurrection begins

1956   2 January: Poujadists gain 12.5 per cent share of the vote in Legislative elections (fifty-two seats)
14 January: Formation of Committee of Action and Defence of French Algeria
19 June: First execution of FLN (Front de Libération Nationale) personnel
15 November: Salan becomes Commander in Chief of the Army in Algeria

1958   13 May: Revolt of army and settlers in Algeria
1 June: National Assembly accepts de Gaulle government
4 July: de Gaulle makes *Je vous ai compris* speech
28 September: Fifth Republic constitution ratified

1960   24 January–1 February: Barricades Week

1961   January: Referendum on Algeria's future
February: Formation of OAS (Organisation Armée Secrète)
22–25 April: 'Generals' Putsch'
6 December: 'Anti-OAS Day' in Paris

1962   March: Evian Accords seal Algerian independence

1965   Tixier-Vignancour wins 5 per cent of the presidential vote

1972   Le Pen founds Front National

1983   Dreux by-election success for the Front National

1984   Front National gains 10 per cent of the vote in the European elections

1986   Front National wins thirty-five seats in the legislative elections

1988   Le Pen wins 14 per cent of the vote in the presidential elections

1989   Front National re-enters parliament on the back of Marie-France Stirbois' by-election victory at Dreux

1993   Front National polls 12 per cent of the vote in legislative elections

1994   Front National wins 10 per cent of the vote in European elections

1995   Le Pen wins 15 per cent in presidential elections

1999   Mêgret leaves Front National to form Front National-Mouvement National [later known as Mouvement National Republicain (MNR)]

Predictably perhaps, the right and the extreme right had a tough time in the immediate post-war years. Laval had been shot, Pétain imprisoned for life and ad hoc 'justice' was being meted out to collaborators. However, as the next decades were to demonstrate, the far-right tradition had certainly not been extinguished. In the 1950s the *Algérie Française* movement and the Poujadist phenomenon were to breathe new life into the right, and in the 1980s and 1990s Jean-Marie Le Pen's FN (Front National) was to dominate French politics – even though it only held a 10–15 per cent share of the national vote. But, in this post-war period, what kind of extreme right are we talking about? What guise did it adopt? What themes did it emphasise? What characteristics did it possess? And what kind of political ideas link *Algérie Française*, *Poujadisme* and *Lepénisme*?

Algérie Française

Of course, there were some early post-war efforts to relaunch the far right – centring mainly on Maurice Bardèche[2] – but it was a full decade before the real 'comeback' began, and when it did it took the form of *Algérie Française*.

This new 'colonial right' emerged during the Algerian War, which began in 1954 and ended eight years later with the Evian Accords, which granted autonomy to Algeria.[3] Historians are in no doubt as to the significance of the conflict:

> The wounds of the war still lie deep, and it was not until April 1975 that the tricolour could fly again in Algiers, with the first state visit of a French President... One reasonable set of figures puts the military cost of the war *per annum* as rising from 2,800 (new) francs in 1955 to 10,000 million by 1960, showing a total of between 50 and 55 milliard for the seven and a half years of war.[4]

It has also been estimated that, between 1954 and 1960, spending on the conflict accounted for 28 per cent of the total French budget.[5] For his part, Marcus regards the war as a stimulus:

The Algerian conflict seemingly provided the far Right with its best mobilising theme since the Liberation, and its best opportunity to influence national political events. A variety of associations were formed to campaign on behalf of keeping Algeria French. Here at last was a contemporary issue capable of raising significant passions. Algeria provided a focus for many of the far Right's concerns: their hostility to the Left, their belief that France's historic destiny was being undermined, and their concern at France's diminishing status in a world increasingly dominated by two rival superpowers.[6]

Commentators agree that the war had a profound effect on the right. Hainsworth says it created a 'reservoir' of ideas, while Winock argues that it fostered a new culture of 'illegality'.[7] Anderson expands on this point:

> The extra-parliamentary organisations of the extreme Right in the years from 1954 to 1962 are cloaked in deep and sometimes inpenetrable obscurity. From the beginning of 1956, when the authority of the regime began to crumble, there were many reports of subversion and plotting. Some conspiracies existed only as far-fetched rumours and, although others had serious implications, there was a very high proportion of 'mythomanes' and of men with an interest in either exaggerating or obscuring their own role in this area of clandestine political activity.[8]

So, the Algerian conflict was a landmark, an event that helped individuals to define themselves politically.

In one sense the decolonisation crisis in Algeria was typical of the post-war period,[9] but the scale of the savagery and the intransigence of the protagonists was unique. Both the French army and the FLN – the Algerian nationalist movement – employed barbaric methods. Historians suggest that over a million Algerians died in the conflict, and ever since the end of the war France has had to fend off accusations that it utilised Gestapo-style torture tactics in North Africa.[10]

The attitude of post-1945 French administrations to the Algeria question was ambiguous, equivocal and sometimes just confused, but they were invariably placed in a difficult situation. Price explains: 'Successive governments were to accept the self-interested advice of colonial administrators and military commanders, and to succumb to pressure from settler opinion and conservative politicians. In so doing they would play into the hands of extreme nationalists.'[11] Throughout the 1950s, governments said one thing and then another. The left believed that independence was inevitable and, somewhat perversely, this seemed to encourage the right. Ultimately the colonial lobby lost the political battle, but not without a fight.

The *Algérie Française* movement has attracted many labels – most notably, 'ultra-nationalist', 'fascist' and 'ultra-rightist'. It incorporated a range of intransigent forces: the army in Algeria, the *pieds noirs* or *colons* (colonial settlers or colonists) and a range of small neo-fascist groupings in Paris.[12] There were natural tensions between the three groups, but they were all working towards the same goal – preventing Algerian independence.

Algeria was colonised in 1830 and in line with France's unique colonial philosophy, which centred on notions of 'integration'[13] and 'assimilation',[14] the army viewed the territory as 'French'. After the 'sell-out' and debâcle of Indo-China,[15] the military was determined to keep hold of Algeria. Clayton depicts the mentality of the army:

> Indochina had been lost to the forces of evil, but the rest of the French Empire must on no account go the same way. Algeria was in any case still regarded as part of France and its defence part of that of the free world. It was argued in a doctrine that primarily represented gut-reaction to defeat, that total revolutionary war, as the Marxists or the FLN envisaged, could only be met by total counter-revolutionary war. In this all means could be justified and order should precede law; military needs must override all legal and political factors, and in the last resort the military might have to dominate the political leadership.[16]

The army in Algeria mistrusted civilian politicians and felt that it alone was the guardian of the country's colonial empire. Price says the officer corps posed as 'the incarnation of France' and argues that their 'patriotism was exceeded only by their arrogance'.[17]

Between 1958 and 1961 the armed forces executed three attempted coups in Algeria. On 13 May 1958 they rose in favour of de Gaulle, an episode that put the final nail in the coffin of the Fourth Republic;[18] in January 1960 they were the fulcrum of 'Barricades Week';[19] and in April 1961 they stood by as four of their leaders – Challe, Jouhaud, Salan and Zeller – launched what became known as the 'Generals' Putsch'.[20] On each occasion top-ranking military personnel were supported by far-right extremists in Paris and Algiers. This was civil war.

Officers and generals shunned the idea of a negotiated peace and campaigned strongly for a military solution. McMillan states:

> From the army's perspective, there could be no question of compromise or any 'sell-out' by cynical politicians, as in Indo-China. Badly in need of a boost to their morale and to their prestige, they convinced themselves that they were engaged above all in an ideological struggle, defending western civilisation against the spread of communism: hence their immense efforts to win the minds of the Arab population through propaganda and genuine efforts to improve schooling, social services and the like.[21]

But it would be wrong to imply that the whole of the army was in the midst of a highly politicised revolt. There was a world of difference between the attitude of senior officials and rank-and-file conscripts. The generals – the key actors in the rebellion – shared a unique psyche and had the confidence to believe that they could alter the course of French political history. But they often had to act alone and maybe this explains why they had such limited success.

In 1961 the anti-Paris revolt took on a new dimension with the birth of the OAS, a movement of far-right 'Ultras' that helped to spread 'apocalyptic neo-fascist views among regular soldiers'.[22] This shady organisation took up an 'extreme position' on the Algeria question, attacked 'French liberals, Left-wing figures and Moslems', and came to be dominated by army 'die-hards', including General Salan.[23] It was renowned for its terror tactics and specialised in 'plastic explosions' and assassination.[24] Simmons says that, by 1962, 'the OAS had moved its operations to France. Bombs were set off in the Arab quarter of French cities, attempts were made to assassinate loyalist army and police officers, and Communist Party offices and buildings were targeted.'[25]

In January 1961 the OAS assassinated one of its key liberal opponents, Maître Popie; in May of the same year it launched a series of explosions in Algiers; and in February 1962 it massacred more than 500 people. Although Anderson describes the movement as the 'apotheosis of the French Algeria extremism',[26] he is sceptical about its overall impact:

> The OAS, like the whole of the extreme Right, laboured under the serious handicaps of sectarianism, lack of able leadership and the usually passive, but very real hostility of the great majority of the French population. Paranoia was a prominent feature in the mental universe of the OAS and of the extreme Right as a whole. Conspiracies, betrayals and persecution were identified in the most unlikely places.[27]

In the end, the relationship between the army and the OAS descended into friction and animosity.[28]

The *pieds noirs* shared similar attitudes to the military and in the view of Behr this 'European minority' had an obsessive outlook:

> Its violence, the tenacity with which it opposed any proposals which would have led to change in time to prevent bloodshed were among the direct causes of the rebellion... The Europeans in Algeria possessed a kind of corporate consciousness. Beneath the braggadocio, the absurd threats, the absolute refusal to consider anything but their own predicament... a sociologist could detect a whole range of psychological problems affecting close on a million people.[29]

Overall, settlers – both French and European – accounted for approximately one in ten of the country's population. Passionate believers in the theory and practice of *Algérie Française*, they had set up home in North Africa and cut ties with mainland Europe. In one of his more cutting, asides de Gaulle said the colonists were still dreaming of the *Algérie du papa*.[30]

The *pieds noirs* had been 'appalled at the weakness and the hesitancy of the successive governments of the Fourth Republic', and during the 1950s they evolved into a hardline political force.[31] A range of 'Ultra' organisations were founded, including Jo Ortiz' Front National Français and the Front de l'Algérie Française.[32] The colonists arranged massed rallies to oppose the Algerian policy of Mollet (appointed prime minister in January 1956) and coordinated a general strike on 13 May 1958 in association with 'extreme right-wing organisations and disgruntled army officers'.[33] They also protested forcefully at de Gaulle's sacking of Massu in January 1960. But although they shared a similar perspective, the colonists and the military did not always get on (in January 1960, for instance, the army did not support the riots organised by the settlers). Not for the first time, the forces of the far right were beset by internal rivalries.

Whatever the tensions, the pro-*Algérie Française* right always had a dangerous weapon up its sleeve: invasion. A pincer movement involving rebel generals in Algeria and far-right activists in Paris had enormous potential. The army used parachute drops to contact rebel troops on the mainland, and in May 1958 there were plans for a 'combined air and armoured assault'.[34] However, in reality these were just rumours and plots:

> These conspiracies and their ramifications were mainly based on Algerian soil, amongst the European settlers and dissident army officers, but they were assisted in metropolitan France by neo-Fascists, Right-wing extremists, ex-servicemen and people carried away by the troubled and sometimes sinister atmosphere of the times.[35]

So, as Anderson notes, a myriad of forces were active in Paris. Although the decade immediately following the war was not conducive to far-right activity, a cluster of small ultra-nationalist groups had begun to germinate by the 1950s: most notably, Jeune Nation, Mouvement National Révolutionnaire, Mouvement Populaire du 13 Mai, Mouvement pour l'Indépendence Nationale, Mouvement pour l'Instauration d'un Ordre Corporatif, Comité de Vigilance pour l'Indépendance Nationale, and Front National des Combattants. There was also a range of newly-formed study groups.[36] For extreme-right activists, in the period after 1954, the colonial issue was a godsend, for it gave them a drum to beat.

Interestingly, many believed that the future of Algeria would not be determined in Algeria but in Paris, the scene of so many previous anti-regime insurrections. That is why individuals like Le Pen and Demarquet spent so much time in the French capital during 1958. Le Pen in fact had a hardline attitude, believing that a revolt had to strike at the heart of Paris and involve the occupation of the Élysée Palace.[37]

A new type of right

In time these three elements – army, settlers and Paris activists – coalesced, uneasily, beneath the banner of *Algérie Française*. Politically and logistically, it was not an easy alliance to manage, but deep down, all three groups shared a similar value-system. Although the tide of post-war decolonisation was gathering momentum, the rebel forces were convinced that Algerian independence would be a betrayal. So, what kind of right did the *Algérie Française* movement represent? What kind of psyche did it possess?

It was, first of all, a far right that clung to a distinct brand of nationalism, for it completely embraced traditional French attitudes to colonialism and, as such, defined the nation as an amalgam of mainland and overseas France. Hence Algeria was not just Algeria, but *Algérie Française*. Via this kind of logic, the 'sell-out' of Algeria was equated to the 'sell-out' of France. It went further and talked about the 'imperial grandeur' of France and peddled a vicious brand of racism and European supremacy. During 'Barricades Week' in January 1960, the Celtic cross symbol was pinned almost everywhere, indicating that the rebels perceived themselves to be part of the French neo-fascist tradition.[38] Moreover, it was an extreme right that aligned itself with the military and at times *was* the military. Anderson argues that the army 'seemed so thoroughly politicised in 1958',[39] and the reverse was also true in that, simultaneously, the far right appeared to be thoroughly 'militarised'. The emergence of the OAS demonstrates this perfectly. The colonists and far-right activists in Paris were deeply attached to the military, and the prestige of the military had now become the central issue.

The ultra-right of the Algerian period also developed strong hatreds. Parliament and the institutions of the Fourth Republic were condemned for their weakness and impotency and it was argued that inertia at the top was to blame for the national 'betrayals' in both Indo-China and Algeria. Paris was viewed as a sitting target – hence the attempted coups of 1958, 1960 and 1961 that ultimately sought to destroy the regime and establish an authoritarian military government in its place.

When the Fourth Republic eventually fell in 1958 under the weight of various political pressures, many related to Algeria, there were no tears shed on the extreme right. If anything though, hostility to de Gaulle – the man brought in to 'save' France – was even more violent. The irony is that, at first, the military viewed the General as a potential saviour. The revolt in 1958 was a clear indication that they regarded him as 'their man' – a soldier, a man of the right, a political figure who almost personified the 'grandeur of France'. When de Gaulle uttered the famous words *Je vous ai compris* ('I understand you'), the far right interpreted his phrase in the way they wanted to – as de Gaulle offering an olive branch to the nationalist community. But by 1962 de Gaulle had granted Algeria its independence, and ever since, movements on the far right have displayed a visceral hatred of the General and all things Gaullist.[40]

Finally, the *Algérie Française* movement was significant on account of its radical political rhetoric. It talked about fundamental change, and in 1958 established a *Comité de Salut Public* to help preserve 'Algeria as an integral part of the mother country'.[41] This was an explicit reference to 1793 and the French Revolution.[42] It was as if the forces of *Algérie Française* were saying they followed in that same revolutionary tradition.

But historians, trying to establish the truth, often refer to the *Algérie Française* movement as a reactionary force. The talk is of 'Ultras' and of 'counter-revolutionary' agitation.[43] The evidence is clear – nostalgia for a long-lost age of French supremacy, belief in authoritarianism and extreme terror tactics – but in the final analysis all we can say is that the combination of arch-revolutionary fervour and intransigent counter-revolutionary tactics established *Algérie Française* as a particularly curious political movement.[44]

Donegani and Sadoun, together with Marcus and Petitfils[45] may argue that Algeria was not the issue to federate or popularise the far right, but it led, nevertheless, to an astonishing upsurge in political agitation. In specific terms, the conflict enabled the extreme right to 'reclaim nationalism following the de facto forfeiture via the Vichy experience'.[46] This was a profound development that paved the way for Le Pen and the FN in the 1970s.

Winock and Milza actually go further, arguing that the period 1954–62 witnessed a process of 'fascistisation' (*fascisation*).[47] It is left to Anderson to offer a more balanced appraisal:

> With the possible exception of the Vichy period, the eight years of the Algerian War were the most favourable historical context which the extreme Right had enjoyed during the twentieth century. Although the fears that it might seize power have, with hindsight, seemed exaggerated, its resources were considerable and its activities alarming.[48]

This is a fair verdict, but with the benefit of greater hindsight it is clear that the key to understanding *Algérie Française* is factionalism. Not only did it encompass scores and scores of new political organisations, but a small number of left-wingers and moderates also gravitated towards the ultra-right.[49] This led to chaos and a range of ineffective political initiatives.

After 1962 the colonists returned to France. They would be a useful asset in the country's drive towards economic modernisation but, politically, they would always resent the 'sell-out' of Algeria. Le Pen's movement – founded in 1972 – would reap the benefits of this enduring bitterness.

Poujade and Poujadism

While *Algérie Française* was gathering steam in North Africa, Poujadism – 'the violent and anarchic protest movement *par excellence*'[50] – was evolving in mainland France. The two factions emerged simultaneously but independently. Anderson argues that the Poujadist movement 'was only loosely involved in the colonial problem, although trying unsuccessfully to make use of it'.[51] There were other connections in the sense that both were fiercely critical of the Fourth Republic, both had dreams of a new authoritarian regime, both embodied a style of nationalism that emphasised the grandeur of France, and at one point Pierre Poujade – the man behind Poujadism – was viewed by *Algérie Française* activists as a potential leader of a post-Fourth Republic France. Price argues that the two groups 'shared a contempt for parliament, an extreme xenophobia, anti-semitism and a visceral anti-communism'.[52]

The Poujadist movement – known more formally as the UDCA – was the ultimate flash-in-the-pan phenomenon. It was born in the early 1950s and won 13 per cent of the national vote and fifty-two seats in the 1956 parliamentary elections.[53] It was particularly strong in the south-west and, in Milza's view, benefited enormously from the post-war agricultural crisis,[54] but by the late 1950s it had disappeared as a political force, undone by an economic upturn that had benefited the socio-economic groups whose hardships it had so gleefully exploited in 1956.[55]

Poujade, the founder of the UDCA, became the personification of the movement. He was a flamboyant and eccentric individual and a man of great political acumen who saw the organisation as a vehicle for protest – against the Republic, post-war economic modernisation and the whole drift of republican politics. In more specific terms, Poujadism portrayed itself as the voice of French shopkeepers. Poujade himself owned a stationery shop in the Lot and feared that post-war economic changes would mean marginalisation and bankruptcy for small-town entrepreneurs across the country. But what significance does the Poujadist phenomenon hold for our investigations? In what sense was it a movement of the far right? And what kind of extreme right did it symbolise?

We should be aware that not all historians consider Poujadism to be a movement of the right, never mind the far right. Most commentators are fascinated by its strangeness rather than its right-wing properties per se, and some even view it as a phenomenon of the left.

Poujade himself had an interesting background. In his early life he had been involved in the PPF and the Vichy youth movement, Compagnons de France; and, just to add to the political mix, his father had supported the AF and his wife was a *pied noir*. In the 1950s Poujade aligned himself with *Algérie Française* and also harangued various politicians on account of their Jewish origins, most notably Prime Minister Pierre Mendès-France. He was also particularly intolerant of homosexuality.[56]

A powerful sense of patriotism lay at the heart of Poujade's right-wing curriculum vitae. Pinol says that Poujadist nationalism was of a 'flag-waving and anti-American' complexion',[57] while Rémond states:

> By its vocabulary, its subject matter, and its phobias, it was indeed the descendant of that form of temperament with which French nationalism

has identified itself since the defeat of 1870 – a defensive and introspective nationalism, a nationalism that a feeling of decadence renders aggressive, an ill-tempered and combative nationalism that turns to chauvinism, xenophobia and anti-Semitism.[58]

Simmons agrees and is in no doubt that the UDCA echoed many important extreme-right themes – including fanatical anti-Semitism and imperialism – and goes on to argue that Poujadism was a significant stepping-stone in the political career of Jean-Marie Le Pen.[59] Gildea puts more emphasis on the Gallic nationalism at the heart of the movement (symbolised by the *coq* it adopted as its main emblem[60]) while Rioux points out that the Algeria issue gave Poujade 'a powerful new rallying cry'.[61]

So nationalism, in all its various guises, was a pillar of Poujadist doctrine. But there was also another Poujade – the man who railed against Paris and privilege, who acted as spokesperson for the 'humble' and 'disenfranchised', who, after 1945, posed as a Resistance hero.[62] His political discourse contained traces of anarchism and radicalism and was littered with references to *fraternité* – a word with explicit revolutionary connotations. As if to emphasise his leftist credentials even more, he called for the Estates General to be reconvened,[63] and for a short period he even attracted communist support.[64] For these reasons and others we should note the view of Declair, who says that the UDCA was in no way conceived as a movement of the far right.[65]

In reality Poujadism was a coalition – of radicals, conservatives, ultra-nationalists, ex-servicemen and neo-fascists, not forgetting the irate shopkeepers and frustrated tax-dodgers.[66] And it was not a very stable coalition at that. But right or left, Poujade presented an acute problem for the French establishment. He was a dangerous rabble-rouser – Winock talks of his 'verbal aggression'[67] – and he did not fit into neat categories.

In some quarters Poujade was billed as a 'French Hitler' (in the 1950s *L'Express* nicknamed him *Poujadolf*)[68] but he never talked seriously about a coup or a putsch. He was content just to disrupt political meetings and act the nuisance. McMillan argues that Poujadism was 'more than a little reminiscent of fascism, with its rallies and recourse to physical as well as verbal violence', but Anderson is probably right when he states that it was 'too ill-disciplined' to be fascist in any authentic sense.[69]

The 'anti-everything' movement

Maybe we should dispense with political labels altogether and just conceive of Poujadism as a prime example of 'anti-system' protest politics.[70] The UDCA was a 'bundle of negatives'[71] and complained so much about so many things that it is difficult to locate a constructive vision at all. Even its main slogan – *Sortez les Sortants* ('Throw the Rascals Out!')[72] – was entirely negative.[73] Gildea says Poujade was 'not impressed by anyone – politicians, intellectuals, bureaucrats, Eurocrats, plutocrats, technocrats'.[74] Winock adds 'men with diplomas, *polytechniciens*, economists, philosophers and other dreamers' to the organisation's blacklist.[75]

The Poujadists viewed Paris with a mixture of jealousy and contempt. The city was a symbol of modernisation, urbanisation and centralisation and, in political terms, of the hated Republic. On a different level, Poujadism singled out supermarkets and hypermarkets as portents of doom for France, and small shopkeepers in particular.[76] Poujade announced that his 'members' were bound to lose out if the obsession with economies of scale was maintained and insisted that the shopkeepers of France had to be protected.

It might sound harsh to say that Poujadism stood for the 'defence of economic backwardness',[77] but this was very close to the truth. Shopkeepers and small traders – all suffering in the post-war period – viewed Poujade as their spokesman. Rioux states:

> Around 1952… conditions began to turn against the retailers: restrictions came to an end, goods were beginning to flood onto a market in which demand was still not fully rekindled, there were the first signs of the changes in production which were to revolutionise distribution and prepare for the supermarkets, and, above all, inflation ended.

Larkin says that inflation had traditionally helped France's small businessmen – they could 'sell at high prices' but 'pay off their debts to wholesalers and other creditors at the level that was current at the time of initial purchase'[78] – and it is clear that their ire only really evaporated when inflation started to rise again in the late 1950s. In the meantime Poujade whipped up discontent.

Supermarkets were only part of the problem but, in Poujadist eyes, they came to represent capitalism at its most intimidating.[79] UDCA discourse was dominated by notions of *les petits et les gros* and in the economic context this translated as unfair competition between small and large traders.[80] It was not just the size or number of supermarkets that bothered Poujade but their modernity, and here we come to a theme of huge importance in Poujadist rhetoric. Simmons explains:

> Poujadism appeared as a reaction against the modernisation of the French economy. Modernisation in the French context meant a continuing depopulation of the countryside as rural masses moved to the burgeoning industries located near or in the cities…; a spurt in industrial production, which leapt 70 percent from 1949 to 1957; and the beginnings of a modern retail sector with the establishment of supermarkets and retail chains such as Uniprix.[81]

Significantly, the basic position of Poujadism – anti-modernisation, anti-modernity – was reflective of general post-war trends, of tension between shopkeeper and technocrat, between 'static' France and the 'new' France.[82] Rioux might suggest that the UDCA was not as anti-progress as it is popularly portrayed, but the same author also states:

> Born of a powerlessness to stem the tide of modernisation, Poujade's revolt was backward-looking, invoking the glories of France and the uncomplicated patriotism of the pre-1914 primary school, coming close to Vichy with its exaltation of a social life based on the family and the small community, a way of life now under attack from the technocrats, the tax inspectors and the politicians.[83]

Interestingly, Pinol plays down the anti-modernisation drive within Poujadism and describes it first and foremost as an 'anti-tax rebellion' (*une révolte antifiscale*), and it would be true to say that *fiscalisme* – a highly pejorative term in Poujadist vocabulary – was viewed as an intrinsic evil.[84] Indeed the UDCA followed in a long line of French political movements that resented the invasion of penny-pinching tax inspectors,[85] and the fact that officials were, in the main, Paris-based added to the Poujadists' distaste. When resistance to tax inspection was outlawed in August 1954, the anger of Poujade and his men reached a new peak. Rioux says, 'this inopportune measure hardened the resolve of all those who had experienced the humiliation of the often brutal inspections by the "polyvalents", the reduction of tax relief, and the clamp-down on fiscal fraud.'[86] In 1955, sickened by tax increases, Poujade and his men caused a rumpus in the public galleries of the National Assembly.[87]

Poujadism was significant for additional reasons. It quickly evolved from pressure group (UDCA) to political party Union et Fraternité Française (UFF), a development that in one sense was unremarkable but in another signified something quite profound. The UDCA had always prided itself on its 'anti-system' persona and, as such, it always said that it did not want to take part in conventional political activity because conventional political activity was its enemy. It could not be 'anti-system' and then join the 'system'.[88] Hence the array of unconventional tactics employed – the public meetings, the street violence, the 'invasion' of parliament. But, by the mid-1950s Poujade had grown tired of the gimmicks and was determined to exert real influence. The UFF was born in 1956 and took part in the elections of that year with astonishing results.

The Poujadist movement also stood as a prime example of populist politics in action. With no discernible ideology and only a rag-bag of policy ideas, UDCA leaders had to mix and match. Rioux talks about the 'almost desperate... mobilisation of any theme likely to make their voices heard: antiparliamentarianism, hostility to Paris and the technocrats, protest over taxation, a defence of *l'Algérie Française*'.[89] More than anything, Poujadism was 'plain speaking' and, in the words of Poujade himself, 'had as much intellectual content as a scream'.[90] We should not exaggerate its cogency, but we should acknowledge its bluntness and, at times, effectiveness.

Unlike almost anything else, the existence of the UDCA helps us to understand the state of France in the 1950s. But how should we interpret Poujadism in the context of right-wing politics? Petitfils argues that the movement was too backward-looking to be regarded as genuine fascism and, as such, it is probably wise to agree with Winock who sees Poujadism as another fleeting manifestation of the national-populist tradition.[91]

For his part McMillan describes Poujadism as 'another negative element in French political life, aggravating the problem of operating a successful parliamentary democracy', and it is true that after the 1956 elections, republican leaders found it acutely disturbing that one in ten voters had put their faith in an 'anti-system' party.[92] However, Poujadism could not be sustained, and in the end 'alarm' turned to 'derision' in rapid time.[93]

Le Pen and the Front National

Veteran far-right activist Jean-Louis Tixier-Vignancour stood for the presidency in 1965 and scored a modest 5 per cent share of the vote.[94] The next key date in the history of extreme-right politics was 1972, the year that Jean-Marie Le Pen's FN was founded.

Le Pen had been a paratrooper in Algeria and a loyal supporter of the anti-independence movement. He also became a leading light in the Poujadist movement and in 1956, on the UDCA ticket, became the youngest-ever parliamentary deputy.[95] In 1972, after a period in the political wilderness, he founded the FN, and in the years that followed it evolved into a significant political force, arguably the biggest and most influential neo-fascist movement in Western Europe.[96] During the 1990s, when Le Pen was at the peak of his powers, the FN posed as the ultimate in modern political formations, boasting an impressive website, a vibrant youth movement – the Front National Jeunesse (FNJ) – and a highly innovative commercial arm that marketed the party via a million and one different gimmicks.[97]

Commentators are agreed on the importance of the FN. Hainsworth claims that 'the emergence of the FN has posed all kinds of problems for political rivals, unsure of how to interpret and respond to the newcomer to the fore of French politics.'[98] Simmons makes a similar point, arguing that the key to understanding the FN is its ambiguity: 'The essential problem is... to determine what side of the amorphous boundary that separates the extreme right from fascism the Front falls. Is it, as some would argue, a neofascist party in disguise?'[99] Marcus is aware of the movement's dubious image but prefers to view the emergence of the FN in a different light. For him, 'the rise of the Front clearly mirrors developments elsewhere in Western Europe.'[100]

The FN had little success until the 1980s.[101] The turning-point came in 1983 when the movement scored an astounding success in a local election in Dreux.[102] Twelve months on, it achieved national prominence when it won 11 per cent of the vote and ten seats in the European elections.[103] In 1985 it published its political programme for the country to inspect – *Pour la France* – and the year after, it captured thirty-five seats on a 10 per cent share of the legislative vote (which set in motion France's first experience of *cohabitation*).[104] In 1988 it maintained its vote in more parliamentary elections but, under new electoral rules, won only one seat; in the presidential poll of the same year Le Pen won 14 per cent of the vote – his best-ever showing at a national level. Soon after, the FN regained a voice in parliament when Marie-France Stirbois gained 42.5 per cent of the vote in the 1989 Dreux by-election. Vaughan states: 'From another *groupuscule* apparently doomed to obscurity, the FN rose to achieve credibility within a decade.'[105]

Throughout the 1980s, politicians, political scientists and media commentators were engaged in a highly emotive debate about the FN breakthrough. At times this debate was about 'origins' and 'causation', but when the point-making became more partisan, the language subtly changed: from 'how and why did the FN emerge?' to 'who or what was to blame?' Some commentators claimed that far-right activity was endemic to France, a component part of national political culture, and here it is argued that the catalyst was the arrival in power of Mitterrand's Socialists in 1981. After a decade of little success under right-wing rule, the FN now had a left-wing government to target and contrast itself with, especially in policy areas such as immigration. This was of vital help to the FN in terms of self-definition.

Mitterrand was a fundamental factor in the rise of the FN. In 1986 he introduced proportional representation (PR) for parliamentary elections; it was well known at the time that PR would help the smaller parties, and so it did. For the first time Le Pen's party won representation in the National Assembly and, in so doing, split the right.[106] This clearly helped the ruling socialists and, not unexpectedly, Mitterrand was accused of cultivating the FN in order to 'divide and rule'. Given the Machiavellian tendencies of the socialist president, it is entirely possible that such a calculation took place. Eatwell argues that Mitterrand even instructed the state media to give 'fringe parties' more access.[107]

However, the central importance of Mitterrand should not obscure the fact that a unique set of circumstances aided, if they did not actually create, the Le Pen phenomenon. In the early 1980s a serious economic downturn had been made more acute by high levels of inner-city crime; France's post-war 'boom' was levelling out and important sections of the population were feeling alienated from the political process. Hainsworth states:

> No single factor will suffice to explain the rise and success of the FN. Rather, the elevation of the movement as a force in contemporary French politics rests upon a complex alchemy and conjuncture of variables... By 1984, the FN was very much the right party in the right place at the right time.[108]

There was nothing inevitable about the rise of Le Pen, but in the early 1980s there was fertile territory to exploit.

It is here that Le Pen – the man and political animal – is crucial. His charisma and charm cannot be understated nor can the simple, populist appeal of the infant party he led. In the 1970s and 1980s there was something refreshing about the FN, for, unlike other politicians, Le Pen – the absolute personification of the movement – was happy to speak his mind and talk in an accessible, down-to-earth language. He also brought a touch of theatre to politics: the stage-managed entrances, the inspirational classical music that accompanied his public appearances, and the *risqué* statements he became famous for. He was wild, flamboyant and unpredictable, and a small but significant proportion of the population was attracted to this. He could also make promises galore to every conceivable social group in the almost certain knowledge that he was never likely to gain any serious power. This gave him a blank cheque.

It was in the mid-1990s that FN support reached its zenith. It polled 12 per cent in the 1993 parliamentary elections and 10 per cent in the 1994 European poll; then Le Pen broke through the 15 per cent barrier in the presidential vote of 1995, which meant in effect that one in seven French people had voted for a man viewed by many as 'racist' and by some as 'fascist'.[109] In the same year the party won three significant mayoral contests – in Toulon, Orange and Marignane – and in 1997 it added Vitrolles to its municipal conquests.[110] For the first time the FN had 'real' power.[111]

But by 1999 the movement had ruptured. One faction, revolving around Le Pen, stayed under the FN banner; the other, led by Bruno Mégret, detached itself from the party and eventually came to call itself the MNR.[112] In the European elections of June 1999 Le Pen won 5.7 per cent of the national vote and Mégret 3.5 per cent.[113] The rump party accused the MNR of 'a betrayal of ideas' and 'existing only to harm the FN'.[114] Nonetheless, the fact remains that in its heyday – the late 1980s and early 1990s – the FN was a profoundly important force, and today the movement is significant for a number of reasons.

More than anything, the FN is a coalition of interests. Neo-fascists, hardened *Algérie Française* veterans, ex-Poujadists, new right activists, disillusioned conservatives, integrist Catholics and former members of the Club de l'Horloge – they all found a home in the organisation, in the years after 1972. This led to fierce internal debate about policy, competition for influence and, ultimately, schism.[115]

At the same time, the overriding importance of Le Pen – the only leader the FN has known – has to be acknowledged. On one level he is a tub-thumping rabble-rouser but on another he is an extremely modern and skilful politician. Vaughan states: 'He is widely held to be a talented demagogue with undoubted debating skills, a love of rhetoric and a keen understanding of TV technique.'[116] Not only was Le Pen able to keep the FN coalition intact for almost three decades but he was also clever enough to keep FN concerns at the top of the political agenda for most of the 1980s and 1990s, a major achievement that owed much to his skills as orator and media manipulator.[117]

Le Pen has also been at the centre of successive political scandals. He provoked outrage when he described the Holocaust as a 'detail' in the history of the Second World War; he was accused of using systematic torture during his *Algérie Française* days; he was forced to defend the FN after a Moroccan drowned in highly suspicious circumstances following a party rally in 1995; and, on a much lighter note, his ex-wife caused him huge embarrassment when she posed naked for *Playboy*.[118] However, the FN leader has always lived to fight another day. One rumour has it that every September – the start of the French political year – he and his advisors meet to plan their next media stunt. The phrase 'all publicity is good publicity' could have been invented for him. Moreover, Le Pen is reluctant to play the 'normal' politician and has made an art form out of smashing taboos. Since the early 1970s he has talked in public about a range of issues that no-one else has wanted to touch: most notably, immigration, AIDS and the Jews. He has made many mistakes and landed himself in a lot of hot water, but the fact is that he has altered the parameters of political debate.

From the outset, the FN was dubbed a 'small', 'fringe' party, and over the years it has grown accustomed to this role. During the mid-1980s and early 1990s – when it was consistently polling 10 per cent, 11 per cent and 12 per cent in elections – it made great play of its 'exclusion' from parliament and the media.[119] Le Pen argued that the French establishment was 'picking on the FN' because it was running scared and did not know how to deal with his movement. He depicted political life as a corrupt 'closed shop'; in the early days he talked about the 'Gang of Four' (political parties) that had captured the French establishment; later he spoke of 'covert total-itarianism'.[120] The FN has always seen itself as the 'underdog' and it has invariably thrived on the role.

In 1991 the movement published its own set of 'New Year' greetings cards. One design was accompanied by the words, '1991: The Year of the Outsider'. This seemed to say it all.

Political ideas

In advance of the 1995 presidential campaign the FN produced a small manifesto-style booklet, *Le Contrat pour la France avec les Français*. It was sixty-four pages long and included five photographs: of Le Pen, a blonde mother and her three blond children, a law-court crest, a piece of classical sculpture, and a *tricolore* flying above the Elysée Palace.[121] These pictures were carefully chosen to indicate the main planks of FN doctrine: strong leadership, reproduction and the future, security and strength, tradition and heritage, and patriotism. There are other 'core values' too: nation, family, religion, and hierarchy.[122] According to Le Pen, these values are permanent and unchanging, and are 'concrete' rather than 'abstract'. As such, the FN is convinced that its doctrine is fully in tune with nature and tradition. But how do all the themes connect? And how is the movement's discourse articulated?

The FN is always proud to proclaim itself as a movement of the right, but at the same time it sees itself as 'transcending the artificial division between left and right'.[123] It has no truck with egalitarian ideas and has put forward various justifications for natural selection and inequality.[124] Furthermore, Le Pen has ridiculed the 'rights of man' and has consistently viewed his values as the antithesis of left-wing values.[125] In particular, he contrasts his brand of nationalism with the 'cosmopolitanism' and 'internationalism' of the Parti Socialiste (PS) and the Parti Communiste (PC). If one attitude has underpinned almost every utterance of the FN leader since 1972 it is hostility to socialism and communism; he argues that the French left is obsessed with the 'rights of man' and that, as a result, institutions like family and nation are being undermined.

At the heart of *Lepéniste* doctrine is belief in the nation or, as Hainsworth puts it, the nation 'as imagined by the FN'.[126] The view is that 'France' is, or should be, the ultimate loyalty for individuals and should 'prevail over all other considerations'.[127] In line with this fundamental attachment, party theorists put enormous emphasis on the notion of 'identity'. In 1989 a whole Institut de Formation Nationale (IFN) lecture series was devoted to the issue, with sessions on *Droit et identité*, *L'Identité en question*, *Identité Européenne*, and *Declin et crise d'identité*.[128] These titles indicate the main thrust of FN thinking. Everybody, the party believes, has a right to express their identity, especially in terms of nationality.

The FN's 1993 'Programme of Government', *300 mesures pour la renaissance de la France*, is split into sections that mirror the five areas in which the national identity is allegedly at stake: *Immigration – Renverser le courant* (Immigration – Reverse the flow); *Famille – Pour la préférence familiale* (Family – In favour of family preference); *Enseignement – Transmettre le savoir* (Education – Transmit knowledge); *Culture – Défendre nos racines* (Culture – Defend our roots); *Environment – Sauvegarder notre patrimoine* (Environment – Safeguard our heritage).[129] For the FN, these are the battlegrounds, and although much of party thinking flies in the face of political correctness, Le Pen is unabashed.

Given these twin emphases – nation and identity – the FN is especially sensitive to forces that, in its view, have the potential to destabilise France and make French nationals feel like second-class citizens in their own country.[130] Not only this, but the movement exaggerates 'national decline' for political effect. It talks about 'decadence' and 'disease', about France 'wasting away' and, of course, only one man is trusted to lead the renaissance: Le Pen.[131]

The movement is obsessed by 'threats' to France, and in recent times it has placed special emphasis on the 'danger' of European integration.[132] In 1991 it declared:

> Our conception is that of a Europe of Nations… founded on the renewal of European nations, with each one guarding its identity and integrity at the heart of a confederal entity. *NON A L'EUROPE BUREAUCRATIQUE*

ET COSMOPOLITE. The Europe of Brussels is constructed around an institutional framework inspired by the American federal model – which will lead to the disappearance of the sovereignty of states and peoples.[133]

Thus, the FN believes in Europe as a historic civilisation founded on Christian values and vital geo-political interests, and it opposes *la vision mondialiste* ('the internationalist vision') and all efforts to 'force' economic or political unity. It believes in a 'French France in a European Europe' and in recent years has campaigned against both Maastricht and the Euro.[134]

In a similar kind of way, the FN is concerned about regionalism. It argues that regionalism is a good, healthy and natural thing, but is afraid of it running wild. Just as European integration could sound the death-knell for the French nation, so, in Le Pen's view, could excessive regional sentiment. The integrity of France is viewed as sacred, and that is why in recent years the party has argued against the staging of an independence referendum in New Caledonia and reacted angrily to any notion of a separate 'Corsican people'.

In terms of manifesto commitments and practical policy ideas, the FN has always been pragmatic and has no hang-ups about the intellectual coherency of its programme. One (perhaps apocryphal) story has it that in the early 1970s party leaders decided to commission an opinion poll; they asked French people for their top ten 'concerns', and then swiftly adopted these concerns as policy! Whether this tale is true or not, it is noticeable how, over the last two decades, the organisation has become more professional and broad-ranging in its policy interests. But that said, France and the protection of France has always been central to what the party has had to say.

In the popular imagination the FN is most famous for its 'discourse of exclusion' and its critique of contemporary immigration, and the party does little to dispel this image.[135] In 1992 it announced:

> The presence on our territory of more and more ethnic groups... poses a problem for civil peace. The history of Europe and the world reveals not one example of long-term peaceful co-existence between different ethnic and religious groups on the same soil... There have already been numerous ethnic and racial conflicts in the cities: French against foreigners, Blacks against Arabs, Jews against Blacks... Turks against Kurds... Could you imagine a better demonstration of the risks involved in a multiracial, multicultural society?[136]

The FN has condemned the extent and make-up of the 'invasion', the cultural dimension to modern-day immigration (in particular, mosque-building and *foulard*-wearing) and the 'terroristic' threat that also lies in wait (it has been especially severe in condemning the Algerian danger).[137] The same theme is evident again: national collapse is imminent.

The movement has responded to the immigration problem in forthright fashion.[138] In 1992 it proposed '50 efficient and humane' policy ideas, including more stringent regulation of population movements, reform of nationality code legislation, better, more 'national' education, and the return and expulsion of illegal immigrants.[139] At the same time, Le Pen's party has condemned the weakness of successive governments on the immigration issue and strongly opposed any moves to grant immigrants the right to vote in national elections.[140]

Interestingly, but not unexpectedly, the FN's discourse on immigration has spawned a new vocabulary: *insecurité* (a word that describes a high immigration–high crime urban mix), *préférence nationale* (a *Lepéniste* policy idea designed to reward 'nationals' over and above 'immigrants'), and *zones du non-droit* (a label now attached to inner-city areas in which the rule of law has ceased).[141] The intensity of this anti-immigration discourse has led some to question whether the FN is now a single-issue movement.[142]

A range of other themes can also be linked to 'nation' and 'identity': the suspicion of Jews, the anxiety about creeping Americanisation, and the support that the FN offers to movements of self-determination around the globe.[143] In the social sphere, the condemnation of divorce, homosexuality, contraception and abortion is based on the premise that the 'French nation' equates to 'French people'.[144] Thus, all obstacles to a healthy indigenous birth-rate must be cleared.[145]

There is also ever-present nostalgia. Although at times the FN would like to define itself as a progressive, forward-thinking movement, it is hampered by its glorification of the 'old France'. There is a longing for the 'good old days' of empire when French grandeur was at its peak, and the memory of *Algérie Française* remains particularly evocative for party officials. It is not just the concept that still excites people, but the history of French rule in North Africa. In 1990 I attended an FN rally at La Mutualité in Paris. There was a specific focus to the event – the 'misrule' of Mitterrand's Socialists – but, nevertheless, many speakers signed off with the magical words, *Vive l'Algérie Française!* And when they did, they were greeted by a cacophony of cheers and applause.

If *Algérie Française* is part of the nation's heritage, so, in a completely different sense, is agriculture and peasant life. Here Le Pen is heir to Pétain and Poujade, speaking on behalf of the 'small man', in favour of a simple, small-town France. In the early 1990s the FN produced a special publicity poster, with a rustic-looking Le Pen pictured amid the picturesque French countryside. The image was accompanied by just four words: LE PEN, LA TERRE (LE PEN, THE EARTH). The subliminal message was simple: Le Pen will stand up for France – all of France.

It is noticeable how party leaders use coded language and over-utilise aphorisms, metaphors and clichés in an attempt to convey their message to ordinary people; what Milza calls the 'euphemisation of discourse' (*euphémisation du discours*).[146] And this is not forgetting the questionable symbolism that is occasionally employed. In the early 1980s the FN co-opted, or 'privatised', the memory and heritage of Joan of Arc and, to the disgust of many, she was upheld by *Lepénistes* as a symbol of 'pure' French nationalism, as someone who had expelled foreign invaders from France in the fifteenth century out of patriotic duty.[147] In FN eyes she was someone who personified 'spiritual renaissance' and her image came to adorn party literature and propaganda posters alike.[148]

However, there was something particularly shallow and shabby about the way in which this 'coup' was executed. The Joan represented on FN posters had been touched up: she was now a dazzling, healthy blonde, not an urchin-like waif, and she was going into battle under the *tricolore*, not the royal crest. The party leadership was playing with history, for in the fifteenth century Joan would have had no conception of 'France' as a national entity, but somehow she had now evolved into a fanatical nationalist (no doubt with far-right sympathies). By the mid-1990s the FN had moved on to Clovis – to the amusement and bemusement of most onlookers.[149]

The FN chief may present himself as a 'man of action', but Eatwell claims that by the 1980s *Lepéniste* discourse was 'remarkably sophisticated'.[150] In its prime the party had a full agenda, cleverly articulated through a pseudo-intellectual journal *(Identité)*, a regular lecture series (hosted by the IFN), and also boasted links with the influential right-wing think-tank, Club de l'Horloge. But if we were being entirely truthful, we would have to call this window dressing. Clearly, it is in Le Pen's interests to 'talk up' his doctrine, to frame it in 'intellectual' terms, to give it the trappings of respectability. Vaughan paints a balanced picture: 'For all its inconsistencies, the message is powerful, precisely to the extent that it is simplistic. It appears to… put forward obvious solutions… to boldly-defined problems.'[151] Le Pen describes his doctrine as 'real politics' or 'common sense' *(le bon sens)*, but it is not the kind of 'common sense' that most French people would recognise.[152]

The wider political context

It is plausible to argue that the main importance of the FN lies in its doctrine, but to acquire a full understanding of *Lepénisme* we need to broaden out the discussion. Political scientists, for example, would argue that the FN's electorate is significant and reveals much about the movement as a whole.

In its discourse the movement rails against left-wing notions of 'class' and 'class struggle' and in electoral terms it does not target specific socio-economic groups. Rather, its populist, nationalist concerns take it in another direction completely, and over time it has developed a cross-sectional, *interclassiste* profile.[153] That said, the party's electorate does have specific traits. Hainsworth claims that in 1984 – the year of the big breakthrough – FN support was predominantly masculine and urban, and goes on to argue that during the 1990s Le Pen's electorate became more 'popular'.[154] Likewise, in the context of the 1995 presidential elections, Eatwell talks about 'significant gains in working-class areas'.[155] But, by 1997 the view was that FN support was more 'balanced' in the sense that it was slightly more 'middle class'.[156] It has also been stated that Le Pen's party scores particularly well with 'first-time and hitherto abstentionist voters'.[157] These insights tell us that the FN does not rely on one single constituency for support and that the movement will always have some kind of future in French politics.

In terms of geography, the FN electorate has a distinct profile. The party gained above-average support in 'left-wing' urban areas throughout the 1980s and 1990s (hence the notion of a Caen–Montpellier 'dividing line').[158] This is no real surprise given the main emphases of FN doctrine. Le Pen has always traded on the inner-city backlash against immigration and crime but, as Hainsworth says, we should not exaggerate the correlation between 'immigrants and votes'.[159] It is a fact nonetheless that the FN does markedly less well in rural zones where there are no 'high urgency' issues to exploit. Thus, Le Pen's party is in no sense a traditional organisation of the right – conservative and backward-looking – but rather a movement with a modern, radical edge and a predominantly urban focus.[160] As a footnote to this discussion, we should note the position of Vaughan who intimates that pollsters and political scientists need not flatter Le Pen by enquiring too deeply into why people vote FN. She says it is fairly straightforward: 'The common denominator to which *Lepénisme* appeals is fear.'[161]

Moving on, we can see that the emergence of the FN has affected French party politics in a variety of ways. On one level, movements have been forced to engage with Le Pen and acknowledge his policy platform. When they have judged that he has captured the public mood, mainstream politicians have aped ideas, copied language or merely pointed out that the FN is a credible voice. From left to right, this category includes individuals such as Mitterrand, Fabius, Giscard, Chirac and Pasqua (Gildea suggests that Pasqua, in government between 1986 and 1993, is the best example).[162]

When this happens Le Pen usually strikes a hard-done-by pose. 'The people of France prefer the original to the copy,' he argues, almost resentfully. But there is no doubt that his party has benefited from this process because it has 'validated the FN's discourse' and 'further legitimated' its programme.[163] The overall effect has been twofold: to shift French party politics to the right and to stir up a hornet's nest on the left, where Socialists, Communists and anti-racist movements have placed themselves in the vanguard of the anti-Le Pen counter-attack.[164]

On another level, the rise of the FN has affected electoral relationships. Plenel and Rollat argue that parties in France have had to decide whether to 'ignore', 'annex' or 'combat' Le Pen's movement.[165] For its part, the FN has a different dilemma. Its general attitude to pacts and alliances is coloured by the belief that the French political system is 'corrupt', that it only operates to the benefit of a 'closed circle' of parties.[166] It has always sought to define itself as the only 'pure' and 'untainted' element in modern French politics. But there is kudos associated with electoral *ententes* and the FN has been quick to realise this. Naturally, Le Pen views the Socialists and Communists as beyond the pale, but there have been many opportunities for understandings with the mainstream right. Marcus highlights two interesting examples: Bouches-du-Rhône in 1988 and 1989 and Languedoc-Roussillon in 1992.[167] In summary, the dilemmas on both sides of the political fence indicate that the FN has emerged as a crucial force in French politics.

It is also significant that since the early 1980s the FN has been able to pose as the ultimate protest party – anti-politics and anti-system – and in so doing it has taken on the mantle of the Communist Party as 'a tribune and protest pole'.[168] Eatwell is right to say that many people voted FN for 'positive' reasons, but the 'negative' appeal of the movement is undeniable. Gildea argues, interestingly, that FN electors are 'not altogether determined to see the party in power'.[169]

So the thesis is that in recent years the FN has acted as a receptacle. Marcus states:

> There has always been a niche in the Fifth Republic's politics for a party attracting a significant protest vote. For much of the period since 1958 this was the part played by the Communist Party. Le Pen's movement, like the Communists of old, seems intent on creating its own counter-culture... But can the Front be anything more than a vehicle for protest?'[170]

The answer to this question has got to be yes. Granted, the FN has been extremely effective at whipping up anti-system agitation, but we would be grossly underestimating it if we viewed it as 'just' a protest party.

Nor should we think of the movement as in any way static. Over the last decade and a half Le Pen has overseen radical changes in the organisation and marketing of his party and has also modernised its doctrine.[171] Since 1972 many policies have remained intact – hostility to immigration and belief in some kind of confederal Europe, for example – but it would again be underestimating the FN if we assumed that it has not reacted to trends. Two examples will be sufficient to demonstrate this fact.

In the realm of economic policy, the FN has gradually shifted from a free-market standpoint to a more statist, corporatist position. In the 1970s and 1980s party theorists had idolised Reaganomics and laissez-faire Thatcherism, but in the 1990s the FN placed increasing emphasis on 'National Preference' and job protection.[172] Descaves, a key FN writer, admits that the movement moved from a 'naïve' position to a 'pragmatic' one.[173] In turn, Hainsworth argues that this change was brought on by political calculations, 'in order to correlate more with its [the FN's] status as France's leading workers' party at the polls'.[174]

Le Pen's movement has also reacted swiftly to the rise of green politics.[175] At its 1990 party congress it unveiled a series of new commitments designed to assuage those with eco-concerns. Since then the party leadership has gone further, claiming that conservation of the environment was more a right-wing than a left-wing concern.[176] The argument is that ecology is about the earth, and the earth is the nation; thus, 'ecology is before everything a national value' and nationalists have a duty to protect and conserve the land.[177] This 'conversion' may have been shallow but it does illuminate the modernity of the FN.

In many ways, the legacy of *Algérie Française* and Poujadism can be seen in the style and discourse of the FN, which has inherited a fanatical anti-Gaullism, a powerful loyalty to the idea of empire, and a strong determination to speak for *les petits* against *les gros*. Le Pen is obviously the link, but the FN is much more than a rehash of previous right-wing currents. It offers the electorate a set of cleverly packaged ideas designed to have widespread appeal. It talks in old-fashioned terms about tradition and Frenchness (*francité*) and also, in more modern terms, parades its ecological credentials and argues that the Fifth Republic should give way to a Sixth.[178]

But how should we categorise the FN? This is an almost impossible question to answer, for at times it is conservative, at other times radical.[179] It can act like a neo-fascist movement and can also come across as the epitome of national-populism.[180] It is, by turn, revolutionary and reactionary, but, more than anything, the party is defensive and protective about the nation, and, as such, is a fine example of 'closed nationalism' in action.[181] And even though schism has ruined the electoral fortunes of the FN, it is certain that Le Pen will keep the flame alive.

Evaluation

The extreme Right has had its own themes expressed continuously but with
varying degrees of vociferousness.[1]

In *Le Fièvre hexagonale* Michel Winock identifies the eight major crises in
France's modern political history.[2] Half of the episodes he chronicles are
related to the extreme right: the Boulanger affair, the Dreyfus case, the riots
of 6 February 1934, and 10 July 1940 – when the French National Assembly
granted full powers to Marshal Pétain. This would seem to say that for
good or for bad the far right has been a major player in French history, and
has often hit the headlines.

So what has this investigation proved? First, developing the point made
by Winock, it is clear that, over the last two centuries, France has been
home to a vigorous extreme-right tradition. Together, our five chapters cover
almost 200 years of French history and – give or take the occasional period
when the forces of the far right have been inactive – the story has been one
of continual protest and agitation. For good reason, this study has kept well
clear of anything approaching comparative analysis, but in the future it
might be pertinent to compare the French experience of far-right politics
with that of Britain, and maybe even Germany and Italy. France would
surely emerge favourably from any comparison – if 'favourably' means that
its tradition has greater longevity.

Second, it is manifest that the extreme right has blossomed in a variety of
guises. There are strong elements of continuity but, at the same time, it is
difficult not to conclude that the far-right tradition is a 'rag bag' of attitudes,
ideas and ideologies. It is not just that the extreme right in one generation is
significantly different from the extreme right in the next (or the previous)
but that different 'extreme rights' can exist side by side. For example, in the
1920s and 1930s, the rarified, elitist, pro-monarchy AF existed in parallel
with the aggressive, populist and thuggish *ligues*. Likewise, the 1790s gave
birth to three different counter-revolutions: popular, violent rebellion in the
Vendée, high-level plotting at Court and theocratic revolt in the form of de
Maistre's writings. And wartime France offered us the ultra-traditionalist

Pétain, the arch-collaborator Laval and the fanatical Paris Nazis. We have attached the 'extreme right' label to all these phenomena but, even with the necessary caveats and qualifications, it will always be problematic to view them as part of the same political family. Debate will continue and generalisations will remain hazardous but, nevertheless, we have been able to identify some universal attitudes and characteristics (though of course these will never be exclusive to the far right).

Third, the extreme right is also topical. In Chapter 6 we demonstrated that far-right politics have flourished in the post-war period in the shape of *Algérie Française*, Poujadism and the FN. Although schism has wrecked Le Pen's chance of exerting influence in the early years of the twenty-first century, it should not be forgotten that he dominated French politics throughout the 1980s and 1990s and was a major force in setting the political agenda. In particular, he thrust the issue of immigration centre-stage and all the mainstream parties were forced to confront it. In 1995 he won 15 per cent of the presidential vote and followed that by winning mayoral elections in Toulon, Marignane, Orange and Vitrolles. The far right may face an uncertain future – the FN and MNR (Mouvement National Républicain) can now manage only 10 per cent of the vote between them – but it is still alive as a political force and relevant to the preoccupations of ordinary French people. Another way to measure topicality is in terms of literature, and the extreme right continues to provoke writers. Whether it is journalists, political scientists, polemicists or historians interested in the lineage of the tradition, it is clear that far-right politics retain their fascination. The present study is just one indication of this.

Finally, the far right is an 'issue' for many people. Over two centuries and more we have seen how extremist movements have trampled over sensibilities and provoked widespread opposition. On more than one occasion the republican left has been challenged, and has responded. In the contemporary era a range of movements has emerged to counter the FN 'threat'. On a national level, SOS-Racisme has come to the fore; on a local level, movements like Alerte Orange have established themselves as counterweights to Le Pen and *Lepénisme*. All this goes to prove that the FN – like the extreme-right tradition in general – cannot be ignored.

What we have also discovered is that the extreme-right tradition is a 'tradition' and not just a set of random events, movements, personnel and ideas. Of course our five main chapters deal with very different 'extreme rights' and in no way can we attempt to link every organisation or ideology examined in this study. However, this should not obscure the fact that there are also important connections within and between eras (and thus important connections within and between sections of this study). We should think in terms of people, events, organisations and ideas.

Perhaps the most obvious and basic continuity emerges in personnel. Over the course of the six chapters we have encountered a range of political leaders, activists and theorists. At this point it would be illustrative to isolate two:

Maurice Barrès
Boulangist Movement (1880s and 1990s)
Anti-Dreyfusard Movement (1890s)
Action Française (*c.* 1899–1901)

Pierre Poujade
Parti Populaire Français (late 1930s)
Compagnons de France (early 1940s)
UDCA/UFF (1950s)

Of course, we could have highlighted many other interesting curriculum vitae – those of Déroulède, Maurras, Pétain and Le Pen, for example – but the case histories of Barrès and Poujade adequately demonstrate the strong sense of progression and fluidity on the far right.

Equally interesting connections can be established at the level of events. To begin with, let us consider the army revolt of 13 May 1958, about which Simmons comments:

> During... May 1958, France hovered on the brink of invasion and civil war as the Fourth Republic government unsuccessfully tried to reassert its authority over the rebel generals. However, Le Pen and his friend and fellow deputy Jean-Marie Demarquet were delighted by the crisis and on May 14, 1958, led a march to the Tomb of the Unknown Soldier at the Arc de Triomphe... This event provokes comparison with a march that had taken place twenty-four years earlier, when on February 6, 1934, extreme right demonstrators tried to cross the Seine from the Place de la Concorde and storm the Chamber of Deputies... Of course, Le Pen's 1958 march was a much less dramatic re-enactment of the 1934 incident, and the marchers were dispersed without incident. Nonetheless, the Fourth Republic had been fatally wounded by the army revolt, and its death throes had begun.[3]

So in Simmons' mind the tactics, approach and style in two different eras bore a significant resemblance, and this puts down an important marker with regard to the mentality of the extreme right across generations.

In a totally different sense, it is clear that events and dates can have a hugely powerful legacy. The riots of 1934 took place on 6 February and, ever since, this date has been intrinsically associated with the rise of fascism. It has acquired almost mythical status, especially for communists fearful of a right-wing resurgence.

This was best illuminated in 1984, fifty years on from the Paris disturbances. Jean-Marie Le Pen was scheduled to make a high-profile television appearance on 6 February, but the PCF (Parti Communiste Français), led by Georges Marchais, objected strongly on the grounds that the feature would hand the FN leader publicity on a 'sensitive' date in the calendar. Le Pen's interview on *L'Heure de vérité* was postponed and the ensuing headlines in the French press told their own story:

ANTENNE 2; 'L'HEURE DE VÉRITÉ' DE LE PEN REPORTÉE D'UNE SEMAINE...
... *pour qu'elle ne corresponde pas au cinquantième anniversaire du 6 février 1934. Le PC avait demandé sa suppression*[4]

'L'HEURE DE VÉRITÉ' AVEC M. LE PEN EST REPORTÉE D'UNE SEMAINE[5]

LE PEN 'DEPROGRAMMÉ'[6]

'L'HEURE DE VÉRITÉ' AVEC LE PEN REPORTÉE D'UNE SEMAINE
Le conseil d'administration d'Antenne 2 a estimé que le leader du Front National ne pouvait pas s'exprimer à la télévision le jour anniversaire du 6 février 1934[7]

LE 6 FÉVRIER: LE PEN VICTIME D'UN SYMBOLE[8]

The message accompanying this last headline was as follows:

L'Heure de Vérité will not sound for Jean-Marie Le Pen on Antenne 2 on 6 February – but on 13 February instead. In deciding on this, against the wishes of the programme's boss François Henri de Virieu, the channel's director has bowed to the pressure of the Communist Party, who wanted to forbid the appearance of Le Pen on the channel. As a result of this decision, the extreme right will not be able to express itself on television exactly 50 years after the date which, for the majority of French people who can remember it, still signifies the moment when the spectre of fascism haunted Paris.[9]

Thus, in the collective French psyche 6 February 1934 is still a date full of resonance. Not only this, but a modern-day 'fascist' like Le Pen has to take the rap for an event that took place in the mid-1930s.

As regards the far-right tradition, there are also important continuities on an organisational level. The AF, for example, was formed in 1899, reached its apogée in the inter-war period, and, in the twenty-first century, continues to believe that a monarchical restoration is on the horizon. Its main publications are unfailingly optimistic and academics remain fascinated by the movement.

In the early 1990s I was sitting in the Bibliothèque National delving into a selection of modern far-right newspapers when I realised that the woman sitting next to me was doing likewise. All the journals laid out on her desk were published by the AF, and she too appeared to be interested in the post-war period. In the hallway of the *bibliothèque* I got chatting to her over a cup of coffee. My first question was a simple one: 'Why are you interested in the modern-day AF when it is so small and insignificant, and when there is absolutely no chance of a monarchical restoration happening in France today?' I will always remember her reply. With a smile on her face, she said: 'I have always been fascinated by people who believe in lost causes.' The AF is a good example of a far-right movement that has survived.

The *ligueur* tradition is another crucial aspect of far-right politics in France. In Chapter 3 we examined the Ligue des Patriotes and also referred to the Ligue Antisémitique and the Ligue de la Patrie Française. In Chapter 4 we turned the spotlight on the extra-parliamentary fascist movements that emerged in the 1920s and 1930s, most notably Croix de Feu, Jeunesses Patriotes, Solidarité Française, the Faisceau and the Camelots du Roi. All these movements described themselves as *ligues* – 'highly disciplined organisations which hoped to act directly on opinion by bringing in the man on the street to exert pressure on parliament and the government. They had nothing in common with political parties.'[10] As we have observed, in the period 1880–1940 France was home to a strong tradition of *ligue*-based protest, and ultimately this current was instrumental in defining what the extreme right was, and what it stood for.

As a footnote to this discussion, it is worth noting Rémond's comments to the effect that the Poujadist movement 'offers more than one common characteristic with the Taxpayers League which made common cause with league agitation in the period around 1934'.[11] Of course the similarity here is about doctrine as much as anything else, but it is not insignificant that a post-war organisation which thrived on direct-action tactics should be linked to a 'single issue' movement of the inter-war period. It is clear, therefore, that a tradition of *ligue*-based protest has enveloped almost a century of French history.

Most significant, however, are the continuities at the level of ideas. Of course there are profound discontinuities in this sphere – most notably, the contrast between 'old' and 'new' right traditions that we examined (mainly) in Chapters 1, 2 and 3[12] – but it would also be true to say that a range of political ideas and attitudes does appear and reappear on the far-right fringes of French politics.

Take the slogan *France pour les Français,* for example. Since the 1880s the far right has regularly utilised this phrase in the interests of self-definition. In simple terms the slogan conveys the essence of closed nationalism and gives the impression that defending and protecting the nation is just 'common sense'. While Le Pen associated himself with the slogan in the 1980s and 1990s, Drumont, a century earlier, had inserted a variation of the phrase as the subtitle of his notorious anti-Semitic journal; thus the masthead read: LA LIBRE PAROLE: LA FRANCE AUX FRANÇAIS! Déroulède used the phrase as well – much to the surprise of some who felt that it had too many 'racial' connotations for a man who was always wary of overstepping the mark.[13]

Other phrases also surface and resurface. In the early twentieth century the AF's integral nationalism gave rise to the slogan 'France First'. Almost a century later, Le Pen penned his political testimony under the title *Les Français d'abord* (*The French First*) and launched a party newsletter of the same name.[14] Similarly, Maurras talked about Jews, Protestants, Freemasons and aliens as *les quatre états confédérés*, and thus as *l'Anti-France*.[15] This last phrase sent out a powerful political message, one that heirs to Maurras have been eager to reiterate. Thus, in 1940, Pétain utilised the phrase in an effort to explain the moral and philosophical impulse at the heart of the National Revolution, stating: 'There is no neutrality possible between right and wrong, good and bad, health and illness, order and disorder, France and Anti-France.'[16] Here the Marshal was outlining his black-and-white value-system and giving notice of his determination to put France on the road to recovery. He used the phrase 'Anti-France' to denote the amalgam of forces that, in some way, threatened the country's future. In the 1980s Le Pen also utilised the term.[17]

Over the years far-right nationalists have also employed common imagery and, in this respect, commentators have pointed to similarities between Boulanger in the 1880s and Le Pen in the 1980s. The two men are characterised by their charismatic personalities, raucous style and unashamed anti-intellectualism, and if we examine their discourse closely we discover another particularly interesting commonality.

Both men talked about France in metaphorical terms, as a living organism that was vulnerable to attack. Both also pinpointed the forces of 'decadence' as the major threat to the nation and, interestingly, both likened the plight of the nation to the plight of a body trying to fight off disease. In the late nineteenth century Boulanger said that his country was suffering from 'syphillis'; in the late twentieth century, Le Pen argued that France was being infected by a political version of AIDS (the main symptoms being *Affairisme*, *Immigration*, *Délinquance* and *Socialisme*).[18] It has been natural for ultra-nationalists to view France as 'ill', 'virus-ridden' and facing 'death', and it is in this way that people like Boulanger and Le Pen have sought to justify and rationalise their political crusades.

Furthermore, in certain periods ultra-nationalism has gone hand in hand with militarism. Over the last 130 years the army has played a central role in the politics of the far right. Boulanger and Pétain were both career soldiers, the Dreyfus Affair centred on the military and its place in French society, and *Algérie Française* was a political slogan devised by disillusioned army generals. The continuities are clear: charismatic soldiers have entered the political arena on the back of their military prowess and viewed themselves as 'national saviours', and the army has invariably seen itself as 'above the nation'. Meanwhile, in the 1920s and 1930s the *ligues* struck a paramilitary pose. The Croix de Feu was home to a significant number of veterans of the First World War and, in its gestures as well as in its political manifesto, it displayed huge loyalty to France's ex-servicemen. Its uniformed parades were especially poignant, and there is a sense in which this particular *ligue* saw itself as some kind of 'unofficial police force' – another bizarre indicator of the *ligues*' self-alignment with the forces of order.

It could be argued, additionally, that those who occupy the far-right 'space' have exhibited similar reflexes. A nostalgia for rural France, a passionate concern about *natalité* (and *denatalité*), and a desire to speak on behalf of 'the people'; these are important instincts and serve to connect many political formations in France's recent history. A single attitude towards parliament has also emerged. In the 1950s Poujade and his cronies proclaimed that parliament would be better off without corrupt, self-serving *députés* – hence, *Sortez les Sortants!* ('Throw the Rascals Out!' or 'Kick the Old Gang Out!') – but this fierce hostility to the national legislature was nothing new, for Boulanger used exactly the same type of language in his tirades of the late 1880s. He felt so strongly about the ineptitude of parliament that he demanded 'revision' of the whole Third Republic constitution. His catchphrase was 'Down with the Robbers!'[19] Given the critique of parliament, it is no surprise that individuals and movements on the far right have advanced an array of blueprints for France's future. It is difficult to generalise, but if there is a common thread to the 'solutions' put forward it is the desire, if not the demand, for strong executive authority to replace 'weak', 'decadent' rule. Moreover, for much of the time the call has been for a charismatic 'saviour figure'.

In the aftermath of the Revolution the right viewed monarchy as the only panacea, with de Maistre concluding that Providence would bring about the return of the Bourbons. A century and more later, Maurras also argued for monarchy. He did not think that a restoration would *just happen* in the way that de Maistre did, but rather that monarchy was the best, most logical solution to the French *malaise*.

Over the last two centuries of extreme-right politics the solution most argued for has probably been some kind of executive republic. Boulanger, Barrès, the *ligues*, Poujade, the supporters of *Algérie Française*, and even Le Pen today, have all indicated an attachment to some form of authoritarianism. Boulanger and Le Pen have spoken in terms of 'direct democracy', of 'referenda' and of restoring power to the people, but, in reality, this 'open' language has concealed a 'closed' agenda. On reflection, it is difficult to disagree with Winock, who says that 'order' and 'authority' are the key to understanding the extreme-right's political philosophy.[20] This, though, does not necessarily mean to say that far-right movements and thinkers are centralisers by instinct, for they have invariably championed some kind of regionalism.[21] Whether it is the Ultras' belief in decentralisation, the AF's attachment to 'provincial liberties' or Vichy's obsession with 'roots' and 'rural customs', there is an important – perhaps curious – alignment with provincial France. Regionalism, in this context, has been viewed as a counterweight to the centralising tendencies of the Jacobin left.

Far-right leaders have also tapped into social conflict and, in particular, the tension between *les petits et les gros*. Invariably there has been sympathy for the 'small man' in French society, whether shopkeeper, taxpayer or peasant: Boulanger staked his reputation on a group of striking miners,

Dorgères helped to radicalise the French peasantry, and Poujade – the man who stood at the apogée of this tradition – gave a voice to anxious shopkeepers, angry taxpayers and anybody else who wished to jump on the UDCA bandwagon. This is certainly a common trait.

Throughout this study we have placed significant emphasis on the fascist tradition in French intellectual history. In every chapter, except the second, we have encountered fascism in some form. We delineated the contours of the tradition in Chapter 1, assessed the nature of 'pre-fascism' in Chapter 3, examined the *ligues* in Chapter 4, analysed the fascist element at play within Pétain's regime in Chapter 5, and in the last section we examined three movements – the UDCA, *Algérie Française* and the FN – that have been branded either 'fascist' or 'neo-fascist', or both.

Here we can make two additional points. First, it is clear that many key figures on the far right – and, indeed, several who have attracted the fascist label – spent their formative political years, or at least some of them, on the left. Boulanger, Barrès, Valois, Déat, Doriot, Laval – they all had either socialist or syndicalist backgrounds. This helps us to understand the impetus behind French fascism and indicates simultaneously the richness and complexity of the far-right tradition. Second, in their own heads if not on paper, Boulanger, Barrès, Valois, Déat and Doriot had thought through the notion of national-socialism and had seized on its essential aim, namely 'the integration of proletariat in the nation'.[22] The dominant view was that the right would rise or fall depending on its ability to bring the people 'on board'. Boulanger and Barrès were attempting to do this in the 'pre-fascist' era, whereas Valois, Doriot and Déat were trying to execute the same task in the 1920s and 1930s, and thus had Mussolini and Hitler as role-models.[23] The national-socialist tradition may not be as strong as either the counter-revolutionary or national-populist strands in French intellectual history, but the country remains a fascinating laboratory for students of fascism.

It is difficult to come to any conclusions about the political 'style' of the extreme right. Rhetoric, invective, emotion, passion and zeal have been commonplace, marking out the extreme right to a degree, but there are other distinctive and defining features.

The hallmark of intransigence is not exclusive to individuals and movements that sit on the extreme right of the political spectrum, but it is certainly more associated with the fringe. De Maistre, the Ultras, Maurras, the collaborationists and the Algerian rebels; these people could all be defined by their inability to compromise and their attachment to absolute values. At other times individuals and movements have been extraordinarily pragmatic in the bedfellows they have chosen.[24] In recent years the FN has formed ententes with the conservative right, whereas a century earlier the Boulangist movement saw the potential in a royalist alliance. Winock argues that far-right politics have always had a cross-sectional appeal, and perhaps this explains to an extent why the political organisations led by Le Pen and Boulanger – among others – have not balked at the prospect of 'controversial' electoral liaisons.[25]

On a different level altogether the far right has shown itself to be highly opportunistic. During the Nazi occupation of France the Vichy regime was happy to use Jews as bargaining chips, and during the Dreyfus Affair of the 1890s Barrès and other leading anti-Dreyfusards had no moral problems with defining 'truth' in a way that would serve France and not an innocent Jew. Here it is not the anti-Semitic impetus that is of paramount significance but the cynical, amoral attitude.

Religion has also conditioned the style of the far right. During the reign of Charles X the relationship between Church and Ultras was so intimate that France evolved into a type of medieval theocracy with the Church not subservient to the State but the State subservient to the Church. In later periods the relationship was more complex.[26] Whereas Boulanger paid lip-service to traditional religion, invoking its patronage whenever politically expedient to do so, Vichy attached itself to the moral teaching of the Church rather than the institution. Most intriguing of all was the AF – a movement that revered Catholicism and its social role, but whose leader was put on the Index of forbidden authors for his outspoken views on religion.

It is a fact that movements on the extreme right have seen political utility in invoking the Church, even if – as is mainly the case – their leaders have displayed very little personal religiosity. It is also true that, with time, new idols have emerged to take the place of those associated with traditional religion. Here we are not just referring to the nation – the crucial icon for the radical right – but also to political figureheads who have cultivated their own personal 'mysticism' and 'spirituality' and have seen themselves as new deities (Pétain is the most obvious example in this context).[27]

In conclusion, it would seem that three points need to be made. First, although Anderson and others are keen to highlight the discontinuities in evidence,[28] the unique fascination of the far right in France is the sense of continuity and tradition that accompanies it. We could illustrate this point in a variety of ways but let us turn to the FN again. On page 135 of its 1991 publication, *Militer au Front*, it identifies Barrès as a man who was the incarnation of the 'national tradition' and who recognised the 'affinities between people of the same soil'.[29] In a similar manner, on page 19 of Marèchal's treatise on ecology – written in the late 1990s – Maurras is acclaimed as one of the first political theorists to 'curse industrial progress'.[30] A number of examples could have been cited here but on the basis of these two alone it is manifest that the FN is conscious of its lineage.

We could go further and suggest that there is a range of crucial influences at work within Le Pen's party. It is simultaneously radical and reactionary, nationalist and European, modern and nostalgic. Hainsworth depicts a movement that in 1972 was home to 'French Algeria die-hards; revolutionary nationalists; wartime Vichyites; Holocaust revisionists; neo-fascists; neo-Nazis; monarchists; Catholic fundamentalists; former members of extreme right *groupuscules*; and so on'.[31] This illustration helps us to understand how the extreme right renews itself in every generation.

In the context of the FN we should not forget the Poujadist connection either. Winock and Milza have both examined the electorates of Le Pen and Poujade and, whatever the similarities and dissimilarities,[32] it would appear that the most obvious continuity lies in the realm of ideas where, in the last quarter of the twentieth century, the FN leader revived:

> ... much of the substance and spirit of Poujadism: anti-intellectualism, anti-technocracy, demagogy, xenophobia, defence of the 'small man', authoritarianism, opposition to 'the political class', anti-statism, anti-bureaucracy, defence of the family, pro-French colonialism, strong law and order, Jeanne d'Arc reverence, rejection of perceived decadence, Vichyite nostalgia, populism, leadership cult, plebiscitarianism and so on.[33]

This, plus the tendency of the French press to talk of Boulangism, the Croix de Feu and Le Pen in the same breath,[34] tends to confirm the view which sees the far-right tradition in France as both deep and complex.

Second, it would be accurate to state that over two centuries the same patterns have accompanied the emergence of the extreme right. 'Crisis conditions' of one kind or another have invariably been central: the Terror in 1793, defeat in war in 1871 and 1940, the rise of socialism in 1924, 1936 and 1981, and moves towards decolonisation in the 1950s.[35] Individuals and movements on the far right have thrived on what they have perceived to be 'emergency situations'.

Finally, we must make reference to the unique psyche of the far right. On reflection, this would seem to be a product of fear, obsession and paranoia. Generalisations are hazardous, but extreme-right movements are quick to identify enemies and eager to establish order, control and authority. As Winock argues, the extreme right is about more than doctrines and organisations. It also spreads doubt, creates anxieties and trivialises the unacceptable.[36]

Today, in the early twenty-first century, the forces of the extreme right may be at a low ebb but the tradition is certainly alive.

Notes

Introduction

1 C. Tilly, *The Vendée*, London, Edward Arnold, 1964.
2 M. Barrès, 'Scènes et Doctrines du Nationalisme', taken from J. S. McClelland (ed.), *The French Right from de Maistre to Maurras*, London, Jonathan Cape, 1971, pp. 189–90.
3 Some of the dates and events chronicled in each timeline might actually be of more relevance to a different chapter, e.g. the AF (Action Française) is dealt with in Chapter 4 (1919–39) but its early history takes place within the parameters of Chapter 3 (1870–1918).
4 J. Roberts, *The Counter-Revolution in France 1787–1830*, London, Macmillan, 1990; J. Godechot, *The Counter-Revolution in France: Doctrine and Action 1789–1804*, London, Routledge & Kegan Paul, 1972; K. Carpenter and P. Mansel (eds), *The French Émigrés in Europe and the Struggle against Revolution, 1789–1814*, London, Macmillan, 1999; Tilly, op. cit.
5 R. Tombs (ed.), *Nationhood and Nationalism in France: From Boulangism to the Great War 1889–1918*, London, HarperCollins, 1991; Z. Sternhell, *La Droite révolutionnaire: les origines françaises du fascisme 1885–1914*; P. Mazgaj, 'The Origins of the French Radical Right: A Historiographical Essay', *French Historical Studies*, 1987, Vol. XV, 2: 287–315.
6 R. Soucy, *French Fascism: The First Wave 1924–33*, New Haven, CT, Yale University Press, 1986; Z. Sternhell, *Ni droite ni gauche*, Paris, Complexe, 1987; R. O. Paxton, *French Peasant Fascism: Henry Dorgères's Greenshirts and the Crises of French Agriculture, 1929–1939*, Oxford, Oxford University Press, 1997; K. Passmore, 'The Croix de Feu and Fascism: a Foreign Thesis Obstinately Maintained', in E. J. Arnold, *The Development of the Radical Right in France: From Boulanger to Le Pen*, London, Macmillan, 2000, pp. 100–18.
7 S. Fishman, L. L. Downs, I. Sinanoglou, L. V. Smith and R. Zaretsky (eds), *France at War: Vichy and the Historians*, Oxford, Berg, 2000; H. Rousso, *The Vichy Syndrome: History and Memory in France since 1944*, London, Harvard University Press, 1994; W. D. Halls, *Politics, Society and Christianity in Vichy France*, Oxford, Berg, 1995.
8 E. G. Declair, *Politics on the Fringe: The People, Policies, and Organisation of the French National Front*, London, Duke University Press, 1999; H. G. Simmons, *The French National Front: The Extremist Challenge to Democracy*, Oxford, Westview, 1996; P. Hainsworth, 'The Front National: From Ascendancy to Fragmentation on the French Extreme Right', in P. Hainsworth (ed.), *The Politics of the Extreme Right: From the Margins to the Mainstream*, London, Pinter, 2000; J. Marcus, *The National Front and French Politics*, London, Macmillan, 1995.

9 J.-F. Sirinelli (ed.), *Les Droites françaises de la Révolution à nos jours*, Paris, Gallimard, 1992.

10 J.-F. Sirinelli and E. Vigne, 'Introduction', in Sirinelli, op. cit., pp. 31–55; see also the structure of the other edition of the book, J.-F. Sirinelli (ed.), *Histoire des droites en France*, Paris, Gallimard, 1992.

11 M. Winock (ed.), *Histoire d'extrême droite en France*, Paris, Seuil, 1994, p. 301.

12 See P. Milza, *Fascisme français*, Paris, Flammarion, 1987, Chapters 4 and 8.

13 J.-C. Petitfils, *L'Extrême droite en France*, Paris, Presses Universitaires de France, 1983.

14 Petitfils, op. cit., p. 125.

15 Simmons, op. cit., pp. 72–6.

16 R. Rémond, *The Right Wing in France*, Philadelphia, University of Pennsylvania Press, 1971.

17 M. Anderson, *Conservative Politics in France*, London, George Allen & Unwin, 1974.

18 McClelland, op. cit.

19 The French version was published in 1990, the English translation in 1998. All endnotes will refer to the French version (see Note 20 below).

20 M. Winock, *Nationalisme, antisémitisme et fascisme en France*, Paris, Seuil, 1990.

21 E. J. Arnold, *The Development of the Radical Right in France: From Boulanger to Le Pen*, London, Macmillan, 2000, pp. xv–xix.

22 See Chapter 1 of the present study.

23 This phrase is often, but not exclusively, used in association with post-1945 movements.

24 This term gained prominence during the 1995 presidential elections when the combined forces of Le Pen, de Villiers and Cheminade were referred to as the 'hard right'.

25 Not to be confused with 'Ultras' – a term used to describe (a) the fanatical royalists of the Restoration era; and (b) the most violent and extreme *Algérie Française* activists in the 1950s.

26 See Chapter 2 of the present study.

1 The extreme right in France: an enduring political tradition

1 A. Thibaudet, quoted in J.-F. Sirinelli and E. Vigne, 'Introduction' in J.-F. Sirinelli (ed.), *Les Droites françaises de la révolution à nos jours*, Paris, Gallimard, 1992, p. 31.

2 M. Winock (ed.), *Histoire d'extrême droite en France*, Paris, Seuil, 1994, p. 14.

3 Winock, op. cit., p. 7.

4 P. Hainsworth (ed.), *The Extreme Right in Europe and the USA*, London, Pinter, 1994, p. 30.

5 R. Eatwell, 'Right or Rights? The Rise of the "New Right" ', in R. Eatwell and N. O'Sullivan (eds), *The Nature of the Right: American and European Politics and Political Thought since 1789*, London, Pinter, 1992, p. 3.

6 Sirinelli and Vigne, op. cit., pp. 9–19; N. O'Sullivan, 'Conservatism' in R. Eatwell and A. Wright (eds), *Contemporary Political Ideologies*, London, Pinter, 1993, p. 54.

7 Winock, op. cit., p. 7; O'Sullivan, op. cit., p. 54; R. Rémond, *The Right Wing in France*, Philadelphia, University of Pennsylvania Press, 1971, p. 21, also pursues this line of thought.

8 Rémond, op. cit., p. 19.

9 See Sirinelli and Vigne, op. cit., pp. 21–5.

10 J. S. McClelland (ed.), *The French Right: From de Maistre to Maurras*, London, Jonathan Cape, 1971, p. 20.
11 McClelland, op. cit., p. 15 and p. 36.
12 M. Billig, 'The Extreme Right: Continuities in Anti-Semitic Conspiracy Theory in Post-War Europe', in Eatwell and O'Sullivan, op. cit., p. 146.
13 Hainsworth, op. cit., p. 3.
14 M. Anderson, *Conservative Politics in France*, London, George Allen & Unwin, 1974, p. 339.
15 Hainsworth, op. cit., p. 30.
16 Winock, op. cit., p. 7.
17 Winock, op. cit., p. 7.
18 McClelland, op. cit., p. 14.
19 Sirinelli, op. cit.; Winock, op. cit.
20 Winock, op. cit., p. 11 and p. 15.
21 Billig, op. cit., pp. 146–8; Hainsworth, op. cit., p. 5, says the extreme right is not synonymous with either 'fascism' or 'new fascism'.
22 Anderson, op. cit., p. 344.
23 Winock, op. cit., p. 16.
24 Winock, op. cit., p. 7 and p. 16.
25 See Eatwell and O'Sullivan, op. cit.
26 Eatwell, op. cit., p. 3.
27 Rémond, op. cit., p. 30.
28 Rémond was also writing pre-FN (Front National).
29 Z. Sternhell, *Ni droite ni gauche*, Paris, Complexe, 1987, p. 29.
30 Sternhell, op. cit., p. 78; see also Z. Sternhell, *La Droite Révolutionnaire*, Paris, Seuil, 1978. Whereas Rémond interprets Boulangism as a pre-industrial phenomenon akin to Bonapartism, Sternhell sees the General and his movement as a product of 'new right' politics and a symptom of 'pre-fascism'.
31 R. Soucy, 'The Nature of Fascism in France', *Journal of Contemporary History*, 1966, Vol. 1: 55.
32 P. Milza, *Fascisme français*, Paris, Flammarion, 1987.
33 E. J. Arnold, *The Development of the Radical Right in France: From Boulanger to Le Pen*, London, Macmillan, 2000.
34 Sirinelli, op. cit.
35 Sirinelli, op. cit.
36 Anderson, op. cit., p. 17 and p. 18.
37 Anderson, op. cit., pp. 339–40.
38 Winock, op. cit., p. 8.
39 Winock, op. cit., p. 9.
40 Winock, op. cit., p 10.
41 See M. Winock, *Nationalisme, antisémitisme et fascisme en France*, Paris, Seuil, 1990; this is also reflected in Winock (1994), op. cit., p. 9.
42 R. Austin, 'The Conservative Right and the Far Right in France: The Search for Power' in M. Blinkhorn (ed.), *Fascists and Conservatives*, London, Hyman, 1990, p. 176.
43 J.-C. Petitfils, *L'Extrême droite en France*, Paris, Presses Universitaires de France, 1983.
44 Petitfils, op. cit., p. 6 and p. 10.
45 McClelland, op. cit., p. 14. By contrast, a survey, conducted by *Le Monde* in 1984, splits the modern extreme right into 'royalists' (who look back to Maurras and the Action Française), 'nationalists' (who are inspired by the memory of *Algèrie Française* and *Pétainisme*) and 'revolutionary nationalists' (who, on the plane of ideas, connect to both anti-Marxist extremists and neo-Nazis).

46 See S. Hazareesingh, *Political Traditions in Modern France*, Oxford, Oxford University Press, 1996.

47 J. S. McClelland, 'The Reactionary Right: The French Revolution, Charles Maurras and the Action Française', in Eatwell and O'Sullivan, op. cit.

48 McClelland, (1971) op. cit., pp. 14–15 and p. 36.

49 J. de Maistre, 'Considerations on France', taken from J. Lively (ed.), *The Works of Joseph de Maistre*, London, George Allen & Unwin, 1965, p. 71.

50 O'Sullivan, op. cit., p. 55.

51 Winock, (1994) op. cit., p. 8.

52 Rémond, op. cit., p. 35.

53 See Winock (1994), op. cit., p. 17; see also G. Steiner, 'Aspects of Counter-Revolution', in G. Best (ed.), *The Permanent Revolution: The French Revolution and its Legacy 1789–1989*, London, Fontana, 1989, pp. 151–2.

54 McClelland (1971), op. cit., p. 36.

55 J.-M. Le Pen, *Les Français d'abord*, Paris, Carrere–Michel Lafon, 1984, pp. 173–4.

56 Hainsworth, op. cit., p. 12.

57 M. Barrès, 'The Nancy Programme, 1898', taken from D. Thomson, *Empire and Republic*, London, Harper & Row, 1968, p. 273.

58 See Front National *Le Contrat pour la France avec les français: Le Pen Président*, Saint-Brieuc, Presses Bretonnes, 1995, p. 5.

59 C. Maurras, 'Dictator and King', taken from McClelland (1971), op. cit., pp. 230–1.

60 P. Claudel, 'Words to the Marshal', taken from McClelland (1971), op. cit., p. 307.

61 One Vichy poster featured two houses: one representative of the old Republic – decrepit and dirty – and the other representative of Vichy – solid and firmly constructed. The message was simple. Also, it goes without saying that, two centuries earlier, the main players in the Counter-Revolution had been provoked into action by the establishment of the First Republic, the political philosophy embodied by the regime, and the various pieces of legislation enacted by it.

62 See R. Woods, 'The Radical Right: The "Conservative Revolutionaries" in Germany', in Eatwell and O'Sullivan, op. cit., pp. 124–45.

63 See G. Boulanger, 'Speech, 2 December 1888', taken from R. Gildea, *The Third Republic 1870–1914*, London, Longman, pp. 96–7; Le Pen, op. cit., pp. 174–6.

64 McClelland (1971), op. cit., p. 15.

65 Anderson, op. cit., p. 341.

66 Winock (1990), op. cit., p. 103, and, more generally, pp. 103–11.

67 See Winock (1990), op. cit., pp. 41–9; and Hainsworth, op. cit., pp. 30–1.

68 Not to be confused with the new right of the 1980s.

69 Winock (1994), op. cit., p. 9.

70 See Woods, op. cit., pp. 124–45.

71 Winock (1990), op. cit., pp. 43–6.

72 Hainsworth, op. cit., pp. 30–1.

73 On anti-Americanisation, see Winock (1990), op. cit., pp. 50–82. Hainsworth, op. cit., pp. 5–7, argues that immigration is the extreme right's issue *par excellence*.

74 Hainsworth, op. cit., p. 33.

75 Boulanger's movement, for which Barrès was a key spokesman, was known officially as the 'Revisionist' movement because it sought to 'revise' the constitutional arrangements of the Third Republic.

76 Hainsworth, op. cit., p. 31.

77 Hainsworth, op. cit., p. 31.

78 Barrès, op. cit., p. 269.
79 Winock (1994), op. cit., p. 9.
80 R. Byrnes, *Anti-Semitism in Modern France*, New Brunswick, NJ, Rutgers University Press, 1950, pp. 152–3.
81 Sternhell (1987), op. cit., p. 78.
82 R. Wistrich, *Anti-Semitism: The Longest Hatred*, London, Mandarin, 1992, p. 126.
83 Wistrich, op. cit., p. 144; for background, see Billig, op. cit., on conspiracy theories and Holocaust denial theories.
84 Hainsworth, op. cit., pp. 9–10.
85 See Rémond, op. cit.
86 R. Eatwell, *Fascism: A History*, London, Vintage, 1996, p.165 and pp. 239–58.
87 See Sternhell (1987), op. cit.; and R. Soucy, *Fascism in France: The Case of Maurice Barrès*, Berkeley, CA, University of California Press, 1972.
88 Milza, op. cit., pp. 442–3.
89 Milza, op. cit., p. 440 and p. 443.
90 Winock (1994), op. cit., p. 302.
91 E. Nolte, *Three Faces of Fascism*, London, Weidenfeld & Nicolson, 1965, p. 26.
92 Winock (1990), op. cit., p. 250.
93 G. Warner, 'France', in S. J. Woolf (ed.), *Fascism in Europe*, London, Methuen, 1981, p. 320.
94 R. Griffin, *The Nature of Fascism*, London, Routledge, 1994, p. 133.
95 Winock (1990), op. cit, p. 246, and, more generally, pp. 231–47.
96 See Rémond, op. cit., p. 224.
97 Anderson, op. cit., p. 24.
98 R. Eatwell, 'Right or Rights? The Rise of the 'New Right'', in Eatwell and O'Sullivan, op. cit., pp. 6–13; see also N. O'Sullivan, 'The New Right: The Quest for a Civil Philosophy in Europe and America', in Eatwell and O'Sullivan, op. cit., pp. 167–91.
99 See D. Johnson, 'The New Right in France', in L. Cheles, R. Ferguson and M. Vaughan, (eds), *Neo-Fascism in Europe*, London, Longman, 1991, pp. 234–44; see also H. G. Simmons, *The French National Front: The Extremist Challenge to Democracy*, Oxford, Westview, 1996, pp. 207–16.
100 The liberal right corresponds to the type of doctrine examined in A. Aughey, 'The Moderate Right: The Conservative Tradition in America and Britain' in Eatwell and O'Sullivan, op. cit., pp. 99–123.
101 Winock (1990), op. cit., pp. 7–8 and pp. 11–40.
102 Sternhell (1987), op. cit., p. 31.
103 Soucy, op. cit.
104 Winock (1994), op. cit., p. 11.
105 Winock (1994), op. cit., p. 12; see also Warner, op. cit.
106 McClelland (1971), op. cit., p. 13
107 Steiner, op. cit., p. 152

2 1789–1830 – the Counter-Revolution: providence and plotting

1 G. Steiner, 'Aspects of Counter-Revolution' in G. Best (ed.), *The Permanent Revolution: The French Revolution and its Legacy 1789–1989*, London, Fontana, 1989, p. 129.
2 M. Péronnet, *Les 50 Mots clefs de la Révolution Française*, Paris, Privat, 1983, pp. 97–104, 137–41 and 281–6.
3 R. Cobb, *Reactions to the French Revolution*, London, Oxford University Press, 1972, p. 31.

4 J. M. Roberts, *The French Revolution*, Oxford, Oxford University Press, 1978, pp. 109–10.

5 J. M. Thompson, *The French Revolution*, Oxford, Oxford University Press, 1969, p. 266.

6 During the Napoleonic period counter-revolutionary activity continued, but it is difficult to count it as a period of concerted agitation. Rather, it was a kind of 'pause', when the traditional left–right conflict was neutralised. With the fall of the Emperor, however, political hostilities swiftly resumed, and then intensified during the reign of Charles X (1824–30).

7 C. Muret, *French Royalist Doctrines since the Revolution*, New York, 1933, p. 11.

8 J. S. McClelland, 'The Reactionary Right: The French Revolution, Charles Maurras and the Action Française' in R. Eatwell and N. O'Sullivan (eds), *The Nature of the Right: American and European Politics and Political Thought since 1789*, London, Pinter, 1992, p. 80; see also R. Rémond, *La Vie Politique en France 1789–1848*, Paris, Armand Colin, 1965, p. 207.

9 J. Roberts, *The Counter-Revolution in France 1787–1830*, London, Macmillan, 1990, p. 1.

10 See A. Forrest, *The French Revolution*, Oxford, Blackwell, 1999, p. 139; and Péronnet, op. cit., pp. 97–104.

11 See M. Winock, *Histoire de l'extrême droite en France*, Paris, Seuil, 1994, p. 19.

12 G. Lewis, *The French Revolution: Rethinking the Debate*, London, Routledge, 1993, p. 46.

13 J. Roberts (1990), op. cit., p. 23.

14 O. Hufton, 'In Search of Counter-Revolutionary Women', in G. Kates (ed.), *The French Revolution: Recent Debates and New Controversies*, London, Routledge, 1998, p. 304.

15 J. M. Roberts (1978), op. cit., p. 109. However, at the same time, Roberts admits that war was a vital catalyst in provoking counter-revolutionary activity (p. 55). See also R. Rémond, *The Right Wing in France*, Philadelphia, University of Pennsylvania Press, 1971, p. 45.

16 M. Anderson, *Conservative Politics in France*, London, George Allen & Unwin, 1974, p. 124.

17 Rémond (1971), op. cit., p. 45; see also Chapter 4 of the present study.

18 W. Doyle, *The Oxford History of the French Revolution*, Oxford, Oxford University Press, 1991, p. 146.

19 Hufton, op. cit., pp. 304–5.

20 D. Woronoff, *The Thermidorean Regime and the Directory, 1794–1799*, Cambridge, Cambridge University Press, 1984, p. 58.

21 See J. Godechot, *The Counter-Revolution: Doctrine and Action 1789–1804*, London, Routledge & Kegan Paul, 1972.

22 Péronnet, op. cit., p. 97.

23 Steiner, op. cit., p. 135.

24 Forrest, op. cit., p. 134.

25 J. Godechot, *Les Révolutions (1770–1799)*, Paris, Presses Universitaires de France, 1970, p. 163.

26 N. Parker, *Portrayals of Revolution*, London, Harvester, 1990, p. 163.

27 See P. Beik, *The French Revolution seen from the Right*, Transactions of the American Philosophical Society, Philadelphia, PA, APS, 1956.

28 R. H. Soltau, *French Political Thought in the Nineteenth Century*, London, Benn, 1931, p. 15.

29 Winock, op. cit., p. 33.

30 J. Hayward, *After the French Revolution*, London, Harvester Wheatsheaf, 1991, p. 44.

31 Bonald, Chateaubriand and Lamennais were probably the most important, with Bonald gaining most attention from historians. For more on Bonald, see C. J. H. Hayes, *The Historical Evolution of Modern Nationalism*, New York, Macmillan, 1948, pp. 95–100; and C. S. Phillips, *The Church in France, 1928*, London, Russell & Russell, 1966, pp. 213–15. For Lamennais, see Phillips, op. cit., pp. 216–29; and for Chateaubriand, see Muret, op. cit., pp. 35–47.

32 See E. Burke, *Reflections on the Revolution in France*, London, Penguin, 1986. See also Hayes, op. cit., pp. 88–95; and Godechot (1972), op. cit., pp. 3–16, 50–66 and 103–19.

33 Godechot (1972), op. cit., p. 384.

34 See Hayward, op. cit., pp. 61–4.

35 Soltau, op. cit., p. 27.

36 J. Murray, 'The Political Thought of Joseph de Maistre', *Review of Politics*, 1949.

37 For good biographies of de Maistre, see J. Lively (ed.), *The Works of Joseph de Maistre*, London, Allen & Unwin, 1965, pp. 1–2; Beik, op. cit., pp. 61–5; and B. Menczer, *Catholic Political Thought in France 1789–1848*, Paris, University of Nôtre-Dame, 1962, pp. 59–61.

38 He spent a lot of time in St Petersburg, Russia.

39 Phillips, op. cit., p. 209.

40 E. Greifer, 'Joseph de Maistre and the Reaction against the Eighteenth Century', *American Political Science Review*, 1961 (Sept.), Vol. 15: 591–8.

41 See Beik, op. cit., p. 66.

42 Murray, op. cit., pp. 63–86.

43 Winock, op. cit., p. 31.

44 J. de Maistre, 'Considerations on France', taken from Lively, op. cit., p. 47.

45 De Maistre, ibid., p. 71.

46 Winock, op. cit., p. 32.

47 De Maistre's religious discourse is distinctly anti-Protestant; see Winock, op. cit., p. 33.

48 The title of one of de Maistre's key works.

49 Soltau, op. cit., p. 15.

50 Muret, op. cit., p. 11.

51 Greifer, op. cit., p. 594.

52 De Maistre, taken from Lively, op. cit., p. 50.

53 Steiner, op. cit., p. 144.

54 Muret, op. cit., p. 17.

55 The King is, of course, human and is restrained by laws, customs, etc.

56 See Muret, op. cit., pp. 24–5; monarchy is not necessarily 'natural' for other countries.

57 See Greifer, op. cit., p. 595.

58 Murray, op. cit., p. 76.

59 Winock, op. cit., pp. 31–2. *Considerations* was aimed directly at the Constitution of Year III.

60 De Maistre, taken from Lively, op. cit., p. 81.

61 De Maistre, taken from Lively, op. cit., p. 49.

62 Lively, op. cit., p. 9.

63 Steiner, op. cit., p. 145.

64 Winock, op. cit., p. 33.

65 Soltau, op. cit., p. 17.

66 R. Lebrun, 'Joseph de Maistre, Cassandra of Science', *French Historical Studies*, 1969 (Fall): 214–31; the point is made in the context of science but it has a more general application.

67 M. Vovelle, *The Fall of the French Monarchy 1787–1792*, Cambridge, Cambridge University Press, 1986.

68 J. Gilchrist and W. J. Murray, *The Press in the French Revolution: A Selection of Documents taken from the Press of the Revolution for the Years 1789–1794*, London, Cheshire & Gihn, 1971, pp. 210–11.
69 'Letter from Louis XVI to Foreign Courts, 23 April 1791', taken from J. H. Stewart (ed.), *A Documentary Survey of the French Revolution*, New York, Macmillan, 1969 (Extract 36). See also later in this chapter.
70 G. Rudé, *Revolutionary Europe*, London, Fontana, 1986, p. 121.
71 For an in-depth review of the Varennes episode, see J. M. Thompson, op. cit., pp. 206–27.
72 See *Journal de Louis XVI*, Paris, Libraire-Editeur, 1873. Not surprisingly, on 14 July of the same year he wrote, *J'avais dû prendre médecine*.
73 Rudé, op. cit., p. 125 and pp. 126–7.
74 Godechot (1972), op. cit., p. 151.
75 See R. R. Palmer, *The World of the French Revolution*, London, Allen & Unwin, 1971.
76 W. J. Murray, *The Right-Wing Press in the French Revolution: 1789–92*, London, Boydell Press, 1986, p. 143.
77 T. C. W. Blanning, *The Origins of the French Revolutionary Wars*, London, Longman, 1986, p. 121.
78 Blanning, op. cit., p. 99. Etienne Dumont's words are quoted by Blanning in this passage.
79 Rudé, op. cit., p. 121.
80 'Extract from the Memoirs of Comtesse d'Adhémar', taken from J. Hardman (ed.), *The French Revolution*, London, Edward Arnold, 1991, p. 90. G. Lefebvre, *The French Revolution: From Its Origins to 1793*, London, Kegan Paul, 1965, p. 193, says they were particularly divided on policy towards the *émigrés*.
81 Vovelle, op. cit..
82 See P. Mansel, 'From Coblenz to Hartwell: The *Émigré* Government and the European Powers, 1791–1814', in K. Carpenter and P. Mansel (eds), *The French Émigrés in Europe and the Struggle against Revolution, 1789–1814*, London, Macmillan, 1990, pp. 1–27.
83 Pillnitz was signed on 27 August 1791, but see Rudé, op. cit., p. 127. F.Furet, *The French Revolution 1770–1814*, Oxford, Blackwell, 1996, p. 105, says Varennes and Pillnitz made the Revolution a 'European question'. See also G. Lefebvre, *The French Revolution: From 1793 to 1799*, London, Routledge & Kegan Paul, 1967, p. 5; and G. Lefebvre (1965), op. cit., pp. 192–4. Lefebvre claims the continental powers 'agreed upon effecting counter-revolution' at Antwerp in 1793 but, for the most part, remained impotent and divided.
84 Gilchrist and Murray, op. cit., p. 214.
85 Thompson, op. cit., p. 262.
86 Chancellor Pasquier, *Memoirs, Volume 1 1789–1810*, London, Fisher Unwin, 1893, p. 64.
87 D. Greer, *The Incidence of the Emigration during the French Revolution*, Cambridge, MA, Harvard University Press, c. 1951., p. 27; October 1791 is the key date here. See also Pasquier, op. cit., p. 66.
88 H. Mason, *French Writers and their Society 1715–1800*, London, Macmillan, 1982, p. 220.
89 Blanning, op. cit., pp. 100–1.
90 For the social consequences of these measures, see N. Hampson, *A Social History of the French Revolution*, London, Routledge, 1995, pp. 250–4; and A. Cobban, *The Social Interpretation of the French Revolution*, Cambridge, Cambridge University Press, 1968, p. 121.
91 'Decree against *Émigrés*', taken from Stewart, op. cit., pp. 414–23.
92 'Decree Ordering *Émigrés* to Return to France', taken from Stewart, op. cit., p. 272.

93   Louis vetoed them; see Stewart, op. cit., p. 272.
94   'Decree Ordering *Émigrés* to Return to France', in Stewart, op. cit., p. 273.
95   Royou in Murray, op. cit., p. 145.
96   Thompson, op. cit., p. 264.
97   Cobb, op. cit., p. 31.
98   Madame de Gontaut extract, taken from G. Pernoud and S. Flaissier (eds), *The French Revolution*, London, Mercury, 1960, p. 233.
99   Godechot (1972), op. cit., pp. 173–200; on p. 158 he says they had three armies; see also Rudé, op. cit., p. 127. Three out of four French officers defected in August 1792 and there were 4,000–5,000 *émigrés* in the Duke of Brunswick's army when it invaded France, see Mason, op. cit., p. 220.
100 Marquis de Falaiseau extract, taken from Pernoud and Flaissier, op. cit., p. 237.
101 Greer, op. cit., p. 22.
102 Greer, op. cit., p. 20.
103 Godechot (1972), op. cit., p. 148.
104 J. F. Bosher, *The French Revolution*, London, Weidenfeld & Nicolson, 1989, p. 162; for more on the clerical emigration, see also N. Aston, *Religion and Revolution in France 1780–1904*, London, Macmillan, 2000, p. 177 and pp. 228–9.
105 Greer, op. cit., pp. 38–62 (geography) and pp. 63–91 (social profile of the emigration).
106 Pasquier, op. cit., p. 66.
107 Godechot (1972), op. cit., p. 142.
108 Winock, op. cit., p. 23.
109 Greer, op. cit., pp. 21, 23 and 29.
110 See Carpenter and Mansell, op. cit.
111 Vergniaud, quoted in Blanning, op. cit., p. 99.
112 C. Hibbert, *The French Revolution*, London, Penguin, 1982, p. 281.
113 Greer, op. cit., p. 24; see also J. Roberts (1990), op. cit., pp. 5–21.
114 Winock, op. cit., p. 21.
115 J. Roberts (1990), op. cit., pp. 46–8
116 Bosher, op. cit., pp. 237–8.
117 Godechot (1972), op. cit., p. 157.
118 Pasquier, op. cit., p. 66.
119 Thompson, op. cit., pp. 262–3.
120 Furet, op. cit., p. 103.
121 Artois letter, taken from Pernoud and Flaissier, op. cit., pp. 240–1.
122 Thompson, op. cit., p. 265.
123 Furet, op. cit., p. 124; see also Hibbert, op. cit., p. 169.
124 See N. Hampson, *The Life and Opinions of Maximilien Robespierre*, Oxford, Basil Blackwell, 1988; Winock, op. cit., p. 19.
125 P. M. Jones, *The Peasantry in the French Revolution*, Cambridge, Cambridge University Press, 1989, pp. 218–19. 'Vendée' is an umbrella term for the following *départements*: Loire-Inférieure, Maine-et-Loire, Deux-Sèvres, Vendée. Furet, op. cit., p. 125, says the Vendée is an 'unknowable story', mainly because of the lack of accurate information available to historians.
126 See Godechot (1972), op. cit., pp. 231–45 for analysis of the revolt in the south-east. More generally, see Hampson (1995), op. cit., pp. 170–5; H. Mitchell, 'The Vendée and Counterrevolution: A Review Essay', *French Historical Studies*, 1968: 405–29.
127 E. Bire, *The Diary of a Citizen of Paris during the Terror, Volume 2*, London, Chatto & Windus, 1896; this is a point made throughout Chapter LXXXIX, pp. 226–37. See also, 'Philippeaux letter on the Vendée, 26 December 1793', taken from Hardman, op. cit., pp. 198–9; F. Furet and D. Richet, *La Révolution*

française, Paris, Hachette, p.225; and M. Bouloiseau, *The Jacobin Republic 1792–1794*, Cambridge, Cambridge University Press, 1983, p. 124.

128 See Woronoff, op. cit., p. 53, and Lefebvre (1967), op. cit., p. 46.

129 Taken from G. Lefebvre, *The Thermidoreans*, London, Routledge & Kegan Paul, 1965, p. 64.

130 *Chouannerie* was characteristic of the region north of the Loire, e.g. a 'series of irregular skirmishes and ambushes'. South of the Loire there was full-scale war. See J. Roberts (1990), op. cit., p. 30.

131 Bosher, op. cit., p. 225; see also Godechot (1972), op. cit., p. 225.

132 M. Bouloiseau, op. cit., pp. 123–4.

133 V. Hugo, *Ninety-Three*, London, Collins' Clear-Type Press, c. 1914, p. 75.

134 Turreau extract, taken from Pernoud and Flaissier, op. cit., p. 299.

135 See Furet and Richet, op. cit., p. 224, and Jones, op. cit., p. 227. However, it wasn't easy to raise an army; see Bire, op. cit.

136 P. Paret, *Internal War and Pacification: The Vendée 1789–1796*, Center of International Studies, Princeton University, Princeton, NJ, p. 1.

137 Bire, op. cit., p. 76.

138 'Philippeaux letter on the Vendée, 26 December 1793', in Hardman, op. cit., pp. 198–9; see also Bire, op. cit., p. 237; Gilchrist and Murray, op. cit., p. 275; and Rudé, op. cit., p. 122. No wonder Furet and Richet talk in terms of *la Vendée maudite* ('the damned Vendée').

139 See J.Roberts (1990), op. cit., p. 23.

140 A. Cobban, op. cit., p. 105.

141 Petitfrère says they accounted for 63 per cent of the rebel force; cited in Jones, op. cit., p. 230; see also Godechot (1972), op. cit., p. 213.

142 See J. Roberts (1990), op. cit., pp. 28–9, for a good definition and description; see also Thompson, op. cit., pp. 391–409 (description) and p. 399 (definition); P. Jones, *The French Revolution in Social and Political Perspective*, London, Arnold, 1996, pp. 358–79; and Godechot (1972), op. cit., p. 217.

143 In mid-1793. See Bosher, op. cit., p. 222; also Cobb, op. cit., pp. 44–62, and 'Philippeaux letter on the Vendée, 26 December 1793', in Hardman, op. cit., pp. 198–9.

144 Woronoff, op. cit., p. 53; see also Jones (1989), op. cit., p. 228.

145 R. Furneaux, *The Bourbon Tragedy*, London, Allen & Unwin, 1968, p. 133.

146 T. Tackett, 'The West in France in 1789: The Religious Factor in the Origins of the Counterrevolution', *Journal of Modern History*, 4 (1982): 715.

147 M. Vovelle, *The Revolution against the Church: From Reason to the Supreme Being*, Cambridge, UK, Polity, 1999, pp. 164 and 166.

148 In terms of historical sites there is, for example, the Mémorial de Vendée at Saint-Sulpice-le-Verdon.

149 Godechot (1972), op. cit., pp. 213–4.

150 Jones (1989), op. cit., p. 228; he quotes Reynald Secher.

151 Winock, op. cit., p. 21; reflected in M. J. Sydenham, *The French Revolution*, London, Batsford, 1969, p. 171.

152 Bire, op. cit., p. 237.

153 A. Cobban, *Aspects of the French Revolution*, London, Jonathan Cape, 1968, p. 133.

154 Mitchell, op. cit., p. 405; see also C. Petitfrère, 'The Origins of the Civil War in the Vendée', in Jones (1996), op. cit., pp. 339–58.

155 Jones (1989), op. cit., p. 225.

156 For more on the Terror-Vendée link, see S. Loomis, *Paris in the Terror: June 1793-July 1794*, London, Jonathan Cape, 1964, p. 288.

157 Godechot (1972), op. cit., pp. 207–12.

158 C. Tilly, 'Local Conflicts in the Vendée before the Rebellion of 1793', *French Historical Studies*, 1961, Vol. 2, No. 2: 209–31.

159 Petitfrère, op. cit., pp. 342–3.
160 Furet, op. cit., p. 125.
161 Mitchell, op. cit., pp. 405–6.
162 Tackett, op. cit., p. 716.
163 Cobban (*Aspects*), op. cit., pp. 131–3.
164 Bire, op. cit., p. 236.
165 H. de Balzac, *The Chouans*, London, Penguin, 1972, p. 77.
166 Aston, op. cit., p. 235; religion was also instrumental in the other counter-revolutionary revolts around France.
167 For background, see C. Tilly, 'Civil Constitution and Counter-Revolution in Southern Anjou', *French Historical Studies*, 1959, Vol. 1, No. 2: 172–99. A. Dansette, *Histoire religeuse de la France contemporaine*, Paris, Flammarion, 1965, pp. 109–24, talks about 'religious anarchy'.
168 Godechot (1972), op. cit., pp. 205–7; J. McManners, *The French Revolution and the Church*, London, SPCK, 1969, p. 82.
169 Tackett, op. cit., p. 717 and p. 745.
170 T. J. A. Le Goff and D. M. G. Sutherland, 'Counter-Revolution in Western France', *Past and Present*, No. 99: 66.
171 For a good summary of the Tilly and Bois approach, see J. Roberts (1990), op. cit., pp. 32–3.
172 C. Tilly, *The Vendée*, London, Edward Arnold, 1964, pp. 1 and 9. Cobban (*Aspects*), op. cit., p. 131, says historians and sociologists are 'natural enemies', but that Tilly and Bois help to break down the barriers.
173 Tilly, op. cit., p. 29.
174 Tilly, op. cit., p. 10.
175 Mitchell, op. cit., p. 418; McManners, op. cit., p. 82.
176 Tackett, op. cit., p. 717.
177 Cobban (*Social Interpretation*), op. cit., p.104; see also J. Roberts (1990), op. cit., pp. 22–43
178 Godechot (1972), op. cit., p. 204.
179 D. P. Jordan, *The Revolutionary Career of Maximilien Robespierre*, Chicago, University of Chicago Press, 1989, p. 134.
180 R. Magraw, *France 1815–1914: The Bourgeois Century*, Oxford, Fontana, 1983, p. 23; P. McPhee, *A Social History of France 1780–1880*, London, Routledge, 1993, p. 116.
181 Phillips, op. cit., p. 189.
182 J. Weiss, *Conservatism in Europe*, London, Thomas & Hudson, 1977, p. 50; see also N. E. Hudson, *Ultra-Royalism and the French Restoration*, Cambridge, Cambridge University Press, 1936, p. 110; Phillips, op. cit., p. 185; F. B. Artz, *France under the Bourbon Restoration*, Cambridge, MA, Harvard University Press, 1931, p. 20; and E. Weber, in H. Rogger and E. Weber, *The European Right: A Historical Profile*, Berkeley, University of California Press, 1965, pp. 71–5. This period also marked the birth of Legitimism.
183 A. Jardin and A.-J. Tudesq, *Restoration & Reaction 1815–1848*, Cambridge, Cambridge University Press, 1988; and Magraw, op. cit., p. 35. See G. de Bertier de Sauvigny, *The Bourbon Restoration*, Philadelphia, University of Pennsylvania Press, 1966, which offers a solid narrative of all periods and is organised around the main ministries.
184 Hudson, op. cit., p. 95; see P. Pilbeam, *Republicanism in Nineteenth-Century France, 1814–1871*, London, Macmillan, 1995, pp. 60–94.
185 V. Hugo, *Les Miserables*, Ware, UK, Wordsworth, 1994, p. 557.
186 I. Collins (ed.), *Government and Society in France 1814–48*, London, Edward Arnold, 1970, p. 10.
187 See Collins, op. cit., pp. 10–15.

188 See for example Hudson, op. cit., p. 48; Artz, op. cit., p. 39; Phillips, op. cit., p. 151.

189 See J. P. T. Bury, *France 1814–1940*, London, Routledge, 1991, pp. 1–9; see also D. M. G. Sutherland, *France 1789–1815: Revolution and Counter-revolution*, London, Fontana, 1985, pp. 432–7; Rudé, op. cit., pp. 280–1; and P. Mansel, *Louis XVIII*, London, Blond & Briggs, 1981, p. 327.

190 Hudson, op. cit., p. 95; the title of one of the book's chapters. The early 1820s witnessed a marked swing to the left – as if in response to the ascendancy of the extreme right.

191 R. Price, *A Concise History of France*, Cambridge, Cambridge University Press, 1993, p. 160; C. Charle, *A Social History of France in the 19th Century*, Oxford, Berg, 1994, p. 30.

192 De Sauvigny, op. cit., p. 378.

193 P.-J. de Béranger, 'The Coronation of Charles X', taken from J. H. Stewart, *The Restoration Era in France 1814–1830*, Princeton, NJ, Van Nostrand, 1968.

194 See Phillips, op. cit., p. 182, 190 and 196; Mansel, op. cit., p.328, says Charles tried to commit himself to *ancien régime* practical politics as well.

195 Weber, op. cit.; Artz, op. cit., p. 14; Rémond (1971), op. cit., p. 52.

196 P. de la Siboutie, 'The Ultra Spirit', taken from Stewart (1968), op. cit.

197 G. Wright, *France in Modern Times*, London, Norton, 1995, p. 96.

198 Rémond, (1971) op. cit., Chapter 1. Wright, op. cit., p. 100, also talks about a subfaction nicknamed the 'Ultra-Ultras'.

199 Weiss, op. cit., p. 45.

200 Artz, op. cit., p. 52.

201 Collins, op. cit., p. 43.

202 Jardin and Tudesq, op. cit., p. 59; Hudson, op. cit., p. 112; and De Sauvigny, op. cit., p. 369.

203 The White Terror, for example This tactic is described as 'aristocratic populism'; see Artz, op. cit., p. 20.

204 See Mansel, op. cit., p. 340; and Artz, op. cit., p. 55 – hence the slogan, 'Long live the King inspite of himself''.

205 E. Bourgeois, *History of Modern France 1815–1913: Volume I 1815–1852*, Cambridge, Cambridge University Press, p. 46.

206 See Collins, op. cit., p. 31.

207 Collins, op. cit., p. 32.

208 See 'Royal Ordinance Concerning the Press, 24 June 1827', in Stewart (1968), op. cit. See also Hudson, op. cit., p. 138, for details of the opposition press legislation provoked; and I. Collins, *The Government and Newspaper Press in France 1814–1881*, London, Oxford University Press, 1959, for general background.

209 Phillips, op. cit., p. 190.

210 Hudson, op. cit., p. 115 and 130; Artz, op. cit., p. 99; Phillips, op. cit., p. 190.

211 See 'The Congregation and its Aims' in Stewart (1968), op. cit.; Hudson, op. cit., p. 116, says Father Ronsin was a key man. The Société des Pères de la Foi was especially influential in propogating Catholicism; see Phillips, op. cit., pp. 156–61.

212 See Magraw, op. cit., p. 301, and D. W. Brogan, *The French Nation: From Napoleon to Pétain 1814–1940*, London, Cassell, 1989, pp. 26–31.

213 Phillips, op. cit., p. 187; Hudson, op. cit., p. 117.

214 Stendhal, 'The Revolution in Literature and the Reaction in Philosophy', taken from M. Williams, *Revolutions 1775–1830*, London, Penguin, 1971, p. 483. This point is also reflected in Stendhal, *Scarlet and Black*. The church was seen as *the* place for ambitious young people.

215 'The Law on Sacrilege, 15 April 1825', taken from Stewart (1968), op. cit.; Jardin and Tudesq, op. cit., say the Ultra party 'forced' Villèle to pass the law.

216 See Phillips, op. cit., p. 192, and also pp. 189–94 for background on the question of why the legislation was never enacted.
217 J. Roberts (1990), op. cit., pp. 101–2.
218 Cited in Artz, op. cit., p. 26.
219 Rémond makes this point (1971), op. cit., pp. 36–7.
220 See J. Roberts (1990), op. cit., pp. 109–10.
221 Phillips, op. cit., pp. 162–3.
222 Artz, op. cit., p. 51.
223 Rémond (1971), op. cit.
224 Collins, op. cit., pp. 85–6.
225 Phillips, op. cit., p. 205.
226 P. Goubert, *The Course of French History*, London, Routledge, 1991, pp. 231–2; see also K. Randell, *France 1814–70*, London, Hodder & Stoughton, 1986, pp. 15–33.
227 Weiss, op. cit., p. 55.
228 J. Roberts (1990), op. cit., p. 3.
229 Steiner, op. cit., p. 133.
230 Thompson, op. cit., p. 267.
231 Hudson, op. cit., p. 141.
232 Steiner, op. cit., p. 135.
233 Tannenbaum, op. cit., p. 267; Rémond (1971), op. cit., p. 30.
234 J. Roberts (1990), op. cit., p. 1.

3 1870–1918 – anti-Third Republic protest: *revanche* and the new nationalism

1 E. J. Arnold, *The Development of the Radical Right in France: From Boulanger to Le Pen*, London, Macmillan, 2000, pp. xii–xiii.
2 B. Jenkins, *Nationalism in France*, London, Routledge, 1990, p. 87.
3 This 'new right' should not be confused with the 'new right' of the 1980s – which was 'new' in a totally different sense. Representatives of the new post-1870 right would have referred to themselves as 'nationalists' or 'revisionists'.
4 J. F. McMillan, *Twentieth-Century France*, London, Arnold, 1992, pp. 31–3.
5 P. Mazgaj, 'The Origins of the French Radical Right: A Historiographical Essay', *French Historical Studies*, 1987, Vol. XV, No. 2: 287–315.
6 See Chapter 4 of this study.
7 W. Buthman, *Integral Nationalism in France*, New York, Octagon, 1970, p. 14.
8 Buthman, op. cit., pp. 13–14.
9 Like Gambetta and Renan, for example. See Buthman, op. cit., pp. 13–22.
10 Z. Sternhell, 'Paul Déroulède and the Origins of Modern French Nationalism', *Journal of Contemporary History*, 1971, Vol.VI: 47.
11 J. Weiss, *Conservatism in Europe 1770–1945*, London, Thomas & Hudson, 1977, p. 107.
12 McMillan, op. cit., p. 31.
13 For background on this, see J. P. T. Bury, *France 1814–1940*, London, Routledge, 1991, pp. 135–49, and F. H. Brabant, *The Beginnings of the Third Republic in France*, New York, Howard Fertig, 1972.
14 See J. Chastenet, *Naissance et jeunesse: histoire de la IIIe République*, Paris, Hachette, 1952, pp. 221–38. G. Wright, *France in Modern Times*, London, Norton, 1995, pp. 205–58, identifies 'The Monarchist Republic, 1870–1879', 'The Opportunist Republic, 1879–1899' and 'The Radical Republic, 1899–1914'.
15 G. Bourgin, *La Troisième République 1870–1914*, Paris, Armand Colin, 1967, pp. 36–51.

16 E. Berl, *Cent ans d'histoire de France*, Paris, Arthaud, 1962, pp. 94–5.

17 Jenkins, op. cit., p. 89.

18 M. Anderson, *Conservative Politics in France*, London, George Allen & Unwin, 1974, pp. 27–8.

19 Interestingly, McMillan argues that the old right almost 'welcomed' the emergence of the new right (op. cit., p. 33).

20 P. M. Rutkoff, *Revanche and Revision*, Athens, OH, Ohio University Press, 1981, p. 11.

21 Jenkins, op. cit., p. 89.

22 G. Le Béguec and J. Prévotat, '1898–1919 – L'Éveil à la modernité politique' in J.-P. Sirinelli (ed.), *Les droites françaises: de la Révolution à nos jours*, Paris, Gallimard, 1992, pp. 384–5.

23 Z. Sternhell, 'The Political Culture of Nationalism', in R. Tombs (ed.), *Nationhood and Nationalism in France: From Boulangism to the Great War 1889–1918*, London, HarperCollins, 1991, p. 27.

24 See G. Boulanger, 'Speech, 2 December 1888', taken from R. Gildea, *The Third Republic 1870–1914*, London, Longman, 1988, pp. 96–7; and M. Barrès, 'Integral Nationalism: The Nancy Programme, 1898', taken from D. Thomson (ed.), *Empire and Republic*, London, Harper and Row, 1968, pp. 268–73. See also Mazgaj, op. cit., p. 297 and P. Milza, *Fascisme français*, Flammarion, Paris, 1987, p. 65.

25 Jenkins, op. cit., pp. 89–90.

26 Sternhell (1971), op. cit., p. 47. See also R. Magraw, *France 1815–1914: The Bourgeois Century*, Oxford, Fontana, 1983, pp. 260–84; R. Soucy, *French Fascism: The Case of Maurice Barrès*, Berkeley, CA, University of California Press, 1972; Milza, op. cit., pp. 70–87; and S. Hood and L. Janz, *Fascism for Beginners*, pp. 10–15. Even they highlight France's contribution to the growth of fascism!

27 McMillan, op. cit., p. 31. There is a very helpful general discussion of the right during the early Third Republic in R. D. Anderson, *France 1870–1914: Politics and Society*, London, Routledge & Kegan Paul, 1977, pp. 100–18.

28 P. Déroulède, 'Quand même' ['All the Same'], refrains militaires, 1888, taken from R. Girardet, *Le Nationalisme français 1871–1914*, Paris, Armand Colin, 1966.

29 'Opportunists' was a pejorative nickname given to the pragmatic coalition-builders of the early Third Republic. See M. Agulhon, *The French Republic 1879–1992*, Oxford, Blackwell, 1995, p. 4; and Wright, op. cit., pp. 223–45.

30 Rutkoff, op. cit., p. 22.

31 Cited in Buthman, op. cit., p. 31.

32 Rutkoff, op. cit., p. 23.

33 See Rutkoff, op. cit., Chapter 2.

34 C. Prochasson 'Les Années 1880: Au Temps du Boulangisme' in M. Winock (ed.), *Histoire de l'extrême droite en France*, Paris, Seuil, 1994, pp. 63 and 65.

35 Buthman, op. cit., p. 30; Rutkoff, op. cit., p. 33. C. Stewart Doty, *From Cultural Rebellion to Counterrevolution: The Politics of Maurice Barrès*, Athens, OH, Ohio University Press (no date), p. 37, says the Ligue had just over 100 members in the town of Nancy (for example).

36 Milza, op. cit., pp. 73 and 75.

37 Magraw, op. cit., p. 261. For more on the distinctiveness of ligues as opposed to political parties, see R. Rémond, *The Right Wing in France*, Philadelphia, University of Pennsylvania Press, 1971, p. 229.

38 P. M. Rutkoff, 'The Ligue des Patriotes: The Nature of the Radical Right and the Dreyfus Affair', *French Historical Studies*, Vol. 8, No. 4, Autumn 1974: 585–603.

39   M. Winock, *Nationalisme, antisémitisme et fascisme en France*, Paris, Seuil, 1990, p. 16; Sternhell (1971), op. cit., p. 70; McMillan, op. cit., p. 31.
40   W. D. Irvine, 'Royalists and the Politics of Nationalism', in R. Tombs, op. cit., p. 111.
41   H. Tint, *The Decline of French Patriotism*, London, Weidenfeld & Nicolson, 1964, p. 43. In essence, revanche or revindication?
42   Mazgaj, op. cit., p. 297.
43   Sternhell (1971), op. cit., p. 51.
44   Prochasson, op. cit, p. 64.
45   Tint, op. cit., p. 44.
46   Buthman, op. cit., p. 30.
47   Z. Sternhell, *Ni droite, ni gauche: l'idéologie fasciste en France*, Paris, Complexe, 1987, p. 75.
48   For more on militarism, see Sternhell (1971), op. cit., p. 55.
49   See later section within this chapter.
50   Tint, op. cit., p. 43; Magraw, op. cit., p. 261, quotes some interesting statistics: in 1869 France had forty gymnastic societies, Germany 2,183. See also P.Arnaud, 'Dividing and Uniting: Sports Societies and Nationalism, 1870–1914', in R. Tombs, op. cit.
51   Buthman, op. cit., pp. 25–6.
52   Jenkins, op. cit., p. 94.
53   'Revisionism' – the desire to revise the constitutional arrangements of the Third Republic – see Bourgin, op. cit., p. 85.
54   Sternhell (1971), op. cit., p. 59.
55   S. Payne, 'Fascism in Western Europe', in W. Laqueur (ed.), *Fascism: A Reader's Guide*, London, Penguin, 1982, p. 301.
56   P. Levillain, '1871–1898: Les droites en République', in Sirinelli, op. cit., p. 402.
57   R. Griffin, *The Nature of Fascism*, London, Routledge, 1994, p. 117; revenge is the 'single issue' he identifies.
58   Jenkins, op. cit., p. 92; Sternhell (1971), op. cit., p. 54.
59   Sternhell (1971), op. cit., p. 51; M. Anderson (1974), op. cit., p. 33, refers to the Jacobin background of some Ligue activists.
60   See A. Dansette, *Le Boulangisme*, Paris, Fayard, 1946.
61   See G. Chapman, *The Third Republic of France: The First Phase 1871–1894*, London, Macmillan, 1962, p. 281.
62   For an almost contemporary account, see E. W. Latimer, *France in the Nineteenth Century 1830–1890*, Chicago, McClurg, 1899, pp. 427–44. See also Chapman, op. cit., pp. 265–74. In P. Ouston, *France in the Twentieth Century*, London, Macmillan, 1972, p. 162, Boulangism is described as 'a complete failure'.
63   Milza, op. cit., p. 65.
64   Winock (1990), op. cit, p. 295.
65   S. Berstein and P. Milza, *Histoire de la France au Xxe Siècle 1900–1930*, Paris, Complexe, 1990, pp. 23–4, make the original comparison. For an in-depth study of the politicians who enabled the Republic to survive, see B. Fulton, 'The Boulanger Affair Revisited: The Preservation of the Third Republic, 1889', *French Historical Studies*, 1991, Vol. 17, No. 2: 310–29.
66   See M. Curtis, *Three Against the Republic*, Princeton, NJ, Princeton University Press, 1959, pp. 27–8; J.-M. Mayeur, *La Vie Politique sous la Troisième République 1870–1940*, Paris, Seuil, 1984, p. 128. For key critiques of Boulangsim, see extracts from J. Ferry, C. Floquet and Challend-Lacour in P. Barral (ed.), *Les Fondateurs de la Troisième République*, Paris, Armand Colin, 1968.

67 Irvine, op. cit., p.108.

68 See Rutkoff, op. cit., Chapter 3.

69 A law was passed on 17 July 1889 to stop it happening again. See 'Law of 17 July 1889 Concerning Multiple Candidatures', taken from Thomson, op. cit., pp. 88–9.

70 Levillain, op. cit., p. 338.

71 Mayeur, op. cit., pp.119 and 135; Levillain, op. cit., p. 338.

72 Jenkins, op. cit., p. 94.

73 Rémond, op. cit., p. 224; J.Rothney, *Bonapartism after Sedan*, New York, Cornell University Press, 1969, p. 280.

74 Berstein and Milza, op. cit., pp. 23–4.

75 Jenkins, op. cit., p. 95; Rémond, op. cit., p. 216, says Boulangism helped to reverse the traditional 'left-urban, right-rural' split in France.

76 See Curtis, op. cit., p. 28. Pro-Boulanger songs were very catchy indeed. See Berl, op. cit., p. 251, and, op. cit., p. 484.

77 R. Tombs, *France 1814–1914*, London, Longman, 1996, p. 450.

78 Jenkins, op. cit., p. 94.

79 P. H. Hutton, *The Cult of Revolutionary Tradition: The Blanquists in French Politics, 1864–1893*, London, University of California Press, 1981, p. 145. For more general analysis of *Boulangisme* and *Blanquisme*, see pp. 143–50.

80 Hutton, op. cit., pp. 143–5.

81 Z. Sternhell, *La droite révolutionnaire: les origines françaises du fascisme 1885– 1914*, Paris, Seuil, 1978, p. 49.

82 See W. D. Irvine, 'French Royalists and Boulangism', *French Historical Studies*, 1988, Vol. XV, No. 3: 395–406.

83 Levillain, op. cit., p. 352.

84 Irvine (1991), op. cit., p. 114.

85 Irvine (1991), op. cit., p. 116. Hence, the title of Chapter 3, 'Boulanger: Saviour of the Monarchy', in W. D. Irvine, *The Boulanger Affair Reconsidered*, New York, Oxford University Press, 1989.

86 Irvine (1991), op. cit., p. 116.

87 Mermeix, 'Plaidoyer pour le Boulangisme', taken from Girardet, op. cit.

88 Buthman, op. cit., p. 39.

89 Hutton, op. cit., p. 143.

90 Buthman, op. cit., p. 32. See also Winock (1990), op. cit., p. 302.

91 See F. H. Seagar, *The Boulanger Affair: Political Crossroad of France 1886– 1889*, New York, Cornell University Press, 1969, pp. 47–69.

92 Mayeur, op. cit., p. 127.

93 See G. Boulanger, 'Address, 1889', taken from Thomson, op. cit., pp. 87–8.

94 Mermeix, op. cit.

95 Jenkins, op. cit., p. 94.

96 Quoted in Bourgin, op. cit., p. 85.

97 Mermeix, op. cit., talks about 'the other form of democracy... the popular form'.

98 Boulanger, 'Speech, 2 December 1888', in Gildea, op. cit. See also Milza, op. cit., p. 65.

99 See Boulanger, 'Address, 1889', in Thomson, op. cit.

100 See Boulanger, 'Speech, 2 December 1888', in Gildea, op. cit.

101 Mayeur is in no doubt that – in Paris especially – his support came mainly from the left and extreme left.

102 Sternhell (1978), op. cit, p. 50. On Boulanger and the legacy of the Paris Commune, see R. Tombs, *The Paris Commune*, London, Longman, 1999.

103 P. G. Nord, *Paris Shopkeepers and the Politics of Resentment*, Princeton, NJ, Princeton University Press, c. 1986, p. 302.

104   See, for example, Curtis, op. cit., p. 25; and Rémond, op. cit., p. 213.

105   Winock (1990), p. 303.

106   See R. Tombs (1996), op. cit., pp. 452–3; Sternhell (1978), op. cit., pp. 36 and 55; and Mayeur, op. cit., p. 135.

107   Sternhell, (1991) op. cit., p.29.

108   Winock (1990), op. cit., pp. 43–5. On p. 298 he says that there was 'ambiguity' about Boulanger's republican sentiments.

109   Levillain, op. cit., p. 337; see also Seagar, op. cit. – this phrase is used in the book's sub-title.

110   Sternhell (1978), op. cit., p. 55.

111   Buthman, op. cit., p. 40; see also D. W. Brogan, *French Personalities and Problems*, London, Hamish Hamilton, 1946, p.101.

112   See M. Barrès, 'The Panama Scandal', taken from *Cosmopolitan*, June 1894, Vol. VXII: 203–10.

113   Weiss, op. cit., p. 103.

114   Milza, op. cit., pp. 71–2.

115   See Soucy, op. cit.

116   Or, with Maurras, as one of the two founding fathers.

117   Magraw, op. cit.; Jenkins, op. cit.

118   See, for example, M. Barrès, 'Integral Nationalism: The Nancy Programme, 1898', in Thomson, op. cit.; see also Stewart Doty, op. cit., for more on Barrès' political career in Nancy.

119   G. F. Putnam, 'The Meaning of Barrèsisme', *Western Political Quarterly*, June 1954, Vol.VII: 165.

120   Brogan, op. cit., p. 113.

121   M. Barrès, 'Young Soldiers of France', taken from *The Atlantic Monthly*, July 1917.

122   Putnam, op. cit., p. 174.

123   M. Barrès, 'Scènes et doctrines du nationalisme', taken from J.S. McClelland (ed.), *The French Right from de Maistre to Maurras*, London, Jonathan Cape, 1971, p. 159 (see also p. 162). But Tint, op. cit., p. 100, says Barrès does not talk excessively about race.

124   M. Barrès, 'Le Cimetière de chambières', taken from Girardet, op. cit.

125   M. Barrès, *The Soul of France: Visits to Invaded Districts*, London, T. Fisher Unwin, 1915, p. 18.

126   Barrès (1917), 'Young Soldiers of France'), op. cit., p. 58.

127   Putnam, op. cit., pp. 177–8.

128   See Soucy, op. cit.

129   Tint, op. cit., p. 98.

130   See Barrès, 'Scènes et doctrines du nationalisme', in McClelland, op. cit., pp. 163–95.

131   Putnam, op. cit., p. 171.

132   Weiss, op. cit., p. 103.

133   Sternhell (1987), op. cit., p. 13.

134   Weiss, op. cit., p. 105.

135   Putnam, op. cit., p. 172.

136   See Brogan, op. cit., p. 106.

137   Putnam, op. cit., p. 179.

138   Putnam, op. cit., p. 171.

139   Barrès, 'Integral Nationalism: The Nancy Programme, 1898', in Thomson, op. cit. See Stewart Doty, op. cit., pp. 36–69.

140   Barrès, 'Integral Nationalism: The Nancy Programme, 1898', in Thomson, op. cit.

141   Barrès, 'Integral Nationalism: The Nancy Programme, 1898', in Thomson,

op. cit. For background, see W. Serman, 'The Nationalists of Meurthe-et-Moselle, 1888–1912', in Tombs (1991), op. cit, pp. 121–35. Serman says (p. 125) that the Comité Révisionniste de la Meurthe-et-Moselle had 1,500 members in February 1889 and 2,500 in July 1889.

142 See Stewart Doty, op. cit., pp. 153–75.

143 Putnam, op. cit., pp. 174–5.

144 McClelland, op. cit., p.143.

145 Barrès, 'Integral Nationalism: The Nancy Programme, 1898', in Thomson, op. cit.

146 Barrès, 'Integral Nationalism: The Nancy Programme, 1898', in Thomson, op. cit.

147 Mazgaj, op. cit., p. 302.

148 For an interesting discussion of Barrèsisme and its relationship to other political creeds, see R. Soucy, 'Barrès and Fascism', *French Historical Studies*, 1967: 67–97.

149 H. Lynch, 'A Political Waiter of France', *Contemporary Review*, 1900, Vol. 78: 385.

150 Nationalist Socialist Republican Committee of Meurthe-et-Moselle.

151 Brogan, op. cit., p. 103.

152 McMillan, op. cit., p. 32. For more on this subject, see Stewart Doty, op. cit., pp. 50–1.

153 For a good discussion, see Brogan, op. cit., pp. 106–7 and p. 115.

154 See Tint, op. cit., p. 97, for more on Barrès' cosmopolitanism.

155 In all kinds of areas. See, for example, M. Grover, 'The Inheritors of Maurice Barrès', *Modern Language Review*, 1961 (July), Vol. LXIV: 329–545; and F. D. Cheydleur, 'Maurice Barrès as a Romanticist', *Publications of the Modern Language Association of America*, 1926, Vol. XLI: 462–87.

156 See Soucy (1967), op. cit.

157 Brogan, op. cit., pp. 102–3.

158 Brogan, op. cit., p. 104.

159 See Mazgaj, op. cit., p. 301.

160 A. L. Guérard, *Five Masters of French Romance*, London, Fisher Unwin, 1916, p. 216.

161 Putnam, op. cit., p. 180.

162 Curtis op. cit., p. 44.

163 For a good narrative of the saga, see J. D. Bredin, *The Affair: The Case of Alfred Dreyfus*, London, Sidgwick & Jackson, 1987; or M. Burns, *Dreyfus: A Family Affair 1789–1945*, London, Chatto & Windus, 1993. For Dreyfus' own view, see A. Dreyfus, *Cinq années de ma vie*, Paris, Maspero, 1982. For another interesting perspective, see L. Blum, *Souvenirs sur l'affaire*, Paris, Gallimard, 1981 (written in 1935). Everything you ever wanted to know about the Affair is contained in M. Drouin, *L'Affaire Dreyfus de A à Z*, Paris, Flammarion, 1994. For a provocative selection of themed essays about the era, see P. Birnbaum (ed.), *La France de l'affaire Dreyfus*, Paris, Gallimard, 1994; and for a retrospective see J. Hue (ed.), *L'Affaire Dreyfus 1894–1910 et le tournant du siècle*, Paris, BDIC, 1994.

164 J. Joll, *Europe Since 1870*, London, Penguin, 1982; see also R. Soltau, *French Parties and Politics 1871–1921*, New York, Russell & Russell, 1965, p. 39; and – for cartoons on the episode – R. Price, *A Concise History of France*, Cambridge, Cambridge University Press, 1993, p. 202.

165 R. Kedward, *The Dreyfus Affair*, London, Longman, 1965.

166 P. Miquel, *L'Affaire Dreyfus*, Paris, Presses Universitaires de France, 1964. For an in-depth study of anti-Semitism, see S. Wilson, *Ideology and Experience: Antisemitism in France at the Time of the Dreyfus Affair*, London, Associated University Press, 1982, Chapters 1 and 2.

167 For more on the shambolic attempted coup, see Buthman op. cit., pp. 94–5.
168 McMillan, op. cit., p. 10.
169 McMillan, op. cit., p. 11.
170 Bredin, op. cit., p. 25; see also Rutkoff, op. cit., pp. 71–4, and Wilson, op. cit. See also R. Byrnes, *Anti-Semitism in Modern France*, New Brunswick, NJ, Rutgers University Press, 1950, pp. 110–36.
171 Z. Sternhell, 'The Roots of Popular Anti-Semitism in the Third Republic' in F. Malino and B. Wasserstein (eds), *The Jews in Modern France*, Hanover, NH, University Press of New England, 1985, p. 103–34. See also J. Jennings, 'Anti-Semitic Discourse in Dreyfus-Affair France', in E. J. Arnold, *The Development of the Radical Right in France: From Boulanger to Le Pen*, London, Macmillan, 2000, pp. 16–32.
172 For more on the book and the reception it got, and on Drumont and his background, see Byrnes, op. cit., Chapter 3.
173 Bredin, op. cit., p. 28.
174 See Byrnes, op. cit., pp. 320–39; B. Joly, 'The Jeunesse Antisémite et Nationaliste 1894–1904' in Tombs (1991), op. cit.; Wilson, op. cit., p. 191 and pp. 213–26; and also S. Wilson, 'The Antisemitic Riots of 1898 in France', *The Historical Journal*, !973, Vol. XVI, No. 4: 789–806.
175 Milza, op. cit., p. 81.
176 R. Wistrich, *Anti-Semitism: The Longest Hatred*, London, Mandarin, 1992, p. 48.
177 Weiss, op. cit., p. 99.
178 E. Drumont, 'La France juive', taken from McClelland, op. cit., p. 92.
179 Drumont, in McClelland, op. cit., pp. 108–9.
180 Sternhell (1987), op. cit., p. 69.
181 Milza, op. cit., p. 82.
182 For more on 'nationalist' anti-Semitism, see Wilson (1982), op. cit., pp. 379–437.
183 For more on 'racial' anti-Semitism, see Wilson (1982), op. cit., pp. 456–95.
184 Brogan, op. cit., p. 11.
185 Sternhell (1985), op. cit., p. 103.
186 Bredin, op. cit., pp. 26–7.
187 Bredin, op. cit., p. 29. But see also Rutkoff, op. cit., pp. 77–8; Byrnes, op. cit., Chapter 2, talks about Drumont in terms of the 'Prologue to the Dreyfus Affair'.
188 Curtis, op. cit., pp. 35–6.
189 See earlier in the present chapter; and also Barrès, 'Scènes et Doctrines du Nationalisme', in McClelland, op. cit., pp. 163–95.
190 D. W. Brogan, *The French Nation: From Napoleon to Pétain 1814–1940*, London, Cassell, 1989, p. 198.
191 Major Marchand, 'Letter from Fashoda', taken from Gildea, op. cit., pp. 106–7.
192 P. Déroulède, 'Vive l'Armée!', taken from Girardet, op. cit.
193 McMillan, op. cit., p. 8.
194 M. Anderson (1974), op. cit., p. 36.
195 C. Charle, *A Social History of France in the 19th Century*, Oxford, Berg, 1994, p. 165.
196 See M. Burns, 'Families and Fatherlands: The Lost Provinces and the Case of Captain Dreyfus' in Tombs (1991), op. cit.
197 For good general background on the church and the Dreyfus Affair, see J. McManners, *Church and State in France 1870–1914*, London, SPCK, 1972, pp. 118–28.
198 Quoted in Bredin, op. cit., p. 29.
199 'Assumptionist statement', taken from E. Cahm (ed.), *Politics and Society in Contemporary France 1789–1971: A Documentary History*, London, Harrap, 1972.

200 'Assumptionist statement', in Cahm, op. cit.
201 Weiss, op. cit., p. 100.
202 McMillan, op. cit., p. 8.
203 Barrès, 'Scènes et doctrines du nationalisme', in McClelland, op. cit., pp. 163–4.
204 G. Cavaignac, 'Ce qui est en Jeu', taken from Girardet, op. cit.
205 See F. Goguel, *La Politique des parties sous la IIIe République*, Paris, Seuil, 1958. In the short term, there was La Patrie Française. For an in-depth study of this movement, see J.-P. Rioux, *Nationalisme et Conservatisme: La Ligue de la Patrie Française 1899–1904*, Paris, Beauchesne, 1977. See also Girardet, op. cit.; and P. Hyman, *From Dreyfus to Vichy: The Remaking of French Jewry 1906–1939*, New York, Columbia University Press, 1979. Longer-term, see Burns, op. cit., pp. 343–492; and Bredin, op. cit., pp. 505–45; also 'Shadow over France', *The Guardian*, 5 January 1995.
206 M. Anderson (1974), op. cit., pp. 40–1; see also Curtis op. cit., pp. 42–3.
207 Milza, op. cit., p. 65.
208 Bourgin, op. cit., p. 106.
209 J. P. Mayer, *Political Thought in France from the Revolution to the Fifth Republic*, London, Routledge & Kegan Paul, 1961, p. 84.
210 Rémond, op. cit., p. 208. He also says that Boulangism drew up the 'birth certificate' of French nationalism and the Dreyfus Affair was its 'baptismal record', p. 208.
211 Irvine (1991), op. cit, p. 108.
212 Curtis, op. cit., p. 37.
213 Wilson (1982), op. cit., p. 737.
214 Bredin, op. cit., p. 28.

4 1919–39 – inter-war fascism: the *ligues* and 6 February

1 G. Warner, 'France' in S. J. Woolf (ed.), *Fascism in Europe*, London, Methuen, 1981, p. 307.
2 See S. Wilson, 'The "Action Française" in French Intellectual Life', *The Historical Journal*, 1969, Vol. XII, No. 2: 328–50.
3 J. S. McClelland (ed.), *The French Right from de Maistre to Maurras*, London, Jonathan Cape, 1971, p. 213.
4 R. Soltau, *French Political Thought*, New York, Russell & Russell, 1965, p. 388.
5 P. Pujo, 'L'Action française devant les droites' in J.-P. Apparu (ed.), *La Droite aujourd'hui*, Paris, Albin Michel, 1979, pp. 184–5.
6 *The Guardian*, 31 May 1991.
7 A cartoon in a 1990s AF journal depicted the movement as a raft, sailing in perilous seas. The message was that allegiance to Maurras' writings would bring safety.
8 *Aspects de la France*, 3 January 1991.
9 See E. Nolte, *Three Faces of Fascism*, London, Weidenfeld & Nicolson, 1965, pp. 65–6; and H. Tint, *The Decline of French Patriotism*, London, Weidenfeld & Nicolson, 1964, p. 150.
10 H. R. Kedward, *Fascism in Western Europe 1900–45*, Glasgow, Blackie, 1969, p. 71; see M. Winock, *Nationalisme, Antisémitisme et Fascisme en France*, Paris, Seuil, 1990, p. 256.
11 P. Mazgaj, 'The Origins of the French Radical Right: A Historiographical Essay', *French Historical Studies*, 1987, Vol. XV, No. 2: 328–50; see also E. Weber, *Action Française*, Stanford, Stanford University Press, 1962, p. 369.
12 On the movement's general organisation, see Weber, op. cit., 172–201.

13 R. Rémond, *The Right Wing in France*, Philadelphia, University of Pennsylvania Press, 1971, p 239. Furthermore, the Camelots du Roi are still active today.
14 Nolte, op. cit., pp. 59–60.
15 Kedward, op. cit., p. 71.
16 Nolte, op. cit., pp. 63–4.
17 Tint, op. cit., p. 146.
18 This is reflected in the AF's membership. See E. R. Tannenbaum, *The Action Française*, New York, Wiley, 1962, pp. 115–35.
19 Nolte, op. cit., p.54.
20 Nolte, op. cit., p. 67.
21 Taken from D. Thomson (ed.), *Empire and Republic*, London, Macmillan, 1968.
22 For background on anti-Semitism, see P. J. Kingston, *Anti-Semitism in France during the 1930s: Origins, Personalities and Propaganda*, Hull, UK, University of Hull, 1983.
23 R. Eatwell, *Fascism: A History*, London, Vintage, 1996, p. 154.
24 J. S. McClelland, 'The Reactionary Right: The French Revolution, Charles Maurras and the Action Française', in R. Eatwell and N. O'Sullivan (eds), *The Nature of the Right: American and European Politics and Political Thought since 1789*, London, Pinter, 1992, p. 79.
25 See M. Curtis, *Three Against the Republic*, Princeton, NJ, Princeton University Press, 1959, p. 242.
26 C. Maurras, 'Dictator and King', taken from McClelland (1971), op. cit., p. 216.
27 Curtis, op. cit., p. 242.
28 Tannenbaum, op. cit., p. 40.
29 See 'Maurice Barrès' Collaboration with the Action Française', *Romanic Review*, 1938 (April), Vol. XXIX: 167–9.
30 R. Girardet, *Le Nationalisme Français 1871–1914*, Paris, Armand Colin, 1966, p. 28.
31 This was a new political term. See Nolte, op. cit., p. 121 and pp. 120–7.
32 D. W. Brogan, *French Personalities and Problems*, London, Hamish Hamilton, 1946, p. 69; see also Nolte, op. cit., p. 104.
33 R. S. Wistrich, *Anti-Semitism: The Longest Hatred*, London, Mandarin, 1992, p. 131.
34 M. Winock, *Histoire de l'extrême droite en France*, Paris, Seuil, 1994, p. 126.
35 Quoted in C. J. H. Hayes, *The Historical Evolution of Modern Nationalism*, New York, Macmillan, 1948, p. 165; see also p.166.
36 McClelland (1992), op. cit., p. 93.
37 Quoted in Girardet, op. cit.
38 McClelland (1992), op. cit., pp. 93 and 95; Curtis, op. cit., p. 250.
39 Curtis, op. cit., p. 251.
40 Brogan, op. cit.
41 C. Maurras, 'The Politics of Nature', in McClelland (1971), op. cit., pp. 264–6.
42 See Nolte, op. cit., pp. 107–13.
43 Maurras, 'Dictator and King', op. cit., pp. 218–20. 'Liberties' are a safeguard.
44 Which are usually associated with the Jacobin, revolutionary left.
45 Soltau, op. cit., pp. 389–90.
46 See S. Wilson, 'History and Traditionalism: Maurras and the Action Française', *Journal of the History of Ideas*, 1968, Vol. 28: 365–80.
47 Rémond, op. cit., pp. 233–53.
48 Nolte, op. cit., p. 100.
49 See W. C. Buthman, *Integral Nationalism in France*, New York, Octagon, 1970, Chapter X, pp. 132–50.

50 Winock (1994), op. cit., p.155.

51 P. Milza, *Fascisme français*, Paris, Flammarion, 1987, p. 119.

52 See Buthman, op. cit., pp. 151–62, for more on Maurras, Mussolini and the 'Latin heritage'.

53 Eatwell, op. cit., p. 155; Nolte, op. cit., classifies the AF as 'early fascism'.

54 See Weber, op. cit., pp. 319–41.

55 Eatwell, op. cit., p. 157. See also J. Levey, 'Georges Valois and the Faisceau: The Making and Breaking of a Fascist', *French Historical Studies*, 1973, Vol. VIII. No. 2: 279–304.

56 Winock (1990), op. cit., p. 256; Tannenbaum, op. cit., p. 226.

57 See A. Werth, *France 1940–55*, London, Robert Hale, 1957, pp. 66–77; also S. M. Osgood, *French Royalism under the 3rd and 4th Republics*, The Hague, Nijhoff, 1960, pp. 182–96; the FN's Georges-Paul Wagner is a particular admirer.

58 Tannenbaum, op. cit., p. 198.

59 McClelland (1992), op. cit., p. 97.

60 J. Weiss, *Conservatism in Europe 1770–1945*, London, Thomas & Hudson, 1977, p. 137.

61 P. Bernard and H. Dubief, *The Decline of the Third Republic 1914–1938*, Cambridge, Cambridge University Press, 1985, p. 211.

62 Winock (1994), op. cit., p. 157.

63 Rémond, op. cit., p. 273.

64 J. F. McMillan, *Twentieth-Century France*, London, Arnold, 1992, p. 103.

65 R. Soucy, 'The Nature of Fascism in France', *Journal of Contemporary History*, 1966, Vol. 1: 53.

66 See Warner, op. cit.; A. Hamilton, *The Appeal of Fascism: A Study of Intellectuals and Fascism 1919–45*, London, Blond, 1971, p. 222.

67 McMillan, op. cit., p. 107; Warner, op. cit., p. 307.

68 Z. Sternhell, *Ni Droite Ni Gauche*, Paris, Complexe, 1987, p. 301.

69 R. Soucy, *French Fascism: The First Wave 1924–33*, New Haven, CT, Yale University Press, 1986, p. 217.

70 M. Anderson, *Conservative Politics in France*, London, George Allen & Unwin, 1974, pp. 199–201.

71 Bernard and Dubief, op. cit., p. 210.

72 G. Warner, 'France' in S. J. Woolf (ed.), *European Fascism*, London, Weidenfeld & Nicolson, 1970, pp. 265–7.

73 Eatwell, op. cit., p. 160

74 Quoted in Warner (1981), op. cit., p. 316.

75 Anderson, op. cit., p. 217.

76 On the Faisceau, see Levey, op. cit. On Defense Paysanne, Parti Agraire and Front Paysan, see R. O. Paxton, *French Peasant Fascism: Henry Dorgères's Greenshirts and the Crises of French Agriculture, 1929–1939*, Oxford, Oxford University Press, 1997; see also Soucy (1986), op. cit., Chapter 2.

77 McMillan, op. cit., p. 106; see also Sternhell, op. cit., pp. 301–2.

78 Tint, op. cit., p. 197.

79 Soucy (1966), op. cit., p.28.

80 S. G. Payne, 'Fascism in Western Europe' in W. Laqueur (ed.), *Fascism: A Reader's Guide*, London, Penguin, 1982, p. 302.

81 Milza, op. cit., pp. 440–1. This point is made throughout his book.

82 R. Griffin, *Fascism: A Reader*, Oxford, Oxford University Press, 1995, p. 196.

83 Soucy (1986), op. cit., p. 1.

84 M. Kitchen, *Europe Between the Wars*, Longman, London, 1993, p. 218.

85 Bernard and Dubief, op. cit., p. 210

86 See Rémond, op. cit.

87 M. Larkin, *France since the Popular Front*, Oxford, Oxford University Press, 1991, p. 49.
88 Anderson, op. cit., p. 196.
89 Eatwell, op. cit., p. 165.
90 Soucy (1966), op. cit., p. 30.
91 See Z. Sternhell, *La Droite révolutionnaire: les origines françaises du fascisme 1885–1914*, Paris, Seuil, 1978; and also Sternhell (1987), op. cit.
92 Rémond, op. cit., p. 282.
93 Sternhell (1987), op. cit., p. 27.
94 Milza, op. cit., p. 440.
95 Soucy (1966), op. cit., p. 31.
96 Warner (1981), op. cit., p. 309; Soucy (1986), op. cit., pp. 218–19.
97 Sternhell (1987), op. cit., p. 270.
98 A general point made by Sternhell (1987), op. cit., pp. 5–6; see also Soucy (1966), op. cit., pp. 32–5, and M. Blinkhorn (ed.), *Fascists and Conservatives*, London, Unwin Hyman, 1990, Chapter 10.
99 See Blinkhorn, op. cit.
100 Hamilton, op. cit., p. 189.
101 Soucy (1986), op. cit., p. 218.
102 Sternhell (1987), op. cit., p. 30.
103 Sternhell (1987), op. cit., p. 7.
104 Soucy (1966), op. cit., pp. 30–1.
105 Weiss, op. cit., p. 137.
106 And means that for France, and the emergence of French fascism, the key date was probably 1871, not 1918. Defeat in the Franco-Prussian War acted as a stimulus to the new-right agitation of the 1880s and 1990s and perhaps we should conclude that, in retrospect, the 'pre-fascist' activity of the late nineteenth century was of more substance and significance than the 'era of the *ligues*'.
107 Sternhell (1987), op. cit., p. 270.
108 See G. Warner, 'The Cagoulard Conspiracy', *History Today*, 1960, Vol. IX, No. 7: 443–50.
109 Kitchen, op. cit., p. 230.
110 L. Trotsky, *On France*, New York, Monad Press, 1979, p. 29.
111 A. Werth, *France in Ferment*, London, Jarrolds, 1934, p. 153.
112 E. Daladier, 1947.
113 See A. Werth (1934), op. cit., Chapter VII, for a good eye-witness account.
114 Eatwell, op. cit., p. 159.
115 Hamilton, op. cit., p. 193.
116 G. Warner, 'The Stavisky Affair and the Riots of February 6th 1934', *History Today*, 1958, Vol. VIII, No. 6: 377–85.
117 See Eatwell, op. cit., p. 160.
118 Warner (*Stavisky Affair*), op. cit., p. 384. He refers to the involvement of the army and even Frot, the Minister of the Interior
119 Trotsky, op. cit., pp. 27, 28 and 31.
120 Trotsky, op. cit., p. 31.
121 L. Blum, 1947.
122 McMillan, op. cit., p. 106.
123 Warner (*Stavisky Affair*), op. cit., p. 385
124 A. Lebrun, 1947.
125 Tint, op. cit., p. 200; however, if you would like to refer to a source that 'plays up' the riot's importance and potential, see L. Ducloux, *From Blackmail to Treason*, London, André Deutsch, 1958 – Ducloux was a senior figure in the Paris police in the 1930s.

126 Tint, op. cit., p. 200.
127 Rémond, op. cit., p. 284.
128 R. Austin, 'The Conservative Right and the Far Right in France: The Search for Power', in Blinkhorn, op. cit., p. 177.
129 Kitchen, op. cit., p. 220.
130 Hamilton, op. cit., p. 194.
131 *Manchester Guardian*, 7 February 1934; *Daily Mirror*, 7 February 1934.
132 Werth, (1934) op. cit., p. 142; see also the map of Paris in M. Beloff, 'The Sixth of February', in J. Joll (ed.), *The Decline of the Third Republic*, St Antony's Papers, No. 5, London, 1959.
133 Warner (*Stavisky Affair*), op. cit., p. 381.
134 Werth (1934), op. cit., p. 142.
135 Beloff, op. cit.
136 Werth (1934), op. cit., p. 144.
137 Kitchen, op. cit., p. 220.
138 See Beloff, op. cit.
139 *Manchester Guardian*, 7 February 1934.
140 See Werth (1934), op. cit., pp. 175–81.
141 Larkin, op. cit., p. 48.
142 Kitchen, op. cit., p. 221.
143 J. Brenda, 1936.
144 Eatwell, op. cit., p. 161; see also Milza, op. cit., p. 141.
145 Warner (*Stavisky Affair*), op. cit., p. 385; see also S. M. Osgood, 'The Front Populaire: Views from the Right', *International Review of Social History*, 1964, Vol. IX: 189–201.
146 Austin, op. cit., p. 178.
147 See Anderson, op. cit, p. 194; and Eatwell, op. cit., p. 154.
148 Soucy (1966), op. cit., p. 53.
149 McMillan, op. cit., pp. 106–7.

5 1940–4 – Vichy: the National Revolution, collaboration and collaborationism

1 S. Fishman and L. V. Smith, 'Introduction', in S. Fishman, L. L. Downs, I. Sinanoglou, L. V. Smith and R. Zaretsky (eds), *France at War: Vichy and the Historians*, Oxford, Berg, 2000.
2 M. Anderson, *Conservative Politics in France*, London, George Allen & Unwin, 1974, p. 269.
3 For a full biography see N. Atkin, *Pétain*, London, Longman, 1998.
4 On the defeat see W. L. Shirer, *The Collapse of the Third Republic*, London, Literary Guild, 1970.
5 'Collaborationists' idolised Nazi ideology and, on the whole, are quite distinct from 'collaborators' – see later in this chapter.
6 D. Thomson, *Democracy in France since 1870*, London, Oxford University Press, 1969, p. 211; P. Novick, *The Resistance Versus Vichy: The Purge of Collaborators in Liberated France*, New York, Columbia University Press, 1968, p. 1.
7 R. Rémond, *The Right Wing in France*, Philadelphia, PA, University of Pennsylvania Press, 1971, p. 311; R. O. Paxton, *Vichy France: Old Guard and New Order 1940–1944*, New York, Columbia University Press, 1982, pp. 138–45.
8 P. Baudoin, *The Private Diaries of Paul Baudoin*, London, Eyre & Spottiswoode, 1948, pp. 145–9.

9   P. Claudel, 'Words to the Marshal', taken from J. S. McClelland, *The French Right from Maurras to de Maistre*, London, Jonathan Cape, 1971, pp. 306–9. S. de Beauvoir, *The Prime of Life*, London, Penguin, 1960, p. 564, said she found Claudel's piece of work 'utterly sickening'.

10   R. Desquesnes, *The Guide to the Memorial*, Caen, Éditions Memorial de Caen, 1994, p. 15.

11   P. Pétain, 'Speech of 11 October 1940', taken from D. Thomson (ed.), *Empire and Republic*, London, Harper and Row, 1968. For a broad-ranging collection of Pétain's speeches in French, see P. Pétain, *Discours aux Français 17 Jun 1940–20 Août 1944*, Paris, Albin Michel, 1989.

12   P. Laval, 'Speech of 10 July 1940', taken from S. M. Osgood, *The Fall of France, 1940: Causes and Responsibilities*, Boston, DC, Heath and Company, 1965, pp. 10–12.

13   Vichy actually labelled 1941 'The Year of the Clean -Up'.

14   Pétain, 'Speech of 11 October 1940', in Thomson, op. cit.

15   R. Bouderon and G. Willard, *De la défaite à la résistance*, Paris, Messidor, 1990, p. 128.

16   Vichy poster, *c.* 1941.

17   Vichy poster, *c.* 1940.

18   See J. Jackson, 'Vichy and Fascism', in E. J. Arnold, *The Development of the Radical Right in France: From Boulanger to Le Pen*, London, Macmillan, 2000, pp. 153–71. See also H. Schnurer, 'The Intellectual Sources of French Fascism', *The Antioch Review*, 1941 (March)

19   P. Farmer, *Vichy Political Dilemma*, London, Octagon, 1977, pp. 216–22.

20   M. Dank, *The French Against the French: Collaboration and Resistance*, Philadelphia, Lippincott, 1974, p. 83.

21   Pétain, 'Speech of 11 October 1940', in Thomson, op. cit.

22   Pétain, 'Speech of 11 October 1940', in Thomson, op. cit.

23   Rémond, op. cit., p. 315.

24   Anderson, op. cit., p. 68; see also H. W. Ehrmann, *Organized Business in France*, Princeton, NJ., Princeton University Press, 1957, p. 63.

25   Bouderon and Willard, op. cit., p. 141.

26   P. Caziot, taken from *France during the German Occupation, 1940–44*, Vol. II, California, The Hoover Institution, c. 1947, p.257.

27   Caziot, op. cit., p. 257.

28   M. Larkin, *France since the Popular Front*, Oxford, Oxford University Press, 1991, p. 95.

29   Rémond, op. cit., p. 315.

30   Larkin, op. cit., p. 94.

31   D. Rossignol, *Histoire de la propagande en France de 1940 à 1955*, Paris, Presses Universitaire de France, 1991, pp. 97–9.

32   Rémond, op. cit., p. 315.

33   R. Kuisel, *Capitalism and the State in Modern France: Renovation and Economic Management in the Twentieth Century*, Cambridge, Cambridge University Press, 1981, p. 131.

34   See Larkin, op. cit., p. 96; and Ehrmann, op. cit., Chapter 2.

35   J. F. McMillan, *Twentieth-Century France*, London, Edward Arnold, 1992, p. 139.

36   See Kuisel, op. cit., pp. 144–56.

37   Pétain, 'Speech of 11 October 1940', in Thomson, op. cit.

38   Ehrmann, op. cit., p. 58.

39   Rémond, op. cit., p. 315; most famously, the Peasant Corporation – see G. Wright, *Rural Revolution in France: The Peasantry in the Twentieth Century*, Stanford, Stanford University Press, 1964, Chapter 5.

40 Pétain, 'Speech of 11 October 1940', in Thomson, op. cit.
41 On 2 December 1940 the Farmers Corporation was founded.
42 McMillan, op. cit., p. 139; see also I. Ousby, *Occupation: The Ordeal of France 1940–1944*, London, John Murray, 1998, p. 94.
43 Rossignol, op. cit., p. 142.
44 M. Pollard, 'Women and the National Revolution' in R. Kedward and R. Austin (eds), *Vichy France and the Resistance*, London, Croom Helm, 1985, p. 38.
45 For other interpretations, see S. M. Osgood, *The Fall of France, 1940: Causes and Responsibilities*, Boston, DC, Heath and Company, 1965.
46 For more on divorce and the regime's attitude to homosexuality, see A. Copley, *Sexual Moralities in France 1780–1980*, London, Routledge, 1992, pp. 192–204.
47 Pollard, op. cit., p. 41.
48 J. Pascot, 'Sports', in Hoover, op. cit., pp. 828–30.
49 See, for example, W. D. Halls, *Politics, Society and Christianity in Vichy France*, Oxford, Berg, 1995; and Paxton, op. cit., pp. 148–53.
50 Pollard, op. cit., p. 39.
51 W. D. Halls, *The Youth of Vichy France*, Oxford, Clarendon, 1981, p. 167.
52 Anderson, op. cit., p. 69; McMillan, op. cit., p. 137; see also N. Atkin, 'Les Maîtres du Maréchal: Catholic Schoolteachers in Vichy France, 1940–44' in F. Tallett and N. Atkin (eds), *Catholicism in Britain and France since 1789*, London, Hambledon, 1996.
53 Rémond, op. cit., p. 316.
54 McMillan, op. cit., p. 136; see also later in this chapter.
55 W. D. Halls, 'Church and State: Prelates, Theologians and the Vichy Regime', in N. Atkin and F. Tallett (eds), *Religion, Society and Politics in France since 1789*, London, Hambledon, 1991, pp. 185–6.
56 Paxton, op. cit., pp. 153–5. See also Pascot, op. cit.
57 Vichy posters *c.* 1940–1.
58 See Rossignol, op. cit., pp. 151–6.
59 Halls (1981), op. cit., p. 148.
60 P. Tissier, *The Government of Vichy*, London, Harrap, 1942, p. 186.
61 Halls (1981), op. cit., p. 166.
62 Halls (1981), op. cit., p. 161.
63 Rossignol, op. cit., p. 117.
64 Vichy poster *c.* 1940.
65 Halls (1981), op. cit., p. 143.
66 See P. Laval, *The Unpublished Diary of Pierre Laval*, London, The Falcon Press, 1948, pp. 70–9, for an interesting perspective on Montoire.
67 'Franco-German Armistice Convention, 1940', taken from Thomson, op. cit., p. 359.
68 For a good analysis, see J. Sweets, *Choices in Vichy France*, New York, Oxford University Press, 1994.
69 See R. Rémond, 'Two Destinies: Pétain and De Gaulle' in H. Gough and J. Horne (eds), *De Gaulle and Twentieth Century France*, London, Arnold, 1994; and also A. Beevor and A. Cooper, *Paris after the Liberation*, London, Hamish Hamilton, 1994, Chapters 1 and 2.
70 For more on Vichy's relationship with the Resistance, see J. E. Talbott, 'Vichy and Resistance France' in W. B. Cohen (ed.), *The Transformation of Modern France*, New York, Houghton Mifflin, 1997, pp. 207–24.
71 H. R. Kedward, *Occupied France: Collaboration and Resistance 1940–1944*, Oxford, Blackwell, 1989, p. 40.
72 See D. Johnson, 'A Question of Guilt: Pierre Laval and the Vichy Regime', *History Today*, 1988 (Jan.), Vol. 38: 17.

73   Kedward, op. cit., p. 33.

74   D. Thomson, *Two Frenchmen: Pierre Laval and Charles de Gaulle*, London, Cresset, 1951, p. 70.

75   S. Hoffman, *Decline or Renewal: France since the 1930s*, New York, Viking Press, 1974, p. 39.

76   P. Webster, *Pétain's Crime*, London, Papermac, 1992, p. 71.

77   On this same theme, see S. Sand, 'A Flirt or a Love Affair? French Intellectuals between Fascism and Nazism', in E. J. Arnold, *The Development of the Radical Right in France: From Boulanger to Le Pen*, London, Macmillan, 2000, pp. 83–99.

78   See *Time*, 4 January 1932.

79   Rémond, op. cit., pp. 316–17.

80   Larkin, op. cit., p. 95.

81   McMillan, op. cit., p. 142.

82   McMillan, op. cit., p. 141.

83   Larkin, op. cit., p. 95.

84   G. Warner, *Pierre Laval and the Eclipse of France*, London, Eyre & Spottiswoode, 1968, p. 299.

85   R. Eatwell, *Fascism: A History*, London, Vintage, 1996, p. 172.

86   Larkin, op. cit, p. 102; based on his 3.3 per cent estimate.

87   Ousby, op. cit., p. 251.

88   See M. R. Marrus and R. O. Paxton, *Vichy France and the Jews*, Stanford, Stanford University Press, 1995, p. 26. But 1930s anti-Semitism was very different from that of the 1890s.

89   X. Vallat, 'Jewish Affairs', in Hoover, op. cit.

90   McMillan, op. cit., p. 138. See also R. Hilberg, *The Destruction of the European Jews*, New York, Holmes & Meier, 1985, p. 399.

91   See *Le Monde*, 3 October 1990; fifty years after its enactment a colloqium on the subject was held.

92   See Y. Cohen, 'The Jewish Community of France in the Face of Vichy-German Persecution: 1940–44' in F. Malino and B. Wasserstein (eds), *The Jews in Modern France*, Hanover, NH, University Press of New England, 1985, p. 200.

93   See G. Reitlinger, *The Final Solution*, London, Vallentine Mitchel, 1968, pp. 333–43; Webster, op. cit., pp. 104–19.

94   J. Defrasne, *L'Occupation Allemende en France*, Paris, Presses Universitaires de France, 1993, p. 95.

95   McMillan, op. cit., p. 138.

96   Larkin, op. cit., p. 101.

97   Warner, op. cit., p. 306.

98   Reitlinger, op. cit., p. 327; McMillan, op. cit., p. 139; Larkin, op. cit., p.101, agrees – his figures.

99   Eatwell, op. cit., p. 173.

100 McMillan, op. cit., p. 139; Larkin, op. cit., p. 101.

101 Reitlinger, op. cit., p. 336.

102 Hilberg, op. cit., p. 400.

103 Eatwell, op. cit., p.172.

104 Halls (1 981), op. cit., p.144.

105 See Y. Cohen, op. cit., pp. 185 and 200; but M. Rajsfus, *Des juifs dans la collaboration: L'UGIF 1941–1944*, Paris, EDI, 1980, argues that many Jews are also to blame for the Holocaust.

106 See J. Defrasne, *Histoire de la collaboration*, Paris, Presses Universitaires de France, 1989.

107 Paxton, op. cit., p. 51.

108 A. Werth, *France 1940–55*, London, Robert Hale, 1957, p. 101.
109 Johnson, op. cit., p. 13.
110 Ousby, op. cit., p. 252.
111 Eatwell, op. cit., p. 172.
112 Laval, op. cit., p. 94.
113 Eatwell, op. cit., p. 172.
114 Werth, op. cit., p. 96.
115 Warner, op. cit., p. 291.
116 See McMillan, op. cit., p. 140. 'Polonisation' meant subjugation to the horrors of direct Nazi rule.
117 Ousby, op. cit., p. 192.
118 Johnson, op. cit., p. 17.
119 McMillan, op. cit., p. 140.
120 Eatwell, op. cit., p. 172.
121 J.-P. Azema, *De Munich à la libération 1938–1944*, Paris, Seuil, 1979, p. 110.
122 A. Cobban, 'Vichy France', in A. Toynbee (ed.), *Hitler's Europe: Survey of International Affairs 1939–1946*, p. 365.
123 Johnson, op. cit., p. 17.
124 See 'Resolution of the Mayors of the Seine, 11 August 1944', reprinted in Laval, op. cit.
125 Werth, op. cit., pp. 107–8.
126 Laval, op. cit., p. 186.
127 R. de Chambrun, … *et ce fut un crime judiciare: le 'procès' Laval*, Paris, France-Empire, 1984, p. 12; see also Josée Laval's introduction to Laval's *Diary*, op. cit.
128 McMillan, op. cit., p. 139.
129 Ousby, op. cit., p. 150.
130 R. Soucy, 'French Fascist Intellectuals in the 1930s: An Old New Left?', *French Historical Studies*, 1974, Vol. VIII, No. 3: 445–58.
131 Werth, op. cit., pp. 119–32.
132 See Larkin, op. cit.
133 Ousby, op. cit., pp. 266–7.
134 McMillan, op. cit., p. 142.
135 Ousby, op. cit., p. 113.
136 See Defrasne (1989), op. cit., pp. 79–82.
137 McMillan, op. cit., p. 142.
138 G. Chauvy, *Histoire secrète de l'Occupation*, Paris, Payot, 1991, p. 21.
139 Ousby, op. cit., p. 140; see R. Cobb, *French and Germans, Germans and French*, Hanover, NH, Brandeis University Press, 1983.
140 Larkin, op. cit., p. 105; Cobb, op. cit., pp. 100–1.
141 Ousby, op. cit., p. 141. However, McMillan estimates that there were probably no more than 15,000 collaborationists *in total*.
142 Werth, op. cit., p. 122.
143 McMillan, op. cit., p. 142.
144 Werth, op. cit., p. 120.
145 Eatwell, op. cit., p. 165.
146 Eatwell, op. cit., p. 165.
147 See Cobb, op. cit., p. 165.
148 McMillan, op. cit., p. 142.
149 Werth, op. cit., p. 126.
150 R. Price, *A Concise History of France*, Cambridge, Cambridge University Press, 1993, p. 258.
151 G. Ragache and J.-R. Ragache, *La Vie quotidienne des écrivains et des artistes sous l'Occupation 1940–4*, Paris, Hachette, 1988, p. 300, make this point with reference to Brasillach, but it is valid across the board.

152 A. Hamilton, *The Appeal of Fascism*, London, Blond, 1971, p. 245.
153 Hamilton, op. cit., p. 248.
154 Hamilton, op. cit., p. 245.
155 P. Drieu La Rochelle, 'Rationalism: voilà l'ennemi!', in Osgood, op. cit., pp. 50–1.
156 Larkin, op. cit., p. 105.
157 See McMillan, op. cit., p. 143.
158 Werth, op. cit., p. 123.
159 Eatwell, op. cit., p. 166. See also W. R. Tucker, 'Politics and Aesthetics: The Fascism of Robert Brasillach', *Western Political Quarterly*, 1962 (Dec.), Vol. 15, Pt 4: 605–17.
160 Hamilton, op. cit., p. 237.
161 Defrasne (1989), op. cit., p. 78.
162 Price, op. cit., p. 257.
163 Eatwell, op. cit., p. 172.
164 Larkin, op. cit.
165 McMillan, op. cit., pp. 142–3.
166 McMillan, op. cit., p. 143.
167 Ousby, op. cit., p. 141.
168 Ousby, op. cit., p. 140.
169 McMillan, op. cit., p. 143.
170 Price, op. cit., p. 258.
171 On Pétain's trial, see J. Roy, *The Trial of Marshal Pétain*, London, Faber & Faber, 1968.
172 Kedward, op. cit., p. 45; Hoffman, op. cit., p. 27; Cobb, op. cit., p. 65.
173 Webster, op. cit., p. 217.
174 E. Conan and H. Rousso, *Vichy, un passé qui ne passe pas*, Paris, Fayard, 1994, p. 268
175 Phrase patented by H. Rousso, *The Vichy Syndrome: History and Memory in France since 1944*, London, Harvard University Press, 1994. Everything seemed to begin with the release of the film *The Sorrow and the Pity* in 1971.
176 See *Le Monde*, 21 and 22 October 1990; R. Gildea, *France since 1945*, Oxford, Oxford University Press, 1996; and Conan and Rousso, op. cit., pp. 109–72. On Mitterrand, see P. Péan, *Une jeunesse française: François Mitterrand 1934–1947*, Paris, Fayard, 1994; see also Annales, *Présence du passé, lenteur de l'histoire Vichy, l'Occupation, les juifs*, 1993 (May–Jun.), No. 3, Paris, Armand Colin, École des Hautes Études en Sciences Sociales.
177 Rousso, op. cit., p. 297.

6 1945–present day – ultra-nationalism and neo-fascism: *Algérie Française*, Poujadism and the Front National

1 E. G. Declair, *Politics on the Fringe: The People, Policies, and Organisation of the French National Front*, London, Duke University Press, 1999, p. 12.
2 See M. Anderson, *Conservative Politics in France*, London, George Allen & Unwin, 1974, pp. 270–1.
3 J.-M. Donegani and M. Sadoun, '1958–1995: Le Jeu des Institutions', in J.-F. Sirinelli (ed.), *Les droites françaises de la Révolution à nos jours*, Paris, Gallimard, 1992, p. 677; see also A. Werth, *De Gaulle*, London, Penguin, 1979, pp. 273–5.
4 A. Horne, *A Savage War of Peace*, London, Penguin, 1985, pp. 17 and 538.
5 D. L. Hanley, A. P. Kerr and N. H. Waites, *Contemporary France: Politics and Society since 1945*, London, Routledge, 1991, p. 13.

6 J. Marcus, *The National Front and French Politics*, London, Macmillan, 1995, p. 15.
7 P. Hainsworth, 'The Extreme Right in Post-War France: The Emergence and Success of the Front National' in P. Hainsworth (ed.), *The Extreme Right in Europe and the USA*, London, Pinter, 1994, p. 33; M. Winock, *Histoire de l'extrême droite en France*, Paris, Seuil, 1994, p. 237; see also M. Winock, *Nationalisme, antisémitisme et fascisme en France*, Paris, Seuil, 1990, p. 425.
8 Anderson, op. cit., p. 280.
9 See R. F. Betts, *France and Decolonisation 1900–1960*, London, Macmillan, 1991; and also A. Clayton, *The Wars of French Decolonization*, London, Longman, 1994.
10 See, for example, H. G. Simmons, *The French National Front: The Extremist Challenge to Democracy*, Oxford, Westview, 1996, pp. 37–41; see also R. Gildea, *France since 1945*, Oxford, Oxford University Press, 1996, p. 24.
11 R. Price, *A Concise History of France*, p. 315; see also P. Morris, *French Politics Today*, Manchester, Manchester University Press, 1994, p. 18.
12 Gildea, op. cit., p. 21, explains the derivation of the phrase *pieds noirs*.
13 See Horne, op. cit., pp. 35 and 37; and E. Behr, *The Algerian Problem*, London, Penguin, 1961, p. 140. Gildea, op. cit., p. 25, says 'integration' equated to 'Francisation'.
14 Simmons, op. cit., p. 40.
15 Horne, op. cit., Chapter 8.
16 Clayton, op. cit., p. 129.
17 Price, op. cit.; Behr, op. cit., p. 315.
18 See J.-P. Rioux, *The Fourth Republic 1944–1958*, Cambridge, Cambridge University Press, 1989, pp. 300–5.
19 Behr, op. cit., pp. 161–72.
20 Horne, op. cit., pp. 436–60.
21 J. F. McMillan, *Twentieth-Century France*, London, Edward Arnold, 1992, p. 162.
22 Betts, op. cit., p. 112; Anderson, op. cit., p. 131. The term Ultras came to describe the most fanatical pro-*Algérie Française* activists.
23 R. Rémond, *The Right Wing in France*, Philadelphia, University of Pennsylvania Press, 1971, op. cit., p. 409; Clayton, op. cit., p. 172; Simmons, op. cit., p. 45; Anderson, op. cit., p. 131. Salan became ex-General Salan.
24 See Werth, op. cit., p. 272. Hainsworth, op. cit, p. 33, talks about its 'scorched earth policy'.
25 Simmons, op. cit., p. 45.
26 Anderson, op. cit., p. 288.
27 Anderson, op. cit., p. 288; Rémond, op. cit., p. 409.
28 Clayton, op. cit., p. 172.
29 Behr, op. cit., p. 212.
30 Cited in Betts, op. cit., p. 109.
31 Betts, op. cit., p. 107. P. Milza, *Fascisme français*, Paris, Flammarion, 1987, p. 317, says Ortiz' movement is the closest to 1930s-style fascism. See also Winock (1994), op. cit., p. 236.
32 Behr, op. cit., p. 162; Clayton, op. cit., p. 162.
33 Gildea, op. cit., p. 25.
34 Simmons, op. cit., p. 42.
35 Anderson, op. cit., p. 87.
36 Anderson, op. cit., p. 281.
37 Simmons, op. cit., pp. 43–4.
38 Simmons, op. cit., p. 44.

39 Anderson, op. cit., p. 280.
40 See M. Winock, 'De Gaulle and the Algerian Crisis, 1958–1962', in H. Gough and J. Horne (eds), *De Gaulle and Twentieth Century France*, London, Arnold, 1994, pp. 71–82; and A. Crawley, *De Gaulle*, London, Literary Guild, 1969, Chapters 19–20, for background.
41 Horne, op. cit., p. 287.
42 See Hanley *et al.*, op. cit., p. 14.
43 Anderson, op. cit., p. 87.
44 Gildea, op. cit., pp. 25–6.
45 Marcus, op. cit., p. 15; Donegani and Sadoun, op. cit., p. 683; J.-C. Petitfils, *L'Extrême droite en France*, Paris, Presses Universitaires de France, 1983, p. 95.
46 Hainsworth, op. cit., p. 32.
47 Winock (1994) op. cit. (*Histoire...*), pp. 234–5; Milza, op. cit., pp. 309–24; it is Winock's phrase.
48 Anderson, op. cit., pp. 287–8.
49 Anderson, op. cit., p. 84.
50 Hanley *et al.*, op. cit., p. 6.
51 Anderson, op. cit., pp. 275–6.
52 Price, op. cit., p. 313; see also Petitfils, op. cit., p. 87.
53 See Milza, op. cit., p. 303, for an electoral map; see also P. Williams, *Politics in Post-War France*, London, Longman, 1958, p. 451, for more on the electoral–legal problems that the Poujadists encountered in 1956.
54 Milza, op. cit., p. 306.
55 See Rioux, op. cit., pp. 248–9.
56 Rioux, op. cit., p. 249.
57 J.-L. Pinol, '1919–1958: Le Temps des droites?', in J.-F. Sirinelli (ed.), op. cit., p. 636.
58 Rémond, op. cit., p. 372.
59 Simmons, op. cit., pp. 27–36. See also Milza, op. cit., pp. 406–12; and Winock (1994), op. cit. (*Histoire...*), pp. 230–1, for UDCA–Le Pen comparisons.
60 Gildea, op. cit., p. 42.
61 Rioux, op. cit., p. 250.
62 After his spell in Compagnons de France, Poujade joined the RAF and worked for the Resistance.
63 R. Eatwell, *Fascism: A History*, London, Vintage, 1996, p. 243.
64 McMillan, op. cit., p. 160.
65 Declair, op. cit., p. 20.
66 Anderson, op. cit., p. 277, implies this; see also Rémond, op. cit., p. 372.
67 Winock (1994), op. cit. (*Histoire...*), p. 227.
68 Reinforced by stereotyping in the British press; see Rioux, op. cit., p. 249.
69 McMillan, op. cit., p. 160; Anderson, op. cit., p. 278.
70 See Eatwell, op. cit., p. 243.
71 M. Larkin, *France since the Popular Front*, Oxford, Oxford University Press, 1991, p. 251.
72 See Simmons, op. cit., p. 27; in Eatwell's words, 'Kick the Old Gang Out!', see Eatwell, op. cit., p. 243.
73 In fact, renegades from other parties seemed to be attracted by the 'protest' element in Poujadism.; see Larkin, op. cit., p. 251; and Anderson, op. cit., p. 278.
74 Gildea, op. cit., p. 41.
75 Winock (1990), p. 109.
76 McMillan, op. cit., p. 196, says France had forty supermarkets in 1960, but over 1,000 in 1970. He also claims that 108,000 *petits commercants* and 18,000 artisans disappeared between 1962 and 1968.

77 Anderson, op. cit., p. 278.
78 Larkin, op. cit., p. 250.
79 Anderson, op. cit., p.276.
80 In addition, Poujade always viewed himself as *un petit gars* – see Eatwell, op. cit., p. 243; there was a political equivalent as well – the provinces battling against Paris.
81 Simmons, op. cit., p. 28.
82 McMillan, op. cit., pp. 170–1.
83 Rioux, op. cit., p. 247–9.
84 Pinol, op. cit., p. 635; see also Gildea, op. cit., p. 41.
85 Simmons, op. cit., p. 28; such as, for example, the Taxpayers League of the 1930s.
86 Rioux, op. cit., p. 248.
87 Gildea, op. cit., p. 42; see also J.G. Andersen and T. Bjørklund, 'Radical Right-Wing Populism in Scandinavia: From Tax Revolt to Neo-Liberalism and Xenophobia' in P. Hainsworth (ed.), *The Politics of the Extreme Right: From the Margins to the Mainstream*, London, Pinter, 2000, p. 202. The Poujadists were radical, even in comparison with their Scandinavian equivalents.
88 Gildea, op. cit., p. 42.
89 Rioux, op. cit., p. 247.
90 Rioux, op. cit., p. 249; Simmons, op. cit., p. 27, Rémond, op. cit., pp. 371–2.
91 This is one of Petifils' main conclusions in his analysis of the Poujadist phenomenon, op. cit. Poujadism could also have hindered the growth of the far right. See Winock (1994), op. cit. (*Histoire...*), p. 225; and Winock (1990), op. cit., p. 108.
92 McMillan, op. cit., p. 160.
93 Rioux, op. cit., p. 260; Hainsworth (1994), op. cit., p. 33; Anderson, op. cit., p. 277. Milza, op. cit., p. 309, says the main legacy of the UDCA was the one word it added to the political vocabulary (*Poujadisme*).
94 Simmons, op. cit., p. 55.
95 For more on Le Pen's early career see M. Vaughan, 'The Extreme Right in France: 'Lepenisme' or the Politics of Fear', in L. Cheles, R. Ferguson and M. Vaughan, (eds), *Neo-Fascism in Europe*, London, Longman, 1991, pp. 218–21; and Simmons, op. cit., pp. 11–70.
96 It could be argued that Haidar's FPÖ (Freihetliche Partei Österreichs, Freedom Party of Austria) in Austria outflanked the FN in the 1990s.
97 Such as, for example, FN bow ties, notepaper and soap.
98 Hainsworth (1994), op. cit., p. 53.
99 Simmons, op. cit., p. 2; see also Milza, op. cit., pp. 398–400 – he sees Dreux as the second stage in the four-stage rise of the FN.
100 Marcus, op. cit., p. 164; see also www.front-national.com/anglais/english.htm (21 June 2001) for a quick guide to the FN's sister youth-movements around Europe.
101 See P. Perrineau, 'The Conditions for the Re-emergence of an Extreme Right Wing in France: the National Front, 1984–98', in E. J. Arnold, *The Development of the Radical Right in France: From Boulanger to Le Pen*, London, Macmillan, 2000, pp. 253–70.
102 See J.-P. Stirbois, *Tonnerre de dreux: l'avenir nous appartient*, Paris, Éditions National-Hebdo, 1988.
103 On the FN's Euro-discourse, see J.-M. Le Pen, *Europe: discours et interventions 1984–1989*, Paris, GDE, 1989.
104 Front National, *Pour la France: programme du Front National*, Paris, Albatros, 1985.

105   Vaughan, op. cit., p. 217. More generally, see P. Perrineau, 'Les Étapes d'une Implantation Électorale (1972–1988)', in N. Mayer and P. Perrineau (eds), *Le Front National à découvert*, Paris, Presses de la Fondation Nationale des Sciences Politiques, 1996.

106   There were also RPR (Rassemblement pour la République) and UDF (Union pour la Democratie Française) blocs.

107   Eatwell, op. cit., p. 253.

108   Hainsworth (1994), op. cit., p. 41.

109   But the FN argues that this 15 per cent is not represented – see www.front-national.com/anglais/english.htm (21 June 2001). It is also important to note that Le Pen and fellow candidates Philppe de Villiers (anti-Europe) and Jacques Cheminade (maverick right-winger) were known as the 'hard right'.

110   On the FN in Toulon, see J.-P. Thiollet, *Le Chevallier à découvert: portrait vérité par son ex-counseiller*, Paris, Laurens, 1998; on Vitrolles, see C. Mégret, *V comme Vitrolles: Histoire d'une Victoire*, Paris, Éditions Nationales, 1997; and also C. Mégret, *Allez Vitrolles: le programme de l'équipe Mégret*, Paris, Équipe Mégret, 1997.

111   See P. Davies, *The National Front in France: Discourse, Ideology and Power*, London, Routledge, 1999, Chapter 4; for the FN's view of itself in local-government power, see *Audit politique des communes de France: à l'usage des conseillers municipaux et des candidats du Front National*, Paris, Éditions Nationales, 1995. The FN in power also produced an enormous counter-response; see, for example, J. Viard (ed.), *Aux sources du populisme nationaliste: l'urgence de comprendre Toulon-Orange-Marignane*, Paris, Aube, 1996.

112   For more on his political philosophy, see B. Mégret et les Comités d'Action Républicaine, *L'impératif du renouveau: les enjeux de demain*, Paris, Albatros, 1986.

113   See www.front-national.com/megret.htm (21 June 2001) for the FN's view of Mégret's new movement.

114   www.front-national.com/megret.htm (21 June 2001); see also P. Hainsworth, 'The Front National: From Ascendancy to Fragmentation on the French Extreme Right' in Hainsworth (2000), op. cit., p. 28. Mégret's movement was initially known as the Front National-Mouvement National (FN-MN).

115   The FN has always seen itself as a movement rather than a party, and thus schism was in a way predictable.

116   Vaughan, op. cit., p. 221.

117   Eatwell, op. cit., p. 253.

118   Eatwell, op. cit., p. 255.

119   Gildea, op. cit., p. 191.

120   Front National (*Pour la France*), op. cit., pp. 17–20; see also www.front-national.com/anglais/english.htm (21 June 2001) and Front National, *Allez la France! Discours intégral de Jean-Marie Le Pen à la Fête des Bleu-Blanc-Rouge 1997*, Paris, Éditions Nationales, 1997, pp. 39–40.

121   Front National, *Le Contrat pour la France avec les Français: Le Pen Président*, Saint-Brieuc, Presses Bretonnes, 1995.

122   Vaughan, op. cit., p. 222.

123   Hainsworth (1994), op. cit., p. 48; see also www.front-national.com/anglais/english.htm (21 June 2001); the FN is influenced by many right-wing thinkers of the past, and even Aristotle! See Y. Blot, *La Politique selon Aristote: leçons du passé pour le present*, Paris, Éditions Nation et Humanisme, 1997. See also Front National, *Militer au front*, Paris, Éditions Nationales, 1991.

124   See Vaughan, op. cit., p. 222.

125   Front National (*Allez la France!*), op. cit., pp. 40–4.

126 Hainsworth (2000), op. cit., p. 23.
127 Front National (*Militer au Front*), op. cit., p. 135.
128 The IFN is the FN's 'study group'. This lecture session ran from 11 January to 28 June 1989.
129 *300 Mesures pour la renaissance de la France: Front National programme de gouvernement*, Paris, Éditions Nationales, 1993, pp. 22–123. The FN has always taken the possibility of taking governmental power very seriously – see B. Mégret, *L'Alternative nationale: les priorities du Front National*, Paris, Éditions Nationales, *c.* 1996 – and there has even been talk of a 'pre-government' era!
130 See, for example, J.-Y. Le Gallou, *Le Racisme antifrançais*, Paris, Club de l'Horloge, 1988. Publications such as this demonstrate the 'overlap' between FN and new right ideas.
131 Vaughan, op. cit., p. 222.
132 See J.-M. Brissaud, *La France en danger: non à l'Europe de Maastricht*, Paris, Éditions Nationales, 1994.
133 Front National (*Militer au Front*), op. cit., p. 116.
134 www.front-national.com/lefn/indexc.htm (21 June 2001); www.front-national.com/anglais/english.htm (21 June 2001); see also J.-C. Martinez, *Maastricht: le non de tous les miens*, Paris, Lettres du Monde, 1992; one FN poster read, *A bas l'Euro, vive le Franc national!*
135 The quote comes from Milza, op. cit., p. 398.
136 J.-Y. Le Gallou and P. Olivier, *Immigration*, Paris, Éditions Nationales, 1992, p. 22.
137 Eatwell, op. cit., p. 257.
138 See, for example, the FN publications *Dossier immigration*, Paris, National Hebdo, 1985; and *Rapport Milloz, le coût de l'immigration*, Paris, Éditions du Centre d'Études et d'Argumentaires, 1990.
139 Le Gallou and Olivier, op. cit., pp. 83–90.
140 Le Gallou and Olivier, op. cit., pp. 49–51. And in its publications the FN has played cleverly on the 'issue' of passports and *cartes d'identité*. See, for example, the FN publication *Passeport pour la victoire*; and J.-Y. Le Gallou and J.-F. Jalkh, *Être français cela se mérite*, Paris, Albatros, 1987.
141 See Eatwell, op. cit., p. 253; and Hainsworth (2000), op. cit., pp. 26–7. On 'national preference' see J.-Y. Le Gallou et le Club de l'Horloge, *La Préférence nationale: réponse à l'immigration*, Paris, Albin Michel, 1985; and Mégret (*L'Alternative Nationale, c.* 1996), op. cit., Chapter 10; see also Milza, op. cit., p. 413.
142 S. Mitra, 'The National Front in France – A Single-Issue Movement?', in K. von Beyme (ed.), *Right-Wing Extremism in Europe*, London, Cass, 1988.
143 This was particularly strong in the late 1980s and early 1990s when Le Pen championed the emerging nation states in Eastern Europe, the former USSR and the former Yugoslavia.
144 See Mégret (*L'Alternative nationale, c.* 1996), op. cit., pp. 99–112.
145 See M. de Rostolan, *Lettre ouverte à mon peuple qui meurt*, Paris, Lanore, 1987.
146 Milza, op. cit., pp. 424, 426 and 428; see also P. Jouve and A. Magoudi, *Les Dits et les non-dits de Jean-Marie Le Pen: enquête et psychoanalyse*, Paris, La Découverte, 1988.
147 See P. Davies, 'Joan of Arc in Front National Discourse', *Politics,* 1993 (Autumn).
148 Front National, *Le Pen 90: analyses et propositions*, Maule, Éditions de Présent, 1991, p. 30.

149   Hence J.-M. Brissaud, *Clovis: roy des Francs: l'album du XVe centenaire*, Paris, Éditions Nationales, *c.* 1996. Also J.-M. Brissaud, *Clovis: premier homme politique français*, Paris, GDE, 1996; interestingly the subtitle of this short booklet was, *Une réponse nationale aux attaques contre Clovis*.

150   www.front-national.com/anglais/english.htm (21 June 2001); see also Eatwell, op. cit., p. 256.

151   Vaughan, op. cit., p. 224.

152   Eatwell, op. cit., p. 258.

153   See Milza, op. cit., p. 410; Hainsworth (2000), op. cit., p. 20.

154   Hainsworth (2000), op. cit., pp.20–1; this is backed up by Milza, op. cit., p. 415, talking about 1986.

155   Eatwell, op. cit., p. 258.

156   Hainsworth (2000), op. cit., p. 22.

157   Hainsworth (1994), op. cit., p. 45.

158   Plenel and Rollat, pp. 137–64; See also Milza, op. cit., pp. 402 and 405 – to the east the FN is generally weak, to the west strong.

159   Hainsworth (1994), op. cit., p.,46.

160   Perrineau, op. cit., p. 57.

161   Vaughan, op. cit., p. 226; see J. Blondel and B. Lacroix, 'Pourquoi votent-ils Front National?' in Mayer and Perrineau, op. cit., pp. 150–72.

162   Hainsworth (2000), op. cit., p. 26; Eatwell op. cit., pp. 256–7; see also Gildea, op. cit., p. 192.

163   Hainsworth (2000), op. cit., p. 26; Hainsworth (1994), op. cit., p. 41.

164   Eatwell, op. cit., p. 255; see also A. Bell, *Against Racism and Fascism in Europe*, Brussels, Socialist Group (European Parliament), 1986

165   Plenel and Rollat, op. cit., p. 289.

166   Eatwell, op. cit., p. 258.

167   Marcus, pp. 145 and 147.

168   Hainsworth (1984), op. cit., p. 45.

169   Eatwell, op. cit., pp. 254–5; Gildea, op. cit., p. 191.

170   Marcus, op. cit., p. 173.

171   See Declair, op. cit., Chapter 6.

172   Eatwell, op. cit., p. 257. For a taste of early FN economic thinking see Front National, *Droite et démocratie économique: docrine économique et sociale du Front National*, Paris, National Hebdo, 1984; for later thinking, see B. Mégret, *La Troisième voie: pour un nouvel ordre économique et Social*, Paris, Éditions Nationales, 1997.

173   P. Descaves, *Pour en finir avec le chômage: les chiffres, les causes, les solutions*, Paris, Coordination des Cercles Nationaux, *c.* 1994, p. 34.

174   Hainsworth (2000), op. cit., p. 28.

175   Front National, *La Charte verte du Front National*, Paris, National Hebdo, 1985, was more about agriculture than ecology.

176   Front National (*Militer au front*), op. cit., p. 112–15.

177   See S. Maréchal, *Écologie: dépolluons les esprits*, Paris, Front National de Jeunesse, *c.* 1998, p. 19; see also J.-M. Le Pen, *L'Éspoir*, Paris, Albatros, 1989, Chapter 5; and P. Routhier, *Contrepoisons: les sciences de la vie et l'histoire parlent pour le Front National*, Paris, Éditions Nationales, *c.* 1998. This kind of discourse also evolves into concern about urbanism and urbanisation – see J.-Y. Le Gallou, *Le Livre bleu blanc rouge: plaidoyer pour une région enracinée*, Paris, Éditions Nationales, 1991; and J.-P. Schenardi and J.-P. Liparoti, *Pour un urbanisme français*, Paris, Éditions Nationales, *c.* 1998.

178   The title of one 1990 IFN lecture featured the word *francité*. When I mentioned this, in passing, to a language specialist I was told that this word was archaic and very rarely used in modern-day France!

179 It also likes to perceive itself as radical. Mégret in Vitrolles and Bompard in Orange have both used the slogan *Le Grand changement* in their campaign literature.
180 Eatwell, op. cit., p. 257.
181 See Winock (1990), op. cit., Chapter 1, for some interesting background.

Evaluation

1 M. Anderson, *Conservative Politics in France*, London, George Allen & Unwin, 1974, p. 344.
2 M. Winock, *Le Fièvre Hexagonale: Les Grandes Crises Politique 1871–1968*, Paris, Calmann-Lévy, 1987.
3 H. G. Simmons, *The French National Front: The Extremist Challenge to Democracy*, Oxford, Westview, 1996, p. 42.
4 *Le Quotidien de Paris*, 25 January 1984.
5 *Le Monde*, 26 January 1984.
6 *Le Figaro*, 25 January 1984.
7 *Le Matin*, 25 January 1984.
8 *Le Quotidien de Paris*, 26 January 1984.
9 *Le Quotidien de Paris*, 25 January 1984.
10 R. Rémond, *The Right Wing in France*, Philadelphia, University of Pennsylvania Press, 1971, p. 275.
11 Rémond, op. cit., p. 371.
12 Even here there are elements of overlap and merger, for example, the AF, Vichy, etc.
13 P. M. Rutkoff, *Revanche and Revision*, Athens, OH, Ohio University Press, 1981, p. 149.
14 J.-M. Le Pen, *Les Français d'Abord*, Paris, Carrere-Michel Lafon, 1984.
15 E. Nolte, *Three Faces of Fascism*, London, Weidenfeld & Nicolson, 1965, p. 121
16 Pétain quoted in R. Bouderon and G. Willard, *De la Défaite à la Résistance*, Paris, Messidor, 1990, p. 131.
17 Le Pen has also called for a 'Ministry of Anti-France' to be created to represent the 'anti-national' interest in contemporary France. He suggested that Harlem Désir, leader of anti-racist group SOS-Racisme, should head it!
18 FN leaflet *c.* 1991.
19 Rémond, op. cit., p. 213.
20 M. Winock (ed.), *Histoire de l'extrême droite en France*, Paris Seuil, 1994, p. 13.
21 See Anderson, op. cit., pp. 342–3.
22 Z. Sternhell, *Ni droite ni gauche*, Paris, Complexe, 1987, p. 54.
23 Déat is generally labelled a 'neo-socialist'.
24 Sometimes intransigence has been mixed with pragmatism, as in the case of the Ultras, who in the 1820s formed a strange alliance with the extreme left, hence the phrase 'aristocratic populism'.
25 Winock, op. cit., p. 13.
26 Anderson, op. cit., pp. 124–7 and pp. 169–73.
27 And are often ridiculed for this.
28 Anderson, op. cit., pp. 344–6.
29 Front National, *Militer au front*, Éditions Nationales, 1991, p. 135.
30 S. Maréchal, *Écologie: dépolluons les esprits*, Paris, Front National de Jeunesse, *c.* 1998, p. 19.
31 P. Hainsworth (ed.), 'The Front National: From Ascendancy to Fragmentation on the French Extreme Right', in *The Politics of the Extreme Right: From the Margins to the Mainstream*, London, Pinter, 2000, p. 18.
32 See P. Milza, *Fascisme Français*, Paris, Flammarion, 1987, pp. 406–12; and Winock, (1994), op. cit., pp. 230–1.

33 P. Hainsworth (ed.), 'The Extreme Right in Post-War France: The Emergence and Success of the Front National', in *The Extreme Right in Europe and the USA*, London, Pinter, 1994, p. 33.
34 *Le Quotidien de Paris*, 14 March 1986.
35 See Hainsworth (1994), op. cit., p.31; and Winock, op. cit., pp.12 and 15.
36 Winock, op. cit., p. 16.

Bibliography

To add to the value of the bibliography it has been divided into secondary and primary sources; the secondary reading list has been further classified into general survey histories and themed material corresponding to the chapter headings.

Secondary sources

General survey histories

Agulhon, M., *The French Republic 1879–1992*, Oxford, Blackwell, 1995.

Anderson, M., *Conservative Politics in France 1880–1958*, London, George Allen & Unwin, 1974.

Apparu, J.-P. (ed.), *La Droite aujourd'hui*, Paris, Albin Michel, 1979.

Arnold, E. J. (ed.), *The Development of the Radical Right in France: From Boulanger to Le Pen*, London, Macmillan, 2000.

Aston, N., *Religion and Revolution in France 1780–1904*, London, Macmillan, 2000.

Beevor, A. and Cooper, A., *Paris after the Liberation*, London, Hamish Hamilton, 1994.

Berl, E., *Cent ans d'histoire de France*, Paris, Arthaud, 1962.

Berstein, S. and Milza, P., *Histoire de la France au xxe siècle 1900–1930*, Paris, Complexe, 1990.

Bourgeois, E., *History of Modern France 1815–1913: Volume I 1815–1852*, Cambridge, Cambridge University Press, 1922.

Brogan, D. W., *French Personalities and Problems*, London, Hamish Hamilton, 1946.

—— *The French Nation: From Napoleon to Pétain 1814–1940*, London, Cassell, 1989.

Bury, J. P. T., *France 1814–1940*, London, Routledge, 1991.

Buthman, W. C., *Integral Nationalism in France*, New York, Octagon, 1970.

Byrnes, R., *Anti-Semitism in Modern France*, New Brunswick, NJ, Rutgers University Press, 1950.

Charle, C., *A Social History of France in the 19th Century*, Oxford, Berg, 1994.

Cobban, A., *A History of Modern France – Volume 1: 1715–1799*, London, Penguin, 1968.

—— *A History of Modern France – Volume 3: 1871–1962,* London, Penguin, 1982.

Cohen, W. B. (ed.), *The Transformation of Modern France,* New York, Houghton Mifflin, 1997.

Collins, I., *The Government and Newspaper Press in France 1814–1881,* London, Oxford University Press, 1959.

Curtis, M., *Three Against the Republic,* Princeton, NJ, Princeton University Press, 1959.

Eatwell, R., *Fascism: A History,* London, Vintage, 1996.

Eatwell, R. and O'Sullivan, N. (eds), *The Nature of the Right: American and European Politics and Political Thought since 1789,* London, Pinter, 1992.

Gildea, R., *France since 1945,* Oxford, Oxford University Press, 1996.

Goubert, P., *The Course of French History,* London, Routledge, 1991.

Gough, H. and Horne, J. (eds), *De Gaulle and Twentieth Century France,* London, Arnold, 1994.

Griffin, R., *The Nature of Fascism,* London, Routledge, 1994.

—— *Fascism: A Reader,* Oxford, Oxford University Press, 1995.

Hamilton, A., *The Appeal of Fascism: A Study of Intellectuals and Fascism 1919–45,* London, Blond, 1971.

Hayes, C. J. H., *The Historical Evolution of Modern Nationalism,* New York, Macmillan, 1948.

Herr, R. and Parker, H., *Ideas in History,* Durham, NC, Duke University Press, 1965.

Hyman, P., *From Dreyfus to Vichy: The Remaking of French Jewry 1906–1939,* New York, Columbia University Press, 1979.

Joll, J., *Europe since 1870,* London, Penguin, 1982.

Laqueur, W. (ed.), *Fascism: A Reader's Guide,* London, Penguin, 1982.

Larkin, M., *France since the Popular Front,* Oxford, Oxford University Press, 1991.

Latimer, E.W., *France in the Nineteenth Century 1830–1890,* Chicago, McClurg, 1899.

Magraw, R., *France 1815–1914: The Bourgeois Century,* Oxford, Fontana, 1983.

Malino, F. and Wasserstein, B. (eds), *The Jews in Modern France* (eds), Hanover, NH, University Press of New England, 1985.

Mayeur, J.-M., *La Vie politique sous la Troisième République 1870–1940,* Paris, Seuil, 1984.

Mayer, J. P., *Political Thought in France from the Revolution to the Fifth Republic,* London, Routledge & Kegan Paul, 1961.

Mazgaj, P., 'The Origins of the French Radical Right: A Historiographical Essay', *French Historical Studies,* Autumn 1987.

McMillan, J. F., *Twentieth-Century France,* London, Edward Arnold, 1992.

McPhee, P., *A Social History of France 1780–1880,* London, Routledge, 1993.

Milza, P., *Fascisme français,* Paris, Flammarion, 1987.

Muret, C., *French Royalist Doctrines since the Revolution,* New York, 1933.

Ouston, P., *France in the Twentieth Century,* London, Macmillan, 1972.

Péan, P., *Une jeunesse française: François Mitterrand 1934–1947,* Paris, Fayard, 1994.

Petitfils, J.-C., *L'Extrême droite en France,* Paris, Presses Universitaires de France, 1983.

Phillips, C. S., *The Church in France,* 1928, London, Russell & Russell, 1966.

Price, R., *A Concise History of France,* Cambridge, Cambridge University Press, 1993.

Prost, A., *Petite histoire de la France au xxe siècle*, Paris, Armand Colin, 1979.

Rémond, R., *La Vie politique en France 1789–1848*, Paris, Armand Colin, 1965.

Rémond, R., *The Right Wing in France*, Philadelphia, University of Pennsylvania Press, 1971.

Rogger, H. and Weber, E., *The European Right: A Historical Profile*, Berkeley, CA, University of California Press, 1965.

Sirinelli, J.-P. (ed.), *Les Droites françaises de la Révolution à nos Jours*, Paris, Gallimard, 1992.

Soltau, R. H., *French Political Thought in the Nineteenth Century*, London, Benn, 1931.

—— *French Parties and Politics 1871–1921*, New York, Russell & Russell, 1965.

Sternhell, Z., *Ni droite, ni gauche: L'Idéologie fasciste en France*, Paris, Complexe, 1987.

Thomson, D., *Democracy in France since 1870*, London, Oxford University Press, 1969.

Tint, H., *The Decline of French Patriotism*, London, Weidenfeld & Nicolson, 1964.

Tombs, R., *France 1814–1914*, London, Longman, 1996.

Weiss, J., *Conservatism in Europe 1770–1945*, London, Thomas & Hudson, 1977.

Werth, A., *France 1940–55*, London, Robert Hale, 1957.

Winock, M., *Nationalisme, antisémitisme et fascisme en France*, Paris, Seuil, 1990.

—— (ed.), *Histoire de l'extrême droite en France*, Paris, Seuil, 1994.

Wistrich, R., *Anti-Semitism: The Longest Hatred*, London, Mandarin, 1992.

Woolf, S. J. (ed.), *Fascism in Europe*, London, Methuen, 1981.

Wright, G., *France in Modern Times*, London, Norton, 1995.

Zeldin, T., *France 1848–1945: Politics and Anger*, Oxford, Oxford University Press.

The Counter-Revolution

Artz, F. B., *France under the Bourbon Restoration*, Cambridge, MA, Harvard University Press, 1931.

Beik, P., *The French Revolution Seen from the Right*, Transactions of the American Philosophical Society, Philadelphia, 1956.

Bertier de Sauvigny, G., *The Bourbon Restoration*, Philadelphia, University of Pennsylvania Press, 1966.

Best, G. (ed.), *The Permanent Revolution: The French Revolution and its Legacy 1789–1989*, London, Fontana, 1989.

Blanning, T. C. W., *The Origins of the French Revolutionary Wars*, London, Longman, 1986.

Bosher, J. F., *The French Revolution*, London, Weidenfeld & Nicolson, 1989.

Bouloiseau, M., *The Jacobin Republic 1792–1794*, Cambridge, Cambridge University Press, 1983.

Carpenter, K. and Mansel, P. (eds), *The French Émigrés in Europe and the Struggle against Revolution, 1789–1814*, London, Macmillan, 1990.

Cobb, R., *Reactions to the French Revolution*, London, Oxford University Press, 1972.

Cobban, A., *The Social Interpretation of the French Revolution*, Cambridge, Cambridge University Press, 1968.

—— *Aspects of the French Revolution*, London, Jonathan Cape, 1968.

Collins, I., *The Government and the Newspaper Press in France 1814–1881*, London, Oxford University Press, 1959.

Dansette, A., *Histoire religeuse de la France contemporaine*, Paris, Flammarion, 1965.

Doyle, W., *The Oxford History of the French Revolution*, Oxford, Oxford University Press, 1991.

Forrest, A., *The French Revolution*, Oxford, Blackwell, 1999.

Furet, F., *The French Revolution 1770–1814*, Oxford, Blackwell, 1996.

Furneaux, R., *The Bourbon Tragedy*, London, Allen & Unwin, 1968.

Gilchrist, J. and Murray, W. J., *The Press in the French Revolution: A Selection of Documents taken from the Press of the Revolution for the Years 1789–1794*, London, Cheshire & Gihn, 1971.

Godechot, J., *Les Révolutions (1770–1799)*, Paris, Presses Universitaires de France, 1970.

—— *The Counter-Revolution: Doctrine and Action 1789–1804*, London, Routledge & Kegan Paul, 1972.

Greer, D., *The Incidence of the Emigration during the French Revolution*, Cambridge, MA, Harvard University Press, c. 1951.

Greifer, E., 'Joseph de Maistre and the Reaction against the Eighteenth Century', *American Political Science Review*, Vol. 15, Sept. 1961.

Hampson, N., *The Life and Opinions of Maximilien Robespierre*, Oxford, Basil Blackwell, 1988.

—— *A Social History of the French Revolution*, London, Routledge, 1995.

Hayward, J., *After the French Revolution*, London, Harvester Wheatsheaf, 1991.

Hibbert, C., *The French Revolution*, London, Penguin, 1982.

Hudson, N. E., *Ultra-Royalism and the French Restoration*, London, Cambridge University Press, 1936.

Jardin, A. and Tudesq, A.-J., *Restoration & Reaction 1815–1848*, Cambridge, Cambridge University Press, 1988.

Jones, P., *The Peasantry in the French Revolution, Cambridge*, Cambridge University Press, 1989.

—— (ed.), *The French Revolution in Social and Political Perspective*, London, Arnold, 1996.

Jordan, D. P., *The Revolutionary Career of Maximilien Robespierre*, Chicago, University of Chicago Press, 1989.

Journal de Louis XVI, Paris, Libraire-Editeur, 1873.

Kates, G. (ed.), *The French Revolution: Recent Debates and New Controversies*, London, Routledge, 1998.

Lebrun, R., 'Joseph de Maistre, Cassandra of Science', *French Historical Studies*, Autumn1969.

Lefebvre, G., *The French Revolution: From Its Origins to 1793*, London, Kegan Paul, 1965.

—— *The Thermidoreans*, London, Routledge & Kegan Paul, 1965.

—— *The French Revolution: From 1793 to 1799*, London, Routledge & Kegan Paul, 1967.

Le Goff, T. J. A. and Sutherland, D. M. G., 'Counter-Revolution in Western France', *Past and Present*, 1983 (May) No. 99: 65–87.

Lewis, G., *The French Revolution: Rethinking the Debate*, London, Routledge, 1993.

Loomis, S., *Paris in the Terror: June 1793-July 1794*, London, Jonathan Cape, 1964.

McManners, J., *The French Revolution and the Church*, London, SPCK, 1969.

Mansel, P., *Louis XVIII*, London, Blond & Briggs, 1981.

Mason, H., *French Writers and their Society 1715–1800*, London, Macmillan, 1982.

Menczer, B., *Catholic Political Thought in France 1789–1848*, Paris, University of Notre-Dame, 1962.

Mitchell, H., 'The Vendée and Counterrevolution: A Review Essay', *French Historical Studies*, 1968, 405–29.

Murray, J., 'The Political Thought of Joseph de Maistre', *Review of Politics*, 1949.

Murray, W. J., *The Right-Wing Press in the French Revolution: 1789–92*, London, Boydell Press, 1986.

Palmer, R. R., *The World of the French Revolution*, London, Allen & Unwin, 1971.

Paret, P., *Internal War and Pacification: The Vendée 1789–1796*, Center of International Studies, Princeton University, Princeton, NJ.

Parker, N., *Portrayals of Revolution*, London, Harvester, 1990.

Péronnet, M., *Les 50 mots clefs de la Révolution Française*, Paris, Privat, 1983.

Pilbeam, P., *Republicanism in Nineteenth-Century France, 1814–1871*, London, Macmillan, 1995.

Randell, K., *France 1814–70*, London, Hodder & Stoughton, 1986.

Resnick, D. P., *The White Terror and the Political Reaction after Waterloo*, Cambridge, MA, Harvard University Press, 1966.

Roberts, J., *The Counter-Revolution in France 1787–1830*, London, Macmillan, 1990.

Roberts, J. M., *The French Revolution*, Oxford, Oxford University Press, 1978.

Rudé, G., *Revolutionary Europe*, London, Fontana, 1986.

Sutherland, D. M. G., *France 1789–1815: Revolution and Counterrevolution*, London, Fontana, 1985.

Sydenham, M. J., *The French Revolution*, London, Batsford, 1969.

Tackett, T., 'The West in France in 1789: The Religious Factor in the Origins of the Counterrevolution', *Journal of Modern History*, Vol. 4, 1982.

Thompson, J. M., *The French Revolution*, Oxford, Oxford University Press, 1969.

Tilly, C., *The Vendée*, London, Edward Arnold, 1964.

—— 'Local Conflicts in the Vendée before the Rebellion of 1793', *French Historical Studies*, 1961, Vol. 2, No. 2: 209–31.

—— 'Civil Constitution and Counter-Revolution in Southern Anjou', *French Historical Studies*, 1959, Vol. 1, No. 2: 172–99.

Vovelle, M., *The Revolution against the Church: From Reason to the Supreme Being*, Cambridge, Polity, 1999.

Woronoff, D., *The Thermidorean Regime and the Directory 1794–1799*, Cambridge, Cambridge University Press, 1984.

Anti-Third Republic protest

Anderson, R. D., *France 1870–1914: Politics and Society*, London, Routledge & Kegan Paul, 1977.

Barral, P. (ed.), *Les Fondateurs de la Troisième République*, Paris, Armand Colin, 1968.

'Maurice Barrès' Collaboration with the Action Française', *Romanic Review*, Vol. XXIX, April 1938.

Birnbaum, P. (ed.), *La France de l'affaire Dreyfus*, Paris, Gallimard, 1994.

Bourgin, G., *La Troisième République 1870–1914*, Paris, Armand Colin, 1967.

Bourne, R. S., 'Maurice Barres and the Youth of France', *Atlantic Monthly*, Vol CXIV, Sept. 1914.

Brabant, F. H., *The Beginnings of the Third Republic in France*, New York, Howard Fertig, 1972.

Bredin, J. D., *The Affair: The Case of Alfred Dreyfus*, London, Sidgwick & Jackson, 1987.

Burns, M., *Dreyfus: A Family Affair 1789–1945*, London, Chatto & Windus, 1993.

Chapman, G., *The Third Republic of France: The First Phase 1871–1894*, London, Macmillan, 1962.

Chastenet, J., *Naissance et jeunesse: histoire de la IIIe République*, Paris, Hachette, 1952.

Cheydleur, F. D., 'Maurice Barrès as a Romanticist', *Publications of the Modern Language Association of America*, 1926, Vol. XLI.

Dansette, A., *Le Boulangisme*, Paris, Fayard, 1946.

Drouin, M., *L'Affaire Dreyfus de A à Z*, Paris, Flammarion, 1994.

Frohock, W. M., 'Maurice Barrès' Collaboration with the Action Francaise', *Romanic Review*, Vol XXIX, April 1938.

Fulton, B., 'The Boulanger Affair Revisited: The Preservation of the Third Republic, 1889', *French Historical Studies*, Vol. 17, No. 2, Autumn 1991.

Gildea, R., *The Third Republic 1870–1914*, London, Longman, 1988.

Goguel, F., *La politique des parties sous la IIIe République*, Paris, Seuil, 1958.

Grover, M., 'The Inheritors of Maurice Barrès', *Modern Language Review*, Vol. LXIV, July 1961.

Guérard, A. L., *Five Masters of French Romance*, London, T. Fisher Unwin, 1916, p. 216.

Hampden Jackson, J., *Clemenceau and the Third Republic*, London, English Universities Press, 1946.

Hue, J. (ed.), *L'Affaire Dreyfus 1894–1910 et le Tournant du Siècle*, Paris, BDIC, 1994.

Hutton, P. H., *The Cult of Revolutionary Tradition: The Blanquists in French Politics, 1864–1893*, London, University of California Press, 1981.

Irvine, W. D., 'French Royalists and Boulangism', *French Historical Studies*, 1988, Vol. XV, No. 3: 395–406.

—— *The Boulanger Affair Reconsidered*, New York, Oxford University Press, 1989.

Jenkins, B., *Nationalism in France*, London, Routledge, 1990.

Kedward, R., *The Dreyfus Affair*, London, Longman, 1965.

Lynch, H., 'A Political Waiter of France', *Contemporary Review*, Vol. 78, 1900.

McManners, J., *Church and State in France 1870–1914*, London, SPCK, 1972.

Miquel, P., *L'Affaire Dreyfus*, Paris, Presses Universitaires de France, 1964.

Nord, P. G., *Paris Shopkeepers and the Politics of Resentment*, Princeton, NJ, Princeton University Press, c. 1986.

Putnam, G. F., 'The Meaning of Barrèsisme', *Western Political Quarterly*, Vol VII, June 1954.

Rioux, J.-P., *Nationalisme et conservatisme: la Ligue de la Patrie Française 1899–1904*, Paris, Beauchesne, 1977.

Rothney, J., *Bonapartism after Sedan*, New York, Cornell University Press, 1969.

Rutkoff, P. M., 'The Ligue des Patriotes: The Nature of the Radical Right and the Dreyfus Affair', *French Historical Studies*, Vol. 8, No. 4, Autumn 1974.

—— *Revanche and Revision*, Athens, OH, Ohio University Press, 1981.

Seagar, F. H., *The Boulanger Affair: Political Crossroad of France 1886–1889*, New York, Cornell University Press, 1969.

Soucy, R., 'Barrès and Fascism', *French Historical Studies*, Spring 1967.

—— *French Fascism: The Case of Maurice Barrès*, Berkeley, CA, University of California Press, 1972.

Sternhell, Z., 'Paul Déroulède and the Origins of Modern French Nationalism', *Journal of Contemporary History*, Vol VI, 1971.

Sternhell, Z., *La Droite révolutionnaire: les origines françaises du Fascisme 1885–1914*, Paris, Seuil, 1978.

Stewart Doty, C., *From Cultural Rebellion to Counterrevolution: The Politics of Maurice Barrès*, Athens, OH, Ohio University Press, (no date).

—— 'Parliamentary Boulangism After 1889', *The Historian*, Vol. 32, Feb. 1970.

Tombs, R. (ed.), *Nationhood and Nationalism in France: From Boulangism to the Great War 1889–1918*, London, HarperCollins, 1991.

Tombs, R., *The Paris Commune*, London, Longman, 1999.

Wilson, S., 'The Antisemitic Riots of 1898 in France', *The Historical Journal*, Vol. XVI, No. 4, 1973.

Wilson, S., *Ideology and Experience: Antisemitism in France at the Time at the Dreyfus Affair*, London, Associated University Press, 1982.

Inter-war fascism: the ligues *and 6 February*

Bernard, P. and Dubief, H., *The Decline of the Third Republic 1914–1938*, Cambridge, Cambridge University Press, 1985.

Blinkhorn, M., (ed.), *Fascists and Conservatives*, London, Unwin Hyman, 1990.

Joll, J. (ed.), *The Decline of the Third Republic*, St Antony's Papers, No. 5, London, 1959.

Kedward, H. R., *Fascism in Western Europe 1900–45*, Glasgow, Blackie, 1969.

Kingston, P. J., *Anti-Semitism in France during the 1930s: Origins, Personalities and Propaganda*, Hull, UK, University of Hull, 1983.

Kitchen, M., *Europe Between the Wars*, Longman, London, 1993.

Levey, J., 'Georges Valois and the Faisceau: The Making and Breaking of a Fascist', *French Historical Studies*, 1973, Vol. VIII, No. 2: 279–304.

Nolte, E., *Three Faces of Fascism*, London, Weidenfeld & Nicolson, 1965.

Osgood, S. M., 'The Front Populaire: Views from the Right', *International Review of Social History*, 1964, Vol. IX.

Paxton, R. O., *French Peasant Fascism: Henry Dorgères's Greenshirts and the Crises of French Agriculture, 1929–1939*, Oxford, Oxford University Press, 1997.

Soucy, R., 'The Nature of Fascism in France', *Journal of Contemporary History*, 1966, Vol. 1, No. 1: 27–55.

—— *French Fascism: The First Wave 1924–33*, New Haven, CT, Yale University Press, 1986.

Sternhell, Z., *La Droite révolutionnaire: les origines françaises du fascisme 1885–1914*, Paris, Seuil, 1978.

Tannenbaum, E. R., *The Action Française*, New York, Wiley, 1962.

Warner, G., 'The Cagoulard Conspiracy', *History Today*, 1960, Vol. IX, No. 7: 443–50.

—— 'The Stavisky Affair and the Riots of February 6th, 1934', *History Today*, 1958, No. 6: 377–85.

Weber, E., *Action Française*, Stanford, CA, Stanford University Press, 1962.

Werth, A., *France in Ferment*, London, Jarrolds, 1934.

Wilson, S., 'History and Traditionalism: Maurras and the Action Française', *Journal of the History of Ideas*, Vol. 28, 1968.

Wilson, S., 'The "Action Française" in French Intellectual Life', *The Historical Journal*, 1969, Vol. XII, No. 2.

Vichy: the National Revolution, collaboration and collaborationism

Annales, *Présence du passé, lenteur de l'histoire Vichy, l'Occupation, les Juifs*, No. 3, May–Jun. 1993, Paris, Armand Colin, École des Hautes Études en Sciences Sociales.

Atkin, N., *Pétain*, London, Longman, 1998.

—— and Tallett, F. (eds), *Religion, Society and Politics in France since 1789*, London, Hambledon, 1991.

Azema, J.-P., *De Munich à la Libération 1938–1944*, Paris, Seuil, 1979.

Bouderon, R. and Willard, G., *De la Défaite à la Résistance*, Paris, Messidor, 1990.

de Chambrun, R., ... *et ce fut un crime judiciare: le 'procès' Laval*, Paris, France-Empire, 1984.

Chauvy, G., *Histoire secrète de l'Occupation*, Paris, Payot, 1991.

Cobb, R., *French and Germans, Germans and French*, Hanover, NH, Brandeis University Press, 1983.

Conan, E. and Rousso, H., *Vichy, un passé qui ne passe pas*, Paris, Fayard, 1994.

Copley, A., *Sexual Moralities in France 1780–1980*, London, Routledge, 1992.

Dank, M., *The French Against the French: Collaboration and Resistance*, Philadelphia, Lippincott, 1974.

Defrasne, J., *Histoire de la collaboration*, Paris, Presses Universitaires de France, 1989.

—— *L'Occupation Allemende en France*, Paris, Presses Universitaires de France, 1993.

Desquesnes, R., *The Guide to the Memorial*, Caen, Éditions Memorial de Caen, 1994.

Ehrmann, H. W., *Organized Business in France*, Princeton, NJ, Princeton University Press, 1957.

Farmer, P., *Vichy Political Dilemma*, London, Octagon, 1977.

Fishman, S., Downs, L. L., Sinanoglou, I., Smith, L. V. and Zaretsky, R. (eds), *France at War: Vichy and the Historians*, Oxford, Berg, 2000.

Halls, W. D., *The Youth of Vichy France*, Oxford, Clarendon, 1981.

—— *Politics, Society and Christianity in Vichy France*, Oxford, Berg, 1995.

Hilberg, R., *The Destruction of the European Jews*, New York, Holmes & Meier, 1985.

Hoffman, S., *Decline or Renewal: France since the 1930s*, New York, Viking Press, 1974.

Johnson, D., 'A Question of Guilt: Pierre Laval and the Vichy Regime', *History Today*, Vol. 38, Jan. 1988.

Kedward, R. and Austin, R. (eds), *Vichy France and the Resistance*, London, Croom Helm, 1985.

Kedward, H. R., *Occupied France: Collaboration and Resistance 1940–1944*, Oxford, Blackwell, 1989.

Kuisel, R., *Capitalism and the State in Modern France: Renovation and Economic Management in the Twentieth Century*, Cambridge, Cambridge University Press, 1981.

Marrus, M. R. and Paxton, R. O., *Vichy France and the Jews*, Stanford, Stanford University Press, 1995.

Novick, P., *The Resistance Versus Vichy: The Purge of Collaborators in Liberated France*, New York, Columbia University Press, 1968.

Osgood, S. M., *The Fall of France, 1940: Causes and Responsibilities*, Boston, DC, Heath and Company, 1965.

Ousby, I., *Occupation: The Ordeal of France 1940–1944*, London, John Murray, 1998.

Paxton, R. O., *Vichy France: Old Guard and New Order 1940–1944*, New York, Columbia University Press, 1982.

Ragache, G. and Ragache, J.-R., *La Vie quotidienne des écrivains et des artistes sous l'Occupation 1940–4*, Paris, Hachette, 1988.

Rajsfus, M., *Des Juifs dans la collaboration: L'UGIF 1941–1944*, Paris, EDI, 1980.

Reitlinger, G., *The Final Solution*, London, Vallentine Mitchel, 1968.

Rossignol, D., *Histoire de la propagande en France de 1940 à 1955*, Paris, Presses Universitaire de France, 1991.

Rousso, H., *The Vichy Syndrome: History and Memory in France since 1944*, London, Harvard University Press, 1994.

Roy, J., *The Trial of Marshal Pétain*, London, Faber & Faber, 1968.

Schnurer, H., 'The Intellectual Sources of French Fascism', *The Antioch Review*, March 1941.

Shirer, W. L., *The Collapse of the Third Republic*, London, Literary Guild, 1970.

Soucy, R., 'French Fascist Intellectuals in the 1930s: An Old New Left?', *French Historical Studies*, 1974, Vol. VIII, No. 3: 445–58.

Sweets, J., *Choices in Vichy France*, New York, Oxford University Press, 1994.

Tallett, F. and Atkin, N. (eds), *Catholicism in Britain and France since 1789*, London, Hambledon, 1996.

Thomson, D., *Two Frenchmen: Pierre Laval and Charles de Gaulle*, London, Cresset, 1951.

Toynbee, A. (ed.), *Hitler's Europe: Survey of International Affairs 1939–1946*.

Tucker, W. R., 'Politics and Aesthetics: The Fascism of Robert Brasillach', *Western Political Quarterly*, Vol. 15, Pt 4, Dec. 1962.

Warner, G., *Pierre Laval and the Eclipse of France*, London, Eyre & Spottiswoode, 1968.

Webster, P., *Pétain's Crime*, London, Papermac, 1992.

Wright, G., *Rural Revolution in France: The Peasantry in the Twentieth Century*, Stanford, Stanford University Press, 1964.

Algérie Française, *Poujadism and the Front National*

Behr, E., *The Algerian Problem*, London, Penguin, 1961.

Betts, R. F., France and Decolonisation 1900–1960, London, Macmillan, 1991.

Clayton, A., *The Wars of French Decolonization*, London, Longman, 1994.

Crawley, A., *De Gaulle*, London, Literary Guild, 1969.

Davies, P., 'Joan of Arc in Front National Discourse', *Politics*, Autumn 1993.

—— *The National Front in France: Discourse, Ideology and Power*, London, Routledge, 1999.

Declair, E. G., *Politics on the Fringe: The People, Policies, and Organisation of the French National Front*, London, Duke University Press, 1999.

Gildea, R., *France since 1945*, Oxford, Oxford University Press, 1996.

Gough, H. and Horne, J., *De Gaulle and Twentieth Century France*, London, Arnold, 1994.

Hainsworth, P. (ed.), *The Extreme Right in Europe and the USA*, London, Pinter, 1994.

—— (ed.), *The Politics of the Extreme Right: From the Margins to the Mainstream*, London, Pinter, 2000.

Hanley, D. L., Kerr, A. P. and Waites, N. H., *Contemporary France: Politics and Society since 1945*, London, Routledge, 1991.

Horne, A., *A Savage War of Peace*, London, Penguin, 1985.

Jouve, P. and Magoudi, A., *Les Dits et les non-dits de Jean-Marie Le Pen: enquête et psychoanalyse*, Paris, La Découverte, 1988.

Marcus, J., *The National Front and French Politics*, London, Macmillan, 1995.

Mayer, N. and Perrineau, P. (eds), *Le Front National à découvert*, Paris, Presses de la Fondation Nationale des Sciences Politiques, 1996.

Mitra, S., 'The National Front in France – A Single-Issue Movement?', in K. von Beyme (ed.), *Right-Wing Extremism in Europe*, London, Cass, 1988.

Morris, P., *French Politics Today*, Manchester, Manchester University Press, 1994.

Rioux, J.-P., *The Fourth Republic 1944–1958*, Cambridge, Cambridge University Press, 1989.

Simmons, H. G., *The French National Front: The Extremist Challenge to Democracy*, Oxford, Westview, 1996.

Thiollet, J.-P., *Le Chevallier à découvert: portrait vérité par son ex-counseiller*, Paris, Laurens, 1998.

Viard, J. (ed.), *Aux sources su populisme nationaliste: l'urgence de comprendre Toulon-Orange-Marignane*, Paris, Aube, 1996.

Werth, A., *De Gaulle*, London, Penguin, 1979.

Williams, P., *Politics in Post-War France*, London, Longman, 1958.

Primary sources and collections of documents

Allez la France! Discours intégral de Jean-Marie Le Pen à la Fête des Bleu-Blanc-Rouge 1997, Paris, Éditions Nationales, 1997.

Allez vitrolles: le programme de l'équipe mégret, Paris, Équipe Mégret, 1997.

Audit Politique des Communes de France: À l'Usage des Conseillers Municipaux et des Candidats du Front National, Paris, Éditions Nationales, 1995.

de Balzac, H., *The Chouans*, London, Penguin, 1972.

Barrès, M., 'The Panama Scandal', *Cosmopolitan*, Vol. XVII, June 1894.

—— *The Soul of France: Visits to Invaded Districts*, London, T. Fisher & Unwin, 1915.

—— 'Young Soldiers of France', *The Atlantic Monthly*, Vol. CXX, July 1917.

Bell, A., *Against Racism and Fascism in Europe*, Brussels, Socialist Group (European Parliament), 1986.

Bire, E., *The Diary of a Citizen of Paris during the Terror*, Vol. 2, London, Chatto & Windus, 1986.

Blot, Y., *La Politique selon Aristote: leçons du passé pour le present*, Paris, Éditions Nation et Humanisme, 1997.

Blum, L., *Souvenirs sur l'affaire*, Paris, Gallimard, 1981 (written in 1935).

Brissaud, J.-M., *La France en danger: non à l'Europe de Maastricht*, Paris, Éditions Nationales, 1994.

—— *Clovis: Roy des Francs: L'Album du XVe Centenaire*, Paris, Éditions Nationales, *c.* 1996.

—— *Clovis: premier homme politique Français*, Paris, GDE, 1996.

Burke, E., *Reflections on the Revolution in France*, London, Penguin, 1986.

Cahm, E. (ed.), *Politics and Society in Contemporary France 1789–1971: A Documentary History*, London, Harrap, 1972.

La Charte verte du Front National, Paris, National Hebdo, 1985.

Collins, I. (ed.), *Government and Society in France 1814–48*, London, Edward Arnold, 1970.

Le Contrat pour la France avec les français: Le Pen Président, Saint-Brieuc, Presses Bretonnes, 1995.

Descaves, P., *Pour en finir avec le chômage: les chiffres, les causes, les solutions*, Paris, Coordination des Cercles Nationaux, *c.* 1994.

Dossier Immigration, Paris, National Hebdo, 1985.

Dreyfus, A., *Cinq années de ma vie*, Paris, Maspero, 1982.

Droite et démocratie économique: docrine économique et sociale du Front National, Paris, National Hebdo, 1984.

Ducloux, L., *From Blackmail to Treason*, London, André Deutsch, 1958.

France during the German Occupation, 1940–44, Vol. II, California, The Hoover Institution, *c.* 1947.

Girardet, R., *Le Nationalisme français 1871–1914*, Paris, Armand Colin, 1966.

Hardman, J. (ed.), The French Revolution, London, Edward Arnold, 1991.

Hugo, V., *Ninety-Three*, London, Collins' Clear-Type Press, (no date).

—— *Les Misérables*, Ware, UK, Wordsworth, 1994.

Laval, P., The Unpublished Diary of Pierre Laval, London, The Falcon Press, 1948.

Le Gallou, J.-Y., *Le Racisme antifrançais*, Paris, Club de l'Horloge, 1988.

—— *Le Livre bleu blanc rouge: Plaidoyer pour une Région Enracinée*, Paris, Éditions Nationales, 1991.

Le Gallou, J.-Y. et le Club de l'Horloge, *La Préférence nationale: réponse à l'immigration*, Paris, Albin Michel, 1985.

Le Gallou, J.-Y. and Jalkh, J.-F., *Être Français cela se mérite*, Paris, Albatros, 1987.

Le Gallou, J.-Y. and Olivier, P., *Immigration*, Éditions Nationales, Paris, 1992.

Le Pen, J.-M., *Les Français d'abord*, Paris, Carrere-Michel Lafon, 1984.

—— *L'Éspoir*, Paris, Albatros, 1989.

—— *Europe: discours et interventions 1984–1989*, Paris, GDE, 1989.

Le Pen 90: Analyses et propositions, Maule, Éditions de Présent, 1991.

Lively, J. (ed.), *The Works of Joseph de Maistre*, London, Allen & Unwin, 1965.

Maréchal, S., *Écologie: dépolluons les esprits*, Paris, Front National de Jeunesse, *c.* 1998.

Martinez, J.-C., *Maastricht: le non de tous les miens*, Paris, Lettres du Monde, 1992.

McClelland, J. S. (ed.), *The French Right from de Maistre to Maurras*, London, Jonathan Cape, 1971.

Mégret, B. et les Comités d'Action Républicaine, *L'Impératif du Renouveau: Les Enjeux de Demain*, Paris, Albatros, 1986.

—— *L'Alternative nationale: les priorities du Front National*, Paris, Éditions Nationales, c.1996.

—— *La Troisième voie: pour un nouvel ordre économique et social*, Paris, Éditions Nationales, 1997.

Mégret, C., *V comme vitrolles: histoire d'une victoire*, Éditions Nationales, Paris, 1997.

Militer au front, Paris, Éditions Nationales, 1991.

Pasquier, Chancellor, *Memoirs, Vol. 1, 1789–1810*, London, Fisher Unwin, 1893.

Pernoud, G. and Flaissier, S. (eds), *The French Revolution*, London, Mercury, 1960.

Pétain, P., *Discours aux français 17 Jun 1940–20 Août 1944*, Paris, Albin Michel, 1989.

Pour la France: programme du Front National, Paris, Albatros, 1985.

Rapport milloz, le coût de l'immigration, Paris, Éditions du Centre d'Études et d'Argumentaires, 1990.

de Rostolan, M., *Lettre ouverte à mon peuple qui meurt*, Paris, Lanore, 1987.

Routhier, P., *Contrepoisons: les sciences de la vie et l'histoire parlent pour le Front National*, Paris, Éditions Nationales, c. 1998.

Schenardi, J.-P. and Liparoti, J.-P., *Pour un urbanisme français*, Paris, Éditions Nationales, c. 1998.

Stewart, J. H. (ed.), *The Restoration Era in France 1814–1830*, Princeton, NJ, Van Nostrand, 1968.

—— (ed.), *A Documentary Survey of the French Revolution*, New York, Macmillan, 1969.

Stirbois, J.-P., *Tonnerre de dreux: l'avenir nous appartient*, Éditions National-Hebdo, Paris, 1988.

Thomson, D., (ed.), *Empire and Republic*, London, Macmillan, 1968.

300 Mesures pour la renaissance de la France: Front National programme de gouvernement, Paris, Éditions Nationales, 1993.

Tissier, P., *The Government of Vichy*, London, Harrap, 1942.

Trotsky, L., *On France*, New York, Monad Press, 1979.

Williams, M., *Revolutions 1775–1830*, London, Penguin, 1971.

Other

Aspects de la France
Daily Mirror
Le Figaro
Guardian
Manchester Guardian
Le Matin
Le Monde
Le Quotidien de Paris
Time
Vendée tourist leaflets
www.front-national.com

Index